Real Indians

Identity and the Survival
of Native America

Eva Marie Garroutte

UNIVERSITY OF CALIFORNIA PRESS

Berkeley / Los Angeles / London

University of California Press
Berkeley and Los Angeles, California

University of California Press, Ltd.
London, England

© 2003 by
The Regents of the University of California

Library of Congress Cataloging-in-Publication Data
Garroutte, Eva Marie.
    Real Indians : identity and the survival of Native America / Eva Marie
Garroutte.
        p.   cm.
    Includes bibliographical references and index.
    ISBN 0-520-21310-6 (alk. paper) — ISBN 0-520-22977-0 (pbk. : alk. paper)
        1. Indians of North America — Ethnic identity.   2. Indians of North
America — Tribal citizenship.   3. Indians of North America — Legal status,
laws, etc.   4. Identification (Psychology).   5. Self-determination,
National—United States.   I. Title.
E98.E85 G37   2003
305.897—dc21   2002152221

Manufactured in the United States of America

11   10   09   08   07   06   05   04   03
10   9   8   7   6   5   4   3   2   1

Real Indians

*This book is dedicated with much love
to my parents, Tom and Patricia Garroutte,
to my husband, Xavier Lopez,
and to American Indian people everywhere*

Contents

Illustrations

Figures

Table

Preface

This book examines some of the many ways that American Indians speak and think about their identity.[1] In one sense, I am just the kind of person who might write this book. I am a light-skinned, mixed-race person. I have been a legal citizen of an American Indian tribe since childhood, one who found her way back, in adulthood, to the Cherokee Nation that her father was born in, grew up in, and left. And I am a sociologist who teaches Native American Studies courses. For these reasons, I know a great deal about scuffles over American Indian identity from both a personal and a scholarly perspective.

In another sense, I am an unlikely person to write this book. It is a book that presumes to suggest to non-Indian and Indian people some ways of thinking about Indianness. As such, perhaps it would more likely have been written by someone who had spent her whole life in a tribal community instead of only a part of it, by someone who spoke her tribal tongue as a first language, not as a language only partially and imperfectly acquired in adulthood. Perhaps it would more likely have been written by someone whose racial ancestry was not divided between European and American Indian: by someone, in short, whose more indisputable racial authenticity seemed to confer upon her a greater authority to speak on such a difficult question as race and identity.

My decision that I *would* write this book was influenced by two considerations. One of these was that the question of racial "authenticity" has been gaining great currency in recent societal debates and needs to be explored, most particularly in the case of American Indians. The other

xi

was that no one else, whatever their identity claims, *had* written this book. So I have written it. It has the benefit of the instruction that I have received from my loved ones and elders in traditional, tribal ways of thought and behavior. It has the benefit of the ceremonies that some of those elders have performed for me, to help me write it in a good way. It is marked by years of living and moving in Indian communities, both professional and personal.

Nonetheless, it is certainly not the final word on how racial identity battles should be resolved or on what the new scholarly perspective on such issues that I suggest might mean for any of the parties involved. Indeed, I hope that this book will be received not as an *answer* but as an *invitation* to further discussion about the meaning of racial identity, particularly in regard to American Indians. I hope, too, that in its argument for the emerging intellectual perspective that I call "Radical Indigenism," it may point to a new way of thinking about a range of issues that concern Indian people, non-Indian people, and the academy. In this regard, if this book does nothing more than open a space for the authors and speakers who will come after me, as further contributors to a fully developed body of thought dedicated to the validation of American Indian (and other indigenous) ways of knowing and of living in the world, I will be satisfied.

Acknowledgments

The irrepressible Ben Ramirez-shkwegnaabi, Department of History, Central Michigan University, gave me the idea to write this book. It is only right to acknowledge that it would not exist but for his suggestion. I also want to emphasize that the ideas expressed here did not emerge in a vacuum. Although I alone bear the responsibility for any difficulties that may attend the arguments, many people have helped me develop my ideas. This is abundantly evident in my discussions of the meanings of American Indian identity claims. I formulated these not only with the help of the individuals interviewed specifically for this book (see appendix for their biographies) but also on the basis of provocative conversations with American Indian relatives, students, friends, elders, and teachers. Many of those conversations occurred years before I knew I would write a book about racial identity.

The collaborative nature of this book is nowhere more evident, however, than in my remarks about the intellectual perspective I call Radical Indigenism. Kathleen Westcott (Anishnabe/Cree), my onetime professor of philosophy at the Institute of American Indian Arts (Santa Fe, New Mexico), was the first to show me that there could be such a way of thinking about the world. Ines Talamantez, a Mescalero Apache professor in the Department of Religious Studies at the University of California, Santa Barbara, shared her vision of an "indigenous theory," which helped to further validate and shape my intellectual process. Friends such as Rayna Green (Cherokee), Larry Emerson (Navajo), Richard Grounds (Yuchi), Joyce Johnson (Cherokee), and Elizabeth

Higgins (Cherokee) each made distinctive contributions to my thinking as they read and made detailed comments on early drafts of the chapters. The same is true of scholars such as Melissa Meyer, Les Field, and George Roth. Angela Gonzales (Hopi) offered much help with my thinking and writing and willingly helped me locate materials. Each one of these generous people has been a priceless advisor.

Others who have influenced my ideas include a group of scholars who participate in the Native Traditions in the Americas Group of the American Academy of Religion, a group for which I serve on the steering committee. The constituents of this group possess conventional academic training, but many are also establishing, reaffirming, or renewing ties to American Indian communities (often their own) as they learn, relearn, or fortify their existing knowledge of languages, cultures, community values, spiritual practices, and so on. This group has provided me with the opportunity for many useful exchanges over the years. These conversations have guided my thinking through the fundamental question around which Radical Indigenism revolves: How can Indian and non-Indian scholars do, *as scholars,* what responsible members and contributors to Native communities always do — use our specialized training and skills to serve the collectively defined concerns and interests of tribes?

While completing the research for this book I seldom lacked for willing assistance. In this regard, Joyce and Ray Johnson deserve special recognition. They encouraged me, helped set up interviews, read drafts of the manuscript, and sometimes even fed my respondents in their Tulsa home. They have put up with my foolishness for years and loved me anyway. Many of my fellow parishioners at the All Tribes Community Church of Tulsa likewise made available their homes, cars, personal possessions, time, prayers, and good thoughts to help me with interviewing and travel related to this book. George Roth, Valerie Lambert, and Lee Fleming generously took time out of their working days at the Branch of Acknowledgment and Research (Washington, D.C.) to grant me interesting and useful interviews about the process by which Indian tribes receive federal recognition. The principal chief of the Cherokee Nation, Chad Smith, devoted part of his first day on the job to an interview.

Finally, I must acknowledge those who have contributed to the physical coming-into-being of the book (a process immensely more complicated than this first-time author had imagined). At University of California Press Doug Abrams (now of Harper Collins) was the editor who got me started on this project, and Monica McCormick was the editor who got me finished. I cannot praise the talents and dedication of either of them highly enough, or their abilities to act as both effective critics and persistent encouragers for someone who required both. Roberta Negrin, Catherine Q. Sullivan, and Jennifer Diaz worked faithfully to transcribe interview tapes. My mother, Patricia Garroutte, typed and retyped the manuscript, checked endnotes ceaselessly, tirelessly tracked down fugitive sources, and also transcribed tapes. My father, Tom Garroutte, cheerfully accepted many dinners of peanut butter sandwiches in order to allow her to do so. On at least one occasion, he defied the local constabulary by driving through an Arkansas snowstorm to deliver my manuscript by deadline, which ought to qualify him for some kind of award. Throughout the whole process of writing, revising, and rewriting, no one was better than my husband, Xavier Lopez, at making me see things clearly and keep on working. He never lets me forget the importance of the issues raised in this book to the well-being and survival of American Indian peoples and communities. My love and appreciation for him, and for all those who have left their intellectual and spiritual impression on this book, can hardly be expressed. Thank you. Thank all of you. *Wado.*

Introduction

The Chief Who Never Was

"The first thing in my life that I can remember is the exciting aftermath of an Indian fight in northern Montana. My mother was crying and running about with me in my moss bag-carrier on her back. . . . Women and horses were everywhere. . . . My mother's hand was bleeding. . . . She handed me to my aunt and jumped on a pony and rode away."[1] These lines introduce the life story of Chief Buffalo Child Long Lance as he himself told it. Earlier in his writing career, Long Lance, whom his recent biographer Donald B. Smith calls "one of the most famous North American Indians of his day," had penned popular newspaper and magazine articles about Indian issues and events.[2] But it was clearly his autobiography that catapulted the man to celebrity in the late 1920s. In it, Long Lance described growing up on the Great Plains as the son of a Blackfoot chief. Long Lance's explanation for his mother's bloody hand in the opening scene was that his mother had just mutilated herself in a ritual of mourning for a brother killed in battle. This exotic vignette was only the first of many. Long Lance went on to relate how he had joined the other small boys in listening outside the tents of the medicine men; how he had seen the hunters return with their gory trophies from the great buffalo chases; how he had trod the circle around a flickering fire beside his father in many war dances, his body daubed with red paint.

American readers embraced the book and its author with equal fervor. In short order, the new literary hero also became a silent film star and a social sensation on both coasts. Men admired his athletic prowess, his roguish humor, his powerful storytelling talents, his ability to deliver a bloodcurdling war cry on request. Women clearly felt they cut a fetching figure dangling from his bronzed and well-muscled arm. The movie magazine *Screenland* reported that "Long Lance, one of the few real one-hundred-percent Americans, has had New York right in his pocket."[3]

But something about Long Lance did not appear quite right. From time to time, observers voiced uncertainties that caused ripples in the high society that had extended its indulgences to him. Could it be that the line of his lower lip was a little *too* full? Was he, perhaps, a trifle *too* swarthy for an Indian? There were rumors about his relatives. Surely that was not a *black* man peeping out from behind Long Lance's carefully groomed presentation of a buckskinned and beaded warrior?

Eventually, such intimations demanded satisfaction. Investigators were dispatched to dig up the roots of Long Lance's family tree — one by the film company that was preparing to release a picture starring the new celebrity, another by a wealthy paramour, both of whom had heard gossip that distressed them. Unfortunately for Long Lance, he *did* have something to hide. In fact, one is hard pressed to know where to begin an enumeration of the things this astonishing man had to conceal.

The Truth about Long Lance

To begin with, his surname was not Long Lance; he had invented this fanciful alternative to his family name, Long. His given name was not Buffalo Child, but — Sylvester. And while his "autobiography" described him as the son of an illustrious Blackfoot chief who roamed the Great Plains, a more accurate job description for Sylvester's father, Joe, was school janitor in Winston, North Carolina.[4] Most damning of all in the eyes of the high society in which he had come to live, at least some of his childhood neighbors and townsmen testified to a belief that his familial bloodlines included African elements.

Once they had this kind of information, most of Long Lance's friends and admirers had little difficulty in determining his "true" racial identity. They were shocked and furious that they had consorted with such a person almost as an equal. "To think that we had him here in this house," the famous short story writer Irvin S. Cobb is said to have expostulated. "We're so ashamed! We entertained a nigger!"[5] The erstwhile paramour was so consumed with bitterness that she had been tricked into a romantic dalliance with a black man that she invented stories that Long had used makeup and chemicals to alter the color of his skin and the texture of his hair and so disguise his African features.

More recent commentators have troubled themselves little more than Sylvester Long's contemporaries did over the question of which racial pigeonhole they should stuff him into. Smith, for instance, subtitles his biography of Long "the true story of an impostor" and writes of how Long, starting from a young age, "*passed* as an Indian, capitalizing on his high cheek bones, straight, jet black hair, and coppery skin."[6] Fellow historian James A. Clifton asserts that Sylvester Long "assumed the identity of an Indian"; that he "became a sham to escape the socially imposed limits and handicaps of being a southern Black boy"; that "his was an adopted ethnic identity pure and simple."[7]

But is Sylvester Long really categorized and disposed of so easily? Certain aspects of his biography complicate the picture at least a little. For one thing, it appears that Long *was* Indian, at least by partial, biological descent — although not Blackfoot, as he had claimed. Biographer Smith describes evidence for Long's being white and Croatan Indian on his mother's side, white and Cherokee on his father's side.[8] He may or may not have possessed black ancestry.

In addition, certain aspects of Long Lance's lived experiences clearly overlapped with those of many unquestionably Indian people of his day. Like men from many tribes, including the famous Hunkpapa Lakota chief Sitting Bull, he traveled in his boyhood as an Indian performer in a Wild West show. Later, he applied to Carlisle Indian School in Pennsylvania, overcoming officials' doubts about his proper race largely by virtue of his demonstrated ability to speak at least some of the language proper to the tribe he claimed at the time (which was Cherokee). He shared the experiences at Carlisle with a vast company of other Indian young people, including the sons of some of the great Indian chiefs, such as Robert Geronimo. In one of Sylvester Long's actually truthful anecdotes he described himself as the good friend and training partner of the world-renowned Indian athlete Jim Thorpe, who was a Carlisle schoolmate.[9]

Some of Long's personal commitments, too, suggest what can be interpreted as strong feelings of connection to Native communities. As a journalist he spent some years traveling about Canada visiting Indian reserves, and his articles in a number of major magazines and newspapers exposed abuses and defended the rights of Indian peoples. In recognition of such efforts, the Blood Indians, a member tribe within the Blackfoot Confederacy, adopted him and invested him with a ceremonial name, one that had been carried before him by an honored warrior. It was the name he always used thereafter: Buffalo Child. Later, Long willed all his assets at his death to the St. Paul's School on the Blood Reserve, where the money provided scholarships for Indian students for many years.[10]

Long Lance and Contemporary Questions of Indian Identity

My intent here is neither to defend nor to vilify a particular historical person or to "prove" his racial identity one way or the other. Whether we choose to arrange the facts of Sylvester Long's life so that they show him as an Indian or as a racial impostor who took advantage of public credulity, his provocative story points to larger issues. How should we think about American Indian identity and its intersections with other racial identities? What assumptions should inform our debates and policies on and off the reservation? This book sets forth the many competing assumptions about Indian identity. Further, it asks why they matter — to Indians, to scholars, to Indian scholars, to individuals involved with Indian communities, and to those who merely observe those communities from afar.

The question of "real Indianness" has more force today than it did even in Long Lance's day — and for a discernible reason. Since the 1960s, a significant subset of the American population has become interested in their own American Indian ancestry. This subset comprises not only some individuals who, like Sylvester Long, were formerly identified as black but also many others formerly identified (by themselves and others) as white, Hispanic, or some other race or ethnicity. The subset embraces two general categories. Some are people whose recent genealogical researches have led them to discover one or more Indian ancestors of whom they were previously unaware. Others have always known that they possessed tribal ancestry but have suppressed or ignored this information to one degree or another. In both of these categories, individuals have often dissociated themselves from the ongoing life of tribal communities; others have moved in and out of them or around their margins.[11]

In recent decades, however, significant numbers of individuals of both descriptions have begun declaring their connections to Indian communities, pressing both tribes and the larger society to respond to them in some way. Many have revised their former racial classification on formal legal documents so as to reflect an Indian identity.[12] Some such individuals have banded together with others like themselves to petition the U.S. government to recognize them as Indian tribes. A few have succeeded.[13]

Such trends have drawn considerable — and often highly charged — attention from a variety of sources. An example is provided by Boston law student Jeff Benedict's recent book, *Without Reservation: The Making of America's Most Powerful Indian Tribe and Foxwoods, the World's Largest Casino*, which examines the legitimacy of the Mashantucket Pequot tribe of Connecticut. The Mashantuckets were formally acknowledged as an Indian tribe by an act of Congress in 1983, and they made use of their new status to establish a fabulously profitable (and tax-exempt) gambling operation on their reservation. The book expresses the author's conviction that the Mashantucket tribe is a band of white Americans who audaciously reinvented themselves as Indians when it became profitable to do so, trampling the rights of their neighbors in the process. Benedict argues that, by his genealogical reckoning, the tribal members share not a scrap of Pequot ancestry and should not be considered real Indians — certainly not for the purpose of enjoying the legal rights reserved for federally recognized tribes. He urges Congress to remember that what it has done it can undo: he hopes to see the Mashantucket's tribal status revoked, along with the attendant privileges. The book has enjoyed tremendous sales, especially in towns near the reservation, where anxiety runs high that the tribe may attempt to expand its current land base.[14]

Benedict's book reads like a novel and is written for a general audience. But debates about Indian identity are equally intense in scholarly contexts, where the material considerations at stake are far less obvious. Clifton, for instance, applies the same straightforward reasoning by which he stigmatized Sylvester Long's identity to many other individuals who assert an Indian identity in our own time. He argues in two recent books (provocatively titled *Being and Becoming Indian* and *The Invented Indian*) that modern America is beset by an epidemic of false claims to Indian identity. These claims emanate, he says, from "hundreds of thousands of . . . [people] with obscure antecedents who, in the past twenty years, have swapped their ethnic identities for Indian." Such individuals seek only "the stamp of federal approval on and specially privileged political economic support of their resuscitated or contrived identities."[15] In this understanding of racial identification, claims to Indian identity function as (to use Clifton's colorful wording) "a sturdy crowbar . . . to gain leverage in the play of interest-group politics."[16]

Ethnohistorian William Quinn, Jr., agrees with his colleague Clifton. He has penned a series of journal articles on what he calls the "Southeast Syndrome," an affliction that he asserts rages throughout a good portion of the American population. It causes its sufferers, some of whom actually possess a modest degree of Indian ancestry but who are (Quinn asserts) by any reasonable standard white, to begin claiming that they are Indians. Quinn argues that these individuals are illegitimately attempting to exchange their true racial identity for what they construe as a more romantic one — and one that may also be more economically profitable in our age of affirmative action.[17]

Nor is it only non-Indians who have become intensely invested in Indian identity claims. The actions of organizations administered by and for Indian people show that Indians, too, have begun taking the issue of racial identity with great seriousness. The Association of American Indian and Alaska Native Professors (AAIANP), the Native American Scholarship Fund, and the National Advisory Council on Indian Education have all recently registered official warnings about university students who dishonestly assert an Indian identity in hopes of gaining access to minority education funding.[18] Even tribes are rethinking the requirements they impose upon petitioners for tribal citizenship. A number of them have been sifting through their membership records and adjusting — sometimes repeatedly — the requirements for citizenship. Some have made their citizenship criteria more stringent, and some have made them less so. Some have closed their rolls altogether so that no new tribal citizens are accepted. Some have even disenrolled, or revoked the membership of, significant numbers of former tribal citizens, charging that they do not meet necessary criteria. The bitterness and anger associated with these decisions frequently reach alarming proportions.

What all these disputes about real Indianness demonstrate is that it is one thing to claim identity as an Indian person, and it is quite another for that claim to be received by others as legitimate. It is my goal in this book to explore the identity-making process among American Indians. This book examines the competing definitions of Indian identity — of which there turn out to be many. It also explores both the ways people move within the available definitions and negotiate (or fail to negotiate) identities to which others consent and the consequences of success or failure in establishing an identity. And it records how people experience and communicate about the issues raised by each definition of identity for themselves and their tribal communities.

America's Shifting Norms of Racialization

What does it profit us to seek a portrait of real Indianness? Why should anyone care about the complexities of racial identification among American Indians in particular? One reason is that Indian people themselves have defined this as an important issue that affects the well-being (perhaps even the survival) of their communities. No one can truly understand the life of those communities without understanding issues related to identity. Another reason is that understanding the controversies about Indian identity can help illuminate important changes in the way American society conceptualizes much broader issues related to race. It offers us a case study in America's dynamic interactions with what sociologists call "norms of racialization."

It is true that Chief Buffalo Child Long Lance belonged to another era in American history. But his existence gave notice of an America that was, even then, coming into being. In the complexity of his racial ancestry Sylvester Long was a living advertisement of a process that America has widely acknowledged only in the past two decades. Interracial unions and their progeny became a reality in the New World with the arrival of Columbus, and estimates suggest that the majority of American Indians — and a very large number of people currently classified as African Americans — possess multiracial ancestry, along with virtually all Latinos, Filipinos, and a large proportion of whites.[19]

Whereas the America of the 1930s knew with great certainty what to do with Sylvester Long once the possibility of African ancestry was revealed, the America of today has less conceptual self-assurance. Certainly strong norms regarding racial boundaries remain in place. But the old, unquestioned confidence that individuals can be classified into one, and only one, racial category is eroding. This new American racial consciousness began to show itself in the 1980s as grassroots organizations sprang up around the country, followed by two powerful lobbying groups, the Association for Multi-Ethnic Americans and Project RACE (Reclassify All Children Equally). All of these defend the rights and interests of people who claim more than one racial identity.

In the 1990s, state after state bowed to the efforts of such groups and changed the official categories of race by adding a "multiracial" option to government forms. Finally, the spearhead of the American demographic enterprise, the U.S. decennial census, also gave formal, governmental recognition to racial hybridity. In the year 2000, for the first time ever, the census allowed people to choose more than one race to describe themselves. By 2003, the new method for classifying race will be required for all federal forms.[20] As the editors of the excellent anthology *The Social Construction of Race in the United States* note, "All this attention to the meaning of race suggests that we are in the midst of a paradigm shift."[21]

The changes in racial categorization lead to issues of much urgency. American civil rights laws and related legislation were created under the assumption that all people can be assigned to a single racial category. The same is true of the formal and informal policies that govern recruitment, hiring, and admissions decisions at universities; the provision of certain educational enrichment opportunities to minority young people in public schools; the distribution of scholarships by private foundations; and the like. Now that a growing number of Americans are choosing, in a variety of contexts, to explicitly claim their multiracial heritage, how will social institutions and practices adjust?

Bureaucratic challenges loom. Federal agencies examine the census statistics to discover and address systematic discrimination against minorities in hiring, housing, banking, or voting practices, as well as racial segregation in public schools.[22] Given the new rules for enumerating racial groups, employers may be required to resurvey their workforce to show compliance with Title VII of the Civil Rights Act of 1964, which guarantees that citizens of all races have equal employment opportunities. Schools may be required to implement new methods for reporting the race of students to show compliance with Title VI of the same act. And — although a government publication predicts that changes will not be "substantial" — some voting districts may have to be redrawn to conform to the requirements of the Voting Rights Act of 1965 and recent Supreme Court decisions.[23]

All of these possibilities are destined to create extremely contentious societal debates. Americans whose lives are affected in material ways by the new norms of racialization will ask whether employers who were in compliance with Title VII under the old classification system can rightly be accused of discriminatory hiring if the new ways produce a different racial count. They will ask whether mixed-race students should properly be treated as minority students for the purpose of assessing school segregation. They will ask whether their city truly requires another majority black ward. They will ask, above all, for assurance that particular groups are not manipulating racial data in self-serving ways.

At bottom, all these demands center on a particular question: Now that people can formally classify themselves in more than one group — can proclaim themselves, for instance, as both black *and* white — who are the "real" minorities? Who are the members of those racial groups for whose protection civil rights laws, and other practices and regulations, were enacted? Who, in short, has a legitimate claim on specific racial identities?[24]

In March 2000, the Office of Management and Budget (OMB) announced a new policy that attempted to formulate a limited answer to the preceding question. It declared that for the purposes of civil rights monitoring and enforcement, any census respondent who says that he or she belongs to the white race and to a minority race must be considered a minority.[25] This decision, however, presently applies *only* to the federal government's handling of civil rights issues. Other institutions (including state and local governments) and other contexts are not bound by it.

More importantly, it is impossible to predict the degree to which Americans confronted with the real consequences of such a policy will deem the policy acceptable. It may well come under fire for overstating the number of minorities, and it may not be adopted for purposes other than civil rights monitoring.[26] Each of the many different strategies that have been proposed for identifying racial groups leads to different enumerations of racial minorities, and therefore to different distributions of opportunities and social resources. It seems likely that American courts and other institutional bodies will soon be asking how we should think about the growing number of individuals who have fought for the right to claim more than one racial identity.[27]

The Example of Indian Identity

American Indians provide a fabulously rich example for considering the implications of the increasingly ambiguous system of racial classification in the United States. They are a group about which the question of racial identification and classification — its legal, social, economic, political, biological, and other dimensions — has been carefully contemplated by a variety of institutions for hundreds of years. Today, as in the past, different definitions of identity are applied to this group in different contexts and with different and profound consequences.

Accordingly, the example of Indian identity provides an instructive study for anyone attempting to think through the issues and consequences associated with various ways of defining racial groups. Examining Indian identity may help us understand how racial identity is asserted and recognized in groups where the possibility of multiple affiliations — and multiple possible bases for affiliation — is explicitly and formally acknowledged. More importantly, it may allow us to assess the consequences of various choices for those most directly affected by them.

The value of the present study for social scientists, who have devoted a great deal of attention to processes of identity, is obvious.[28] But what does it do for Indian people and Indian communities? Older social scientific approaches to studying Indian (and other minority) communities have been strongly challenged in recent years, as those communities began to protest that they were tired of being perennial objects of scientific inquiries from which they seldom benefited. The academy has responded with new philosophies of research, especially "participatory research," which requires scholars to pursue work which grows out of the expressed concerns of communities and furthers their self-defined goals.[29] But I argue that if scholars hope to participate meaningfully in the discussion of such issues as the identity concerns of American Indian communities, an entirely new scholarly perspective is required. I attempt to formulate such an approach and to show how it may offer something to both Indian communities and to the academy — and indeed, to all those who are interested in learning about different ways of encountering the world.

An essential part of my analysis is to flesh out the emerging theoretical perspective that I call "Radical Indigenism" by applying it to issues of racial identification. Stated very simply, Radical Indigenism assumes that scholars can take philosophies of knowledge carried by indigenous peoples seriously. They can consider those philosophies and their assumptions, values, and goals not simply as interesting objects of study (claims that some people *believe* to be true) but as intellectual orientations that map out ways of discovering things about the world (claims that, to one degree or another, *reflect* or *engage* the true).

By applying Radical Indigenism to the study of American Indian identity, I intend to refine our understanding of the perspective itself. I use this perspective to consider how indigenous philosophies of identity and community allow us to reframe the questions we ask about Indianness and to guide our inquiries in different directions. I argue, moreover, that this approach can lead us to new fundamental understandings of what it means to do scholarship — about racial identity or anything else. And I argue that this new perspective opens up dramatically different ways for American Indian people to interact with the academy and to accomplish goals they define for their own communities.

Road Map for the Journey

The plan of this book is straightforward. I begin by exploring, in some detail, four definitions of American Indian identity that are used in various contemporary contexts. Each one assigns divergent meanings to the label "Indian," and each one sets a framework of rules within which the legitimacy of specific "identity claims" may be determined. In chapter 1, I examine legal definitions of Indianness, while in chapters 2, 3, and 4, I turn to biological, cultural, and personal definitions, respectively.

Significant questions for these chapters include: How does each definition establish and delimit Indian identity? How does each definition offer both opportunities for and constraints upon identification? Why do the "Indians" and "non-Indians" who emerge from these definitions sometimes look surprisingly unlike what most of us expect? What happens to those who can establish a legitimate identity within each definition and to those who cannot? Finally, what issues do each of these definitions raise for the individuals and communities who adopt them, or are the object of them? What benefits does each definition confer and what hazards does each entail, from the perspective of those most intimately affected by it?

These four chapters, in short, provide detailed portraits of the many ways that meanings about Indian identity are made. I have drawn these portraits by listening to the voices of people who identify themselves as Indian. I have found these voices in published sources — journal articles, autobiographies, works of fiction, and newspaper articles. And I have found them, as well, in unpublished sources — particularly the personal interviews I conducted with people who are part of one or another of the Indian communities with which I personally identify. Data from a published source is presented according to customary stylistic conventions. In most cases, data from my own interviews is presented with the speaker's given name and the first initial of the surname. Interviews with public officials are an exception to this rule; given that readers may recognize the respondents' full names in such cases, I have attached the full name to their comments. Readers who desire more information about each interview respondent may look up these names in the appendix, which includes two sections with short biographies of each speaker.

Chapter 5 takes up a different sort of question. It acknowledges the devastating consequences that many Indian communities suffer because of conflict over identity issues and asks if there is a way for them to move beyond those conflicts. In particular, it explores the question of whether scholars can properly have any part in that movement. I begin to sketch out the perspective of Radical Indigenism and to argue that it provides possibilities for addressing questions of identity — or anything else — in ways that open up new possibilities for the academy and for Indian communities.

In chapter 6, I apply the perspective of Radical Indigenism to a specific issue, exploring how it can help American Indian communities think about what new definitions of identity might look like and how they would function. And I consider what it might mean for the academy to accept such perspectives as "genuine scholarship" — a distinctively American Indian scholarship.

In the conclusion I examine what the issue of Indian identity, when viewed from the perspective of Radical Indigenism, can tell us about broader issues of race in America. And I offer some final thoughts on the implications of Radical Indigenism, as I have attempted to develop it, for the academy and for Indian people.

A number of the issues raised in connection with the matter of identity take us to some of the most contested terrain both in the academy and in Indian country — racial identity, "ethnic switching," "ethnic fraud," the relationship of Americans of remote Indian ancestry to Indian communities, the essential nature of the scholarly endeavor, and so on. If the ride through these issues sometimes turns bumpy and uncomfortable, perhaps readers will wish to think of their efforts to endure its rigors as a small tribute to the unfortunate Buffalo Child Long Lance, the chief who never was. His story, whatever one makes of it, cannot fail to compel. He was no doubt a devious character, yet I imagine him also as a soul genuinely tormented about his racial identity. His concern and confusion, and his efforts to resolve these, make him closer kin to many people today than the dramatic elements of his autobiography first suggest. If the America of his day was too steeped in racial stereotypes to see the complexity of American Indian identity and the complexity of the ways meaningful identities come into being, perhaps we modern observers can use his example more profitably.

I hope that my exploration of Long Lance's story and the many other stories in the subsequent chapters suggests to Indian communities new ways to respond to identity issues with the seriousness they merit yet without being destroyed by the increasingly acrimonious arguments that surround them. I hope that it also helps individuals who are considering reestablishing their own lapsed ties with Indian communities to formulate a clearer understanding of the costs and consequences, for themselves and for others. I hope that it suggests to the academy a new vision of scholarship that extends the horizon of intellectual possibility beyond what it has imagined before. And I hope that this book assists members of all racial groups to participate in more sophisticated ways in the unfolding process through which our nation is rethinking old ideas about racial identity and creating new norms of racialization. With these goals in mind, let us turn to consideration of the various definitions within which today's candidates for real Indianness must negotiate their identities.

CHAPTER ONE

Enrollees and Outalucks

Law

"I am not a real Indian," writes the acclaimed Choctaw/Cherokee novelist Louis Owens. "Not a real, essential Indian because I'm not enrolled. . . . Because growing up in different times I naively thought that Indian was something we were, not something we did or had or were required to prove on demand. Listening to my mother's stories about Oklahoma, about brutally hard lives and dreams that cut across the fabric of every experience, I thought that was Indian." A childhood friend, Owens notes, *was* an enrollee — invested with formal citizenship in his tribe — and was "somewhat smug about that fact, though it meant little to me then. Now I know better."[1]

Readers familiar with Owens's work — his popular novels that artfully and sensitively reflect familiarity with the cultural knowledge of both Cherokees and Choctaws, his intelligent contributions to American Indian literary criticism — may find themselves a bit taken aback at his disavowal of his Indian identity.[2] The definitions of identity within which Owens sardonically locates himself are sets of legal rules that distinguish Indians from non-Indians. They create another category of people, as well. This is a group to which one historian refers, half-jokingly, as the "outalucks," people of Indian ancestry who are nevertheless unable to negotiate their identity as Indians within the available legal definitions.[3]

These legal definitions are many. Some of them operate on an individual level, defining either who is a citizen in the eyes of a specific tribe, or who is an Indian person in the eyes of the federal government. Others operate at the collective level, defining what groups constitute an Indian tribe. The definitions Owens refers to are the rules that tribes use to determine citizenship, so I turn first to these.

Individual Legal Definitions: Contexts and Consequences

Many people imagine that the American government sets the legal criteria for tribal citizenship. However, tribes have the exclusive right to create their own legal definitions of identity and to do so in any way they choose.[4] The most common tribal requirement for determining citizenship concerns "blood quantum," or degree of Indian ancestry, a concept that receives fuller treatment in the next chapter. About two-thirds of all federally recognized tribes of the coterminous United States specify a minimum blood quantum in their legal citizenship criteria, with one-quarter blood degree being the most frequent minimum requirement.[5] (In the simplest instance, an individual has a one-quarter blood quantum if any one of her four grandparents is of exclusively Indian ancestry and the other three are non-Indian.) The remaining one-third of Indian tribes specify *no* minimum blood quantum. They often simply require that any new enrollee be a lineal (direct) descendant of another tribal member.

Tribal legal definitions may take into consideration other factors besides biological descent, however. Certain tribes require that citizens not only possess tribal ancestry but that this ancestry come from a *particular* parent. Thus, the Santa Clara Pueblo (New Mexico) requires paternal descent, and the Seneca tribe (New York) requires maternal descent. By contrast, the Tohono O'Odham (Arizona) consider residency definitive, automatically admitting to citizenship all children born to parents living on the reservation. The Swinomish (Washington) take careful stock of various indicators of community participation, ignoring blood quantum, while the Lower Sioux Indian Community (Minnesota) requires a vote of the tribal council. In still other tribes, community recognition or parental enrollment may also be a means to or a prerequisite for enrollment, and a few tribes only accept applicants whose parents submit the necessary paperwork within a limited time after their child's birth. Some tribes also require members to fulfill certain minimal duties, such as maintaining annual contact with the tribal council, for their citizenship to remain in good standing.[6]

Legal definitions of tribal membership regulate the rights to vote in tribal elections, to hold tribal office, and generally to participate in the political, and sometimes also the cultural, life of the tribe. One's ability to satisfy legal definitions of identification may also determine one's right to share in certain tribal revenues (such as income generated by tribally controlled businesses). Perhaps most significantly, it may determine the right to live on a reservation or to inherit land interests there.

The tribes' power to determine citizenship allows them to delimit the distribution of certain important resources, such as reservation land, tribal monies, and political privileges. But this is hardly the end of the story of legal definitions of identity. The federal government has many purposes for which it, too, must distinguish Indians from non-Indians, and it uses its own, separate legal definition for doing so. More precisely, it uses a whole array of legal definitions. Since the U.S. Constitution uses the word "Indian" in two places but defines it nowhere, Congress has made its own definitions on an ad hoc basis.[7] A 1978 congressional survey discovered no less than *thirty-three* separate definitions of Indians in use in different pieces of federal legislation.[8] These may or may not correspond with those any given tribe uses to determine its citizenship.

Most federal legal definitions of Indian identity specify a minimum blood quantum — frequently one-quarter but sometimes one-half — but others do not. Some require or accept tribal citizenship as a criterion of federal identification, and others do not. Some require reservation residency, or ownership of land held in trust by the government, and others do not. Other laws affecting Indians specify *no* definition of identity, such that the courts must determine to whom the laws apply.[9] Because of these wide variations in legal identity definitions and their frequent departure from the various tribal ones, many individuals who are recognized by their tribes as citizens are nevertheless considered non-Indian for some or all federal purposes. The converse can be true as well.[10]

There are a variety of contexts in which one or more federal legal definitions of identity become important. The matter of economic resource distribution — access to various social services, monetary awards, and opportunities — probably comes immediately to the minds of many readers. The legal situation of Indian people, and its attendant opportunities and responsibilities, are the result of historic negotiations between tribes and the federal government. In these, the government agreed to compensate tribes in various ways for the large amounts of land and other resources that the tribes had surrendered, often by force.[11] Benefits available to those who can satisfy federal definitions of Indian identity are administered through a variety of agencies, including the

Bureau of Indian Affairs, the Indian Health Service, the Department of Agriculture, the Office of Elementary and Secondary Education, and the Department of Labor, to name a few.[12]

Legal definitions also affect specific economic rights deriving from treaties or agreements that some (not all) tribes made with the federal government. These may include such rights as the use of particular geographic areas for hunting, harvesting, fishing, or trapping. Those legally defined as Indians are also sometimes exempted from certain requirements related to state licensure and state (but not federal) income and property taxation.[13]

Legal identity also determines the applicability of a number of protections available to individual Indians from the federal government. Notable among these are an Indian parent's rights under the Indian Child Welfare Act of 1978 (25 U.S.C. 1901 et seq.). Before the passage of this act, as many as 25 to 35 percent of Indian children in some states were being removed from their homes and placed in the care of non-Indians through such means as adoption and foster care. In one state (Wisconsin), the likelihood of such an eventuality was 1600 times greater for an Indian than a non-Indian child.[14] Many commentators have suggested that a number of Indian families lost their children less because they were genuinely unsuitable parents and more because they refused to abandon traditional cultural values in favor of those enforced by the essentially white, middle-class, social service bureaucracy. A 1974 Senate subcommittee hearing revealed another reason why social workers were sometimes overactive in removing Indian children: testimony suggested a "gray market" for Indian infants, fueled by white couples' inability to secure white infants for adoption and their lack of interest in black infants.[15] The Indian Child Welfare Act was passed to stem the wholesale transfer of children out of their families, tribes, and cultures. It requires that, where Indian children must be removed from their homes, efforts be made to place them with another family member, or at least with another Indian family, rather than a non-Indian one.

Just as importantly, federally specified legal definitions provide for certain religious freedoms. For one thing, they allow Indian people to seek protection from prosecution for the possession of specific ceremonial objects, otherwise restricted by law. For instance, many Indian people own eagle feathers, which they use in prayer and ceremonies, although non-Indians are not permitted to possess any part of this endangered species. Similarly, Indian members of the Native American Church ingest peyote, legally classified as a hallucinogen, as a sacramental substance in closely controlled worship settings. Non-Indians are forbidden to possess it. Since the passage of the Native American Graves Protection and Repatriation Act of 1990, federal legal definitions also allow Indian people to claim sacred ceremonial objects, as well as to receive and rebury the remains of their ancestral dead, if these are being held in federally funded museums for display or study (as they very frequently are).

Federal legal definitions of Indian identity can even affect some individuals' ability to pursue their livelihood. A particularly controversial protection that has recently become available to those legally defined as Indians revolves around the Indian Arts and Crafts Act of 1990. Arguments for this legislation started from the recognition that many buyers consider artwork more desirable and valuable if it is created by an Indian person and that a great deal of art was therefore being falsely labeled as Indian-made. The same arguments concluded that such misrepresentations were seriously reducing the revenues of artists who were, in fact, Indian.[16] The cartoon in figure 1.1 satirizes the attempt to pass off cheaply manufactured, foreign goods as Indian-madeThe Arts and Crafts Act forbids any artist who is not a citizen of a federally recognized or state-recognized tribe to market work as "Indian produced." Penalties for violation of the act include large fines and imprisonment. Certain galleries and organizations have also voluntarily chosen to restrict exhibitions and art commissions to people who can demonstrate that they are Indians by reference to formal, legal criteria.[17]

Finally, the invocation of legal definitions has allowed Indian people, collectively, to claim certain privileges that other minorities do not enjoy. One such privilege is the right to benefit from "Indian preference" in federal employment. More specifically, the Bureau of Indian Affairs and the Indian Health Service are permitted a bias in favor of Indian applicants. This policy has helped to ensure a significant presence of Indian employees in those government bodies that are primarily responsible for administering tribal programs.

The courts have ruled that Indian preference does not imply racial discrimination because "Indian" refers, in this context, to a political rather than to a racial status. That is, it refers to rights and obligations vis-à-vis the United States that an individual possesses not by virtue of his specific biological characteristics but by virtue of his meeting a particular set of legal criteria.[18] (In the case of Indian preference, these criteria include being enrolled in a federally recognized tribe, showing descent from an individual who lived on a reservation in 1934, or demonstrating a blood quantum of at least one-half.)[19]

FIGURE 1.1. The Bering Strait. Before the passage of the Indian Arts and Crafts Act of 1990, foreign-produced goods were often marked as "Indian-made." (Source: Drawn by Jeff Kerr, a Texas physician whose cartoon series "The Promised Land" is published weekly in the newspaper *Indian Country Today*. Printed in *Indian Country Today*.)

Negotiating Individual Legal Identities

All the legal rights and protections sketched earlier offer their significant advantages only to those who can successfully claim Indianness within particular definitions of identity. However, many Indian people cannot meet the definitions of identity imposed by the federal government or even by their own tribes. (As noted before, there is no guarantee that those definitions correspond.) By what process is the legitimacy of claims to Indian identity asserted and evaluated within the definitions of law? Who is able to negotiate a legal identity and who is not? How is it that people with seemingly identical characteristics can meet with very different outcomes within legal definitions? The answers to such questions are frequently astonishing.

Let us begin with a consideration of tribal citizenship requirements in relation to the most common criterion, blood quantum. This apparently straightforward measure of Indianness runs aground quite quickly when it comes to the common phenomenon of intertribal families. Consider, for instance, the hypothetical case of a child possessing one-half Indian ancestry and one-half white ancestry, meaning that she has one parent who is exclusively white and one parent who is exclusively Indian. Her identity claim will likely get a green light from both the federal government and her tribe — so long as her Indian ancestry comes from a single tribe.

But compare her potential fortunes with those of a child whose half-Indian heritage derives from several different tribes. Let us say that this second child, in addition to her one-half white ancestry, is also one-eighth Lower Brule Sioux, one-eighth Cheyenne-Arapho, one-eighth Blackfoot, and one-eighth Turtle Mountain Chippewa. She is, like the first child, one-half Indian. But each tribe of her ancestry requires its citizens to document a one-quarter blood degree *from that tribe only*. From the perspective of each of her tribes, therefore, this child is ineligible for citizenship; she is simply non-Indian.

Indeed, even children of exclusively Indian ancestry can find themselves denied citizenship due to similar circumstances. The repeated intertribal marriages implied by the foregoing example of a child with fractionated blood quantum are not even necessary. A mother with exclusively Indian ancestry in one tribe and a father with exclusively Indian ancestry in another tribe can produce legally non-Indian children when the two tribes reckon descent differently. In such cases, legal criteria can tear apart families by pushing certain members off the reservation while allowing others to stay.

For instance, in 1997, an *Indian Country Today* article reported the following family scenario: "Mr. Montoya has lived at Santa Clara Pueblo, his mother's home, his whole life. He raised his four children at the pueblo and now has grandchildren there."[20] But Mr. Montoya cannot be enrolled at Santa Clara because, since 1939, the pueblo has operated by a tribal law that allows for enrollment only on the basis of paternal descent — and his father was not from Santa Clara but from the nearby Isleta Pueblo. Montoya has inherited rights to his mother's property in Santa Clara, but his ability to exercise those rights remains uncertain.[21]

Families in the Montoyas' situation sometimes cannot tolerate the tenuousness of their position and choose to abandon the community, their relatives, and their intimate participation in the culture in which they were born and raised. And in some cases family dissolution by legal definition has occurred by force; that is, mixed-race children have been actively expelled from the reservation, even though the children had been living there under the care of a relative enrolled in the tribe.

Such an event occurred on the Onondaga reservation in the recent past. The Onondaga — by a law that is the reverse of the Santa Clara Pueblo law — are matrilineal. They permit tribal citizenship only to children who can trace Onondaga ancestry through their mothers. In 1974, the tribal council ordered all noncitizens to leave the reservation or face ejection. This order included even noncitizen spouses (who were mostly women) and the children born to Onondaga men by such women. The

Onondaga men could stay, of course — but only if they chose to live apart from their wives and mixed-race children. The national journal of Native news and issues, *Akwesasne Notes,* reported the rationale behind the expulsion: Over a period of years, a large number of non-Indians had moved onto Onondaga land, and the council feared that the federal government might consequently dissolve the reservation.[22] Most individuals affected by the ruling left peaceably; others had to be forcibly removed. One family burned down its home before leaving.[23]

Some people of Indian ancestry fall into still another legal identity snare. Although a few tribes have no written records of citizenship even today — some of the Pueblos, for instance, depend upon oral traditions — the majority of tribes maintain written documents, usually called "tribal rolls."[24] Present-day applications for citizenship are usually evaluated with reference to certain "base rolls," or written records of tribal membership in a specific year.[25] Individuals seeking tribal identification as Indian must typically establish that one or more of their ancestors appears on one of these rolls.

Unfortunately, many people who clearly conform to any other definition of Indian identity do not have ancestors listed on the base rolls — and for a multitude of reasons. Historians agree that the process by which many tribal rolls were initially compiled was almost unbelievably complicated. The compilation of some tribal rolls — including the Dawes Rolls (1899–1906), from which all of today's enrolled Oklahoma Cherokees (and a number of other tribes) must show descent — took so long that a significant number of registrants died before the paperwork was completed. This meant that their descendants would be forever barred from tribal citizenship. Even when an applicant did manage to live long enough to complete the entire process of enrollment, she frequently found herself denied. Attorneys retained by the tribes (which were concerned that the commission might pack their rolls with unqualified applicants) made objection to nearly every application, seeking to limit enrollments as much as possible.[26] Dawes commissioners enrolled only a small fraction of all those who applied, and they readily agreed that they had denied many people of indubitable tribal ancestry.[27]

Other Indian people actively resisted registration on the Dawes Rolls, either individually or collectively. For instance, among Oklahoma Creeks, Cherokees, Chickasaws, and Choctaws conservative traditionalists or "irreconcilables" fought a hard fight against registration with the Dawes Commission. The reason was that the Dawes Roll was the first step in what President Theodore Roosevelt had rapturously declared (in his first annual address to Congress in 1901) "a mighty, pulverizing engine to break up the tribal mass."[28] The effort, in a nutshell, was to destroy indigenous cultures by destroying their foundation — their collective ownership of land — and then to integrate the Indians thus "liberated" into the dominant American culture. Through a process of land allotment, Indians were to be remade into individual, private owners of small farms who would quickly become independent of government attention and expenditures.

Probably no one could have foreseen all of the catastrophic results that would befall tribes with the destruction of the old, traditional system of land tenure. The irreconcilables, however, had at least intuited the outlines of the coming disaster. In the words of historian Angie Debo, they "clung to the old order with the stubbornness of despair."[29] In many tribes opposition to land allotment ran high. In some, leaders arose who used all their resources, from cunning to force, to discourage their fellows' enrollment and subsequent allotment.[30]

Government patience with conservative obduracy soon wore thin, and the more influential and uncooperative leaders and their families were hunted out and forcibly enrolled. Cherokee leader Redbird Smith consented to his own enrollment only after he was finally jailed for his refusal. Others who shared his anti-enrollment sentiments managed to elude capture altogether and so their names were never entered onto the census document.

The stories of the irreconcilables are narratives of determined and principled resistance to a monumental step toward Indians' forced acculturation to the dominant American culture. Yet ironically the descendants of those traditionalists find themselves worse off, in the modern, legal context, for their forebears' success in the fight to maintain cultural integrity. By the criteria their tribes have established, they can never become enrolled citizens.[31] This fact frequently affects, in turn, their ability to satisfy federal definitions. Like Louis Owens, whose remarks opened this chapter, according to many or most legal definitions, they are not "real Indians." They are simply "outaluck."[32]

Far more contemporary events can also impinge upon an individual's ability to establish an Indian identity. Legal identities, being strictly documentary, are open to manipulation by corrupt interests. Sometimes those interests work from within the tribes themselves. In figure 1.2, a cartoonist imagines a humorous scenario of "downsizing" carried out at the behest of an economy-minded tribal government. But accusations of illegal revocation of citizenship do occur in real life. For instance, a 1994 by Richard MacPhie

Encouraged by the successful management of the casino by non-Indians, the tribal council lets a corporate entity run their administration...

NEXT!

Due to a shaky fiscal forecast for the next two quarters, we are 'downsizing' the tribe.... Your name came up in a random draw, kinda like 'Bingo'

But, I was in here last wee— —BOOP— What was that? Your tribal ID number has been erased from the data base.

But...but...I own land! Yes, we know, lot 471. Its being clear-cut as we speak.

I've lived here my whole life. I work here, my kids go to school here...what am I gonna do?!

D.Do you have any advice for me? Yes, be off the reservation by sundown... NEXT!

FIGURE 1.2. Tribal "downsizing." Adjustments to tribal enrollment requirements generate suspicion and criticism. (Source: Drawn by Richard MacPhie,
a Minnesota Chippewa, who publishes his cartoons in *Indian Country Today*
and in the *Minneapolis Star Tribune*. Printed in *Indian Country Today*.)

general election in the Keeweenaw Bay Indian Community in Michigan
produced a tie vote for tribal judge — an office for which the son of
Chairman Fred Dakota was running. It also replaced several council
members who had supported the chairman, although Dakota himself
remained in power. Subsequently, approximately two hundred tribal citizens (a substantial percentage of the electorate) were disenrolled. The
majority of these were reported to be supporters of Fight for Justice
(FFJ), a tribal faction that opposed the chairman. The original election
was then nullified. A second election brought significantly revised vote
counts, reinstating the original council members and confirming
Dakota's son as chief judge.

A portion of the disenfranchised individuals were later re-enrolled as
adopted citizens. As such, however, they were forever barred from voting or holding political office in the tribe. As the chairman's critics
pointed out, "Once [the chairman] . . . manipulates the 'adoption'
process in his favor, he will be politically situated to banish his opponents
permanently, effectively foreclosing even the possibility of political
change."[33] In 1999, the Bureau of Indian Affairs determined that the dis-
enrollments and denial of voting rights were violations of the Indian
Civil Rights Act. By this time, Mr. Dakota had already been convicted on
various federal charges.[34]

All of the foregoing demonstrate that tribal legal definitions of identity can spawn any number of peculiarities of exclusion. Conversely, a number of people who may have *no* ancestral connections to tribes have been, or are, defined as Indian in the legal sense alone. In some places and times, non-Indian spouses were allowed to become citizens of Indian nations. Even in instances where an adopted white spouse was subsequently widowed, remarried, and had children by a non-Indian, the children (who had no tribal ancestry at all) were sometimes recognized as tribal citizens.[35] And following the Civil War, certain African-American slaves formerly owned by members of Oklahoma tribes were made, by due legal process, into tribal citizens officially called "freedmen." Their new status did not depend upon their possessing any Indian ancestry.[36] Finally, where census registration implied eligibility for distribution of tribal lands, as it did in Oklahoma, it was not uncommon for individuals with no Indian ancestry, but with active homesteading ambitions and perhaps an unscrupulous lawyer in tow, to seek a place on the rolls through dishonest means. Thousands of them succeeded,[37] thus earning for themselves the name "five-dollar Indians," presumably referring to the amount required to bribe the census enumerator.

This discussion would not be complete without the acknowledgment that it is not only non-Indian people who have made their way onto the tribal census lists and thus legally "become" Indian; *nonexistent* people sometimes did so, as well. An amusing example comes from the 1885 census of the Sicangu Lakota (South Dakota). As historian Thomas Biolsi records, census takers at the Rosebud Agency "recorded some remarkable English translations of Lakota names." Nestled in among the common and dignified appellations — Black Elk, Walking Bull, Dull Knife — are a more colorful class of personal names: Bad Cunt, Dirty Prick, Shit Head.

"What happened," Biolsi notes, "is not difficult to unravel: Lakota people were filing past the census enumerator, and then getting back in line — or lending their babies to people in line — to be enumerated a second time using fictitious and rather imaginative names."[38] Since this particular census was taken for the purpose of distributing rations, the ploy had the very practical goal of enhancing survival — and the Lakota apparently felt that even such serious work need not be undertaken without humor.

At least some of the historic oddities of the Indian census rolls have continued to create more of the same — forever. That is, while the nonexistent Indians of Rosebud clearly could not have produced children, the many living, breathing "five-dollar Indians" who bought their way onto the Oklahoma census rolls certainly could. It is impossible to estimate the number of modern-day descendants of those non-Indian "Indians," but it could be quite large. Probably at least some descendants have maintained tribal enrollment and its privileges, even while many people of actual, Indian descent were — and are — unable to acquire the same.

Collective Legal Definitions: Contexts and Consequences

We have spoken so far as if identity definitions are an issue of concern only to individuals. They are, however, also a concern to entire groups. Both federal and state governments formally classify certain groups as "recognized" or "acknowledged" Indian tribes and invest them with specific rights and responsibilities not shared by other groups.[39] While the consequences of state recognition of a tribe are highly variable, the consequences of federal acknowledgment are always profound.[40] By acknowledging a group of claimants as an Indian tribe, the federal government extends "government-to-government" relations to it, legally constituting that group as a sovereign power and as a "domestic dependent nation."[41] These are extremely powerful statuses. In fact, the legal case of *Native American Church v. Navajo Tribal Council* (1959) made it clear that tribes enjoy a governmental status higher than that of states. It is argued that they retain all national powers that they have not explicitly been required to surrender by the United States.[42]

Federal acknowledgment is also important because it extends government "trust responsibility" to the tribe. The precise interpretation of this concept has changed significantly over time, and continues to change, but one current definition describes trust responsibility as "the responsibility to act in the best interests of Indians in managing Indian-owned land and other resources."[43] In present practice, the extension of trust responsibility usually implies, among other things, that the group's members become individually eligible for certain U.S. government services and programs and the tribe collectively becomes eligible for others. In some cases, acknowledgment creates a government obligation to provide land for a reservation or allows the tribe to seek compensation for land judged as having been improperly taken from it. Federally acknowledged tribes have the right to establish political and legal institutions, and they are exempt from various kinds of taxation and legislation (including certain environmental protection laws) on the reservation. In addition, they can operate businesses that others cannot (such as gambling operations).[44]

Federal acknowledgment of tribes helps prevent non-Indian groups from exploiting the just-named advantages of tribal status. This is an effort in which certain claimants have shown themselves to be quite ambitious, with consequences that range from the appalling to the bizarre. For instance, the subject of a recent Senate subcommittee hearing was a company claiming the title of the Sovereign Cherokee Nation Tejas and using a seal easily mistaken for that of the federally acknowledged Cherokee Nation (Oklahoma). The subcommittee alleged that the company had misrepresented itself as an Indian tribe for the purpose of perpetrating a variety of massive business frauds.

The company's head, "Chief Bear Who Walks Softly" (also known as William M. Fry, Jr.), testified that the Sovereign Cherokee Nation Tejas had been created by an act of God. The subcommittee offered the somewhat humbler interpretation that it was more likely the product of one Colonel Herbert M. Williams, a retired U.S. Air Force officer. He had birthed the idea of creating an (as he put it) "offshore tax haven" on a sandbar in the middle of the Rio Grande, to which he could lure a variety of businesses. By the time of the "tribe's" encounter with the Senate subcommittee, it had contracted to underwrite a number of corporate insurance policies, though its assets were inadequate to guarantee them.

Some of these assets were dubious in an ordinary sort of way. These included a large quantity of treasury bills, which according to the subcommittee, one of the group's officials had "issued" himself with nothing more than a typewriter and some attractive bond paper. Other assets were a little more unusual, including a gold mine, a collection of cassette tapes, and a Marlon Brando "life mask" for which the group's financial statements claimed a $1.5 million value.

When questioned by the Senate subcommittee, this "Cherokee" nation's representative indicated that the company had lost or misplaced its assets (including, sadly, the intriguing mask). The gold mine (being harder to misplace) was investigated and was judged difficult to distinguish from a parking lot. The subcommittee expressed concern that the Sovereign Cherokee Nation Tejas had the potential to cause massive business failure and large-scale economic disruptions because some of America's largest corporations, such as Dow Chemical, had had business dealings with it.[45]

This case clearly illustrates the need for legal definitions to protect recognized tribes, the federal government, and ordinary citizens from illegitimate attempts to procure the rights and resources of Indian tribes. But what happens to groups of people who believe themselves to be a tribe but cannot establish the claim to the satisfaction of the federal government? A report by the American Indian Policy Review Commission stated: "The results of nonrecognition on Indian communities and individuals have been devastating. . . . [They include] the continued erosion of tribal lands, or the complete loss thereof; the deterioration of cohesive, effective tribal governments and social organization; and the elimination of special Federal services, through the continued denial of such services which Indian communities in general appear to need desperately."[46]

In addition, lack of federal acknowledgment has been shown to affect a group's ability to preserve or maintain its culture. It means that groups do not have access, for instance, to monies that can allow recognized tribes to establish language or cultural programs, museums, and the like. Similarly, it can prevent Indian people who have been dispersed from their traditional lands from regaining a land base where they can reestablish community bonds. It can prevent others from resurrecting, or even maintaining, traditional practices. For instance, when the Samish tribe (Washington) was declared formally "extinct" by the federal government, its remaining citizens (who, in the face of the official pronouncement, declared themselves very much alive) lost access, formerly guaranteed by treaty, to their ancestral fishing grounds. These rights were given over to the nearby Tulalip tribes. Samish tribal chairwoman Margaret Green subsequently reported that the Tulalips denied her tribe even the small privilege of taking ten salmon from the fishing grounds as the indispensable component of its traditional potlatch ceremony, which is central to its religious practice.[47]

Negotiating Collective Legal Identities

As at the individual level, there are many difficulties that a group faces in establishing a legitimate definition of itself as an Indian tribe. The application of the federal criteria for recognizing a group of claimants as a tribe is frequently described in scholarly literature with words such as "woefully inconsistent," "serendipitous," and "an accident of history."[48] Until quite recently, the federal government did not even have a formally or universally applied criterion for distinguishing between recognized and unrecognized tribes. It simply issued lists, from time to time, of tribes that it defined as such, but the list could change on the basis of congressional or executive decision. On occasion, the list changed without notice. Indian people sometimes woke up one morning to discover that their tribe had mysteriously been dropped for reasons unclear to them, and that they and their fellow tribesmembers had suddenly and unceremoniously become non-Indians, at least for a range of legal purposes.[49] In general, tribal groups that were large, showed serious resistance to white settlement, signed treaties with the U.S. government, or were otherwise hard to ignore have historically been treated as tribes by the federal government. They now enjoy unquestioned recognition status. They have not been required to formally demonstrate the legitimacy of their collective identity. By contrast, smaller, less aggressive groups, groups that moved around a great deal, and many groups that were colonized early (including many in the eastern United States) have been much easier to neglect. They have frequently remained unrecognized into modern times.

Since the mid-1970s, there has been a mechanism by which nonrecognized tribal groups may create or establish a legal definition of themselves as an Indian tribe. Called the Federal Acknowledgment Process (FAP), it requires that petitioners satisfy the seven criteria set out in part 83 of title 25 of the Code of Federal Regulations (25 CFR 83). These criteria occupy twenty single-spaced pages and are accompanied by a set of "official guidelines" consisting of another eighty pages.[50] They can be briefly summarized as requiring "that a single Indian group has existed since its first sustained contact with European cultures on a continuous basis to the present; that its members live in a distinct, autonomous community perceived by others as Indian; that it has maintained some sort of authority with a governing system by which its members abide; that all its members can be traced genealogically to an historic tribe; and that it can provide evidence to substantiate all of this."[51]

Though these criteria sound relatively straightforward and sensible, not all petitioners — even those who seem to have a reasonable claim on a tribal identity — can satisfy them. And some tribal groups lack formal acknowledgment because they decline to seek it. In an interview, George Roth, a cultural anthropologist for the Branch of Acknowledgment and Research (BAR), described to me his agency's extensive efforts to contact tribal groups that might be eligible to petition for acknowledgment: "We [have] talked to some groups that weren't really sure they *wanted* recognition. . . . Not everyone wants to get involved with the federal government."

One thing that can discourage some petitioners is that the process of filing an application is expensive, potentially requiring the hiring of genealogists, historians, anthropologists, and other experts. It is also lengthy; ten years or more can elapse between the time a petitioner submits a letter of intent to petition and a decision.[52] And those tribal groups who do file may confront difficulties in meeting the FAP criteria for historical reasons beyond their control. For instance, the BAR acknowledges that it will deny tribal recognition to groups on the basis of characteristics or conditions that the federal government itself deliberately created. The requirement that a group has maintained a continuous community is a case in point. Tribes have been refused recognition on this ground, even when the reason for their dispersion clearly lies not with members' insufficient desire to live together in a community but with the federal government's failure to follow through on explicit promises to take land into trust for the tribe. As the BAR states in its instructions to petitioning groups, for the purpose of determining the continuous existence of a tribal community, it makes no distinction between "people who left [the community] voluntarily and those who were forced to leave."[53]

Evaluating Legal Definitions

Having considered the many ways that legal definitions — tribal and federal, individual and collective — may either create or constrain opportunities to make meaningful claims to identity, we can now examine an additional set of issues. How do people who must move within legal definitions on a daily basis respond to them? What larger concerns do these definitions raise for tribal communities? What are the benefits and hazards of legal definitions from the perspective of those whom they affect? To find answers to these questions, I draw upon the words of Indian people themselves.

Indian people are often heard to complain that they constitute the only racial group that is required to produce documentation of their identity — a standard that many or most members of other racial groups need not (or could not) meet. A friend of mine sometimes announces, with a broad wink, that besides being an enrolled Ojibwe, he is also "part white, but I don't have the papers to prove it." The significant difference between Indians and other racial minorities, of course, is that legally defined Indian people enjoy rights and privileges which other racial groups do not. Melvin B., honorary chief of the Creek Nation (Oklahoma), explains the importance of documentation:

The story about that is: A young man [was] fishing one day and the game warden caught him, and said, "Hey, you're not allowed to do that. . . . Where's your license?" So he [the young man] said, "I'm an Indian." So he [the warden] said, "Where's your card?" Well, he didn't *have* a card, but he *was* an Indian. He [the warden] said, "Well, prove that you're an Indian and you can go ahead and fish." So, that is one of the many reasons why they issued Indian cards.

Billy S., an Eastern Delaware and Peoria tribal member, comments on a topic where legal definitions can become tremendously salient: the weighty issue of Indian land claims against the U.S. government:

For example, the Lakotas [or Sioux tribe] have a clear claim to the Black Hills [tribal land that the U.S. government has conceded was illegally taken from the tribe in the nineteenth century]. . . . I think if we pull away from some sort of *structure* that, in fact, clarifies who *is* Native and who isn't, we're going to lose claim to some of these things that I hope, someday, are going to be resolved.

My interview respondents mentioned many of the other rights they enjoy in relation to tribal and federal governments, many of which I have discussed earlier. But some also pointed out more subtle implications of legal identification. For instance, Julie M., a citizen and employee of the United Keetoowah Band of Cherokee Indians (Oklahoma), observed that legal documentation can provide important psychological validation. A full blood who has lived in rural Cherokee communities all her life, Julie is nevertheless sensitive to the profound meaning of legal documentation for those who meet no other criterion of identity:

There are a lot of people that *I* see . . . who didn't grow up around Cherokee [culture], but *know* they're Cherokee or *learned* they're Cherokee. [And they] *have* something. . . . A lot of people who are what I call marginal Cherokees in terms of [having] that [traditional] culture . . . really are in pain from not having that in their lives. It's kind of like a search that lasts all your life. . . . And for *those* people . . . having that tribal membership, having *some* kind of a connection, even if it's by paper, to the tribe, is *tremendously* significant.

Indeed, the remarks of a correspondent to an Oklahoma tribal newspaper exemplify the foregoing observation perfectly. The author writes that although she is of mixed ancestry and was raised away from the tribe, her grandmother pressed her to become tribally enrolled:

Everybody talks of all you can get with an Indian card. Well I didn't want to take anything, but I wanted to make my Grandmother happy. I was totally unprepared for the gift I received with the arrival of my card. I felt such a [sense] of homecoming and belonging; it was incredible. I actually stood at my mailbox crying with joy. It was so much more than a piece of paper; it was my heritage. I could actually feel it in my very soul.[54]

Legal definitions provide tangible, external proof of a personal racial identification. And once established, legal definitions also have the virtue of being easily verifiable: to determine whether a particular person satisfies a legal definition, a shuffling of papers is generally sufficient. As chief of the Cherokee Nation (Oklahoma), Chad Smith, said in an interview, legal definitions of identity are a "safe harbor of being Indian. . . . There's really not a lot of question about it. . . . If you're a tribal citizen, you're an Indian."

Legal definitions in many cases allow for a bureaucratic, impersonal — and therefore relatively efficient — processing of claims. Legal definition reduces the possibility of arguments about tribal status between individuals formally identified as Indian and the various agencies with which they must deal — both tribal and federal. They may even settle squabbles at a more personal level. Many Indians are suspicious or dismissive of those who cannot show documentary evidence that they satisfy legal definitions of identity. As Cornelia S., a Cherokee tribal member, says:

I think that a person who says that they're Indian that does not have their CDIB [Certificate of Degree of Indian Blood] card — they don't know if they're Indian or not, so . . . they shouldn't be saying that they're Indian. And it could be true [that they are Indian. . . . But] I think that if it's not that important to him to go and see about getting his Indian card, his CDIB card, then to him it's really not that important for him to be an Indian, so he doesn't need to be telling people that he is an Indian.[55]

Bill T., a Wichita and Seneca minister, has seen legal documentation cut arguments about identity short:

It [legal documentation] does give proof. . . . It proves to me that that person has a degree of Indian blood. . . . [That claim] is accepted and recognized by the government, so it must be true. . . . I have seen people challenged [by other

Indian people]: "Show me your CDIB card." And so the person did show it to prove that they were [Indian]. . . . Well, then they were accepted. So I think it does help in being accepted into the Native community.

A Yuchi elder, Mose C., concurs: "If a person has a Certificate of Degree of Indian Blood from the BIA [Bureau of Indian Affairs], that person is okay."

Though many Indian people approve of and have confidence in legal definitions of identity, others have little regard for them. One young correspondent to *Indian Country Today* newspaper writes that "I have a tribal ID. This is similar to a license to drive. Only very useless. This is a license to be Indian."[56] Interview respondent Billy S. is less willing to dismiss the significance of legal documentation, but he points out its limitations:

I think one of our elders, my adopted grandmother, put it real well. [She] said, "Unless a person knows their language, and they know the songs and they know their *culture*, they can have all the pieces of paper in the world and still not be Native American. Because it [identity] is not just a legal document; it's a way of *life*, it's a way of *thinking*, a way of *living*, a way of worship that you can't instill on someone with a notarized legal document." And I feel that too many times we get into looking at things from a legalistic standpoint and really *lose* the idea of what it is to be Native.

Other Indian people feel that the issuing of CDIBs is an intrusion by the federal government into tribal affairs. One complaint is that such legal documentation creates a class of people who enjoy, and even exploit, formal connection to a tribe but have no other relationships to it. For instance, though she herself is a tribal citizen with a CDIB card, Cherokee and Choctaw great-grandmother Joyce J. disparages legal mechanisms for identification: "I don't think it [legal documentation] is important to the Indian. I think it's important to the white person. Because I think that a person that's not Indian at heart thinks that if they've got a white card [CDIB] and a tribal dress, they can go out and play Indian. And that, to them, is being Indian."

Some Indians are less troubled by issues of potential exploitation than they are by the concern that some legal definitions facilitate the attenuation of tribal blood quanta. For example, Martha S., a full-blood elder of the Yuchi tribe (Oklahoma), opposes a proposed revision of tribal legal definitions, which she sees as creating an artificial group: "I don't think they [the Yuchi tribe] should lower [the blood quantum requirement to one quarter degree]. . . . Even that would be wrong, [to include] the quarter bloods. . . . They'll be mixed up with different tribes and with the non-Indians. That one-quarter blood quantum — it's not going to mean a thing."

In other tribes, Martha's concern can be greatly magnified. Indeed, by the enrollment criteria of approximately one-third of all tribes in the lower forty-eight states, there is *no* theoretical or practical limit to the diminution of a potential citizen's genetic connection to the tribe.[57] This means, for instance, that a person who can document only that her ancestor ten generations earlier, or an even more distant relative, appeared on a tribal roll can be legally recognized as a citizen of any of the numerous tribes that do not have a blood quantum requirement.

For example, in an interview BAR branch chief R. Lee Fleming told a story from the days when he worked as registrar for his own tribe, the Cherokee Nation: "All of the Five Eastern Tribes [of Oklahoma] have people on the original Dawes Rolls [of the early twentieth century] with blood degrees as low as 1/256. I remember the day when the fourteen-year-old girl came in [to the tribal registration office] with her parents. She was descended from one of those people who was 1/256. Her blood degree was 1/2048 [Cherokee]. And I enrolled her."[58]

Fleming accepts this circumstance with equanimity. As he explains, "That enrollment was based on the Cherokee [tribal] constitution's provision, which is based on that person's legal-historical relationship to the tribe, and on the fact that she is a descendant of ancestors who also maintained that legal-historical relationship. Nothing else matters. What matters is that *relationship.*"

When asked his opinion about why the modern-day Cherokee tribal constitution, ratified by voters in 1975, chose to define citizenship in the way he describes, rather than by reference to a blood quantum standard, Fleming answered:

The original Cherokee constitution, passed in 1827, did not have a blood quantum requirement. And our second [constitution], the Constitution of 1839, didn't have one, either. The drafters of our current, third, constitution, put a lot of thought into it. When they were done, they were satisfied that they had created a standard that was well grounded in our tribe's law, our tribe's culture, and our tribe's history. People might find this standard surprising if they don't understand the whole context of how it was created, and our tribe's history. But our reasons for crafting it were sound reasons, reasons that come from who we are as a people.

While Fleming's logic is coherent, not everyone can accept it. Cornelia S. remains firm in her conviction that people should have a blood quantum of at least one-quarter or one-half in order to be considered Indians:

if an individual has a lower blood quantum, they "can still say [they] are Indian, but you know, it's not really like it would be . . . if [they're] a full blood or half or even a quarter. . . . If it [blood quantum] is underneath a quarter, it's kind of like, you know, it's kind of like [the heritage] is more to the *other* side than the Indian side."

Others who object to legal standards of identity ignore the ways that these may affect tribal blood quanta. Instead, they complain that legal mechanisms for establishing connections to tribal communities are culturally foreign. Even those who have been granted the privileges of Indian identity by both federal and tribal governments may protest that legal definitions are in no way faithful to tribal history and traditions. Melvin B. states his firm conviction: "You don't have to have a [CDIB] card to be an Indian. I think it's a wonderful thing that they have those cards. But those rules and regulations of an Indian card wasn't made by the Indian. They were made by the federal government." Anishnabe and Cree grandmother Kathleen W. is more vehement in her assessment. She feels "outraged by the fact that [a legal document] has become a criteria for identifying who's Native and who isn't. Because I *am* very much aware that that was never a criteria employed by Native people before [European] contact."

Julie M. feels that

for people like us, who are just *here,* who grew up in this [Cherokee community], it's kind of like, at least for me . . . that whole idea of having to *document* who we are — well, I *know* who I am! It was an insult to me to *have* to get a CDIB. . . . I felt like, why do I need the federal government to tell me what the definition of Indian is? Why do I have to be the one to go out and get a card that says I'm Indian to meet *their* requirements? Because *I* don't have any requirements in my community. Or if there *are* requirements, I meet 'em. And I don't have to have the federal government saying . . . that I'm Cherokee to *know* who I am.

Billy S. makes the same point more briefly, "It's kind of a joke that the federal government has to certify us as to whether or not we are who we are."

Traditional Native societies certainly possessed shared understandings of group belonging; some of these form the subject of chapter 6, but suffice it to say here that the means for making those determinations were not the legal-bureaucratic ones described in this chapter. These are creations of the dominant, American society, even though modern tribes have, in recent times, adopted legal definitions similar in form to those used in the dominant society.[59]

Moreover, the strictly rational-bureaucratic character of the identities brought into being by legal definitions also makes them open to manipulation in various ways. Some observers notice that the formal, documented membership of tribes tends to vary between periods when the larger society perceives Indianness as a valuable commodity and periods when it considers Native ancestry an unimportant or embarrassing aspect of family history. Osage and Cherokee elder Archie M. comments that "there are sometimes those that *may* want to become Indian *because* it's popular to be an Indian. . . . As opposed to when I was growing up, in my family. We grew up as — you were Indian, that was it."

Nancy C., a Navajo artist living in Oklahoma, offers an example of the way that specific practical considerations can affect the size of tribal membership:

Oklahoma has many tribes, and a number of them can issue their own [automobile] license tags. These tribal tags cost a *lot* less than the tags issued by the state of Oklahoma, but you have to be a tribal member to get one. I noticed a new surge of "Indians" when these cheaper tags became available to tribal members. People who never claimed to be Indian started to research their genealogy so they could get the cheaper tags.

Similarly, Lakota/Dakota elder Joe B. notes:

A lot of people jump on the bandwagon [of obtaining legal recognition as Indian]. You know, especially when . . . Indians gets a settlement of some kind, they all jump on the wagon. They come up with papers, too. Whether they're forged or not, I don't know. Other times they don't want to be an Indian. They're kind of ashamed of it. . . . They *are* part Indian, but they don't claim it. But this come along — big settlement come — and, oh gosh — they even end up talkin' [Indian] sign language! [laughs]

The cartoonist whose work is shown in figure 1.3 further highlights the absurdity of some attempts to claim Indian citizenship. Such individual machinations aside, the operations of governments in relation to the creation and re-creation of Indian identity should not escape our notice. The instance of the Keeweenaw Bay Indian community, described earlier, exemplifies the way that tribal governments may manipulate legal definitions. But the federal government, too, has had many opportunities to tailor the legal definitions of Indianness to its own advantage. For instance, in 1892, President Benjamin Harrison's Commissioner of Indian Affairs, Thomas Jefferson Morgan, urged the federal government to adopt "a liberal and not technical or restrictive construction" of Indian identity when distributing property and other government benefits.[60] Morgan's proposal allowed many individuals of

FIGURE 1.3. Bob Tworabbits. Some people have practical motivations for seeking legal identification as Indian. (Source: Drawn by Richard MacPhie, a Minnesota Chippewa, who publishes his cartoons in *Indian Country Today* and in the *Minneapolis Star Tribune*. Printed in *Indian Country Today*.)

varying degrees of ancestry to qualify for these benefits. His stance, however, did not originate strictly in generosity of spirit.

Prior to 1892, agents of American government had judged mixed bloods more cooperative than full bloods on a variety of issues, particularly in the signing of legal documents allowing for land cessions. The agents had therefore specifically sought them out for such purposes.[61] By the end of the nineteenth century, to deny the Indian status of mixed bloods, Morgan argued, would have been disastrous to government interests:

Where by treaty or law it has been required that three-fourths of an Indian tribe shall sign any subsequent agreement to give it validity, we have accepted the signature of mixed bloods as sufficient, and have treated said agreements as valid for the purpose of relinquishment of the rights of the tribe. . . . To decide at this time that such mixed bloods are not Indian . . . would unsettle or endanger the titles to much of the lands that have been relinquished by Indian tribes and patented to citizens of the United States.[62]

Once the specific question of legitimate landownership — still open to debate in the nineteenth century — was more settled, the federal government found it useful to formulate more restrictive legal definitions. It often insisted on a standard of one-quarter, or even one-half, blood quantum before it would legally define individuals as Indians. It has similarly vacillated over the categorization of mixed bloods, depending on particular pragmatic goals, and continues to do so.[63] It appears, in short, that institutions are no better able to resist the temptation to manipulate legal definitions of Indian identity than are individuals.

CHAPTER TWO

"If He Gets a Nosebleed,
He'll Turn into a White Man"

Biology

North American Indians who successfully negotiate the rigors of legal definitions of identity at the federal level can achieve what some consider the dubious distinction of being a "card-carrying Indian." That is, their federal government can issue them a laminated document (in the United States, a CDIB; in Canada an Indian status card) that certifies them as possessing a certain "degree of Indian blood."

Unlike Louis Owens, of the previous chapter, Canadian-born country music singer Shania Twain has what it takes to be a card-carrying Indian: she is formally recognized as an Anishnabe (Ojibwe) Indian with band membership in the Temagami Bear Island First Nation (Ontario, Canada). More specifically, she is legally on record as possessing one-half degree Indian blood. Given this information, one might conclude that Twain's identity as an Indian person is more or less unassailable. It's not.

Controversy has engulfed this celebrity because of an anonymous phone call to a Canadian newspaper a few years ago that led to the disclosure of another name by which Shania was once known: Eileen Regina Edwards. Eileen/Shania was adopted by a stepfather in early childhood and took the surname of Twain at that time. So far well and good — except for one thing. Both sides of her *biological* family describe themselves not as Indian but as white. It is only Jerry Twain, her late stepfather, who was Indian.

As the adopted child of an Anishnabe man, Shania Twain occupies an unusual status. Though the U.S. government allows for the assignment of blood quantum only to biological descendants of Indian people,

Canada allows for the naturalization of non-Native children through adoption.[1] Although Twain has stated that her white mother (now deceased) had told her, in childhood, that her biological father (also deceased) had some Indian heritage, his family denies the suggestion entirely. They say they are French and Irish. Ms. Twain explains: "I don't know how much Indian blood I actually have in me, but as the adopted daughter of my father Jerry, I became legally registered as 50-percent North American Indian. Being raised by a full-blooded Indian and being part of his family and their culture from such a young age is all I've ever known. That heritage is in my heart and my soul, and I'm proud of it."[2]

Twain has been sharply criticized, in both the United States and Canada, for not making the full details of her racial background clearer, especially to awards-granting agencies such as the First Americans in the Arts (FAITA), which honored her in February 1996 as a Native performer. FAITA itself has made no such complaint. The group states that it is satisfied that "Ms. Twain has not intentionally misrepresented herself." And more importantly, her adopted family defends her. An aunt observes: "She was raised by us. She was accepted by our band. If my brother were alive, he'd be very upset. He raised her as his own daughter. My parents, her grandparents, took her into the bush and taught her the [Native] traditions."[3]

Twain's case shows with uncommon clarity that legal and biological definitions are conceptually distinct. It is the task of this chapter to examine the latter.

In their modern American construction, at least, biological definitions of identity assume the centrality of an individual's genetic relationship to other tribal members. Not just any degree of relationship will do, however. Typically, the degree of closeness is also important. And this is the starting point for much of the controversy that swirls around issues of biological Indianness.

Closeness of biological or blood relationship can be conceived in a fairly mechanical fashion, as suggested in the diagram provided by a Bureau of Indian Affairs training handbook and shown in figure 2.1. It graphically illustrates the amount of blood that should be attributed to a child born to one parent of four-fourths (full-blood) Indian ancestry and one parent of one-quarter Indian ancestry: this child is shown to be filled up to the level of five-eighths with Indian blood.

Some Indian people accept a similar construction of blood relationship. Interview respondent Donald G., a Cherokee full blood, explained

FIGURE 2.1. Visualizing blood quantum. Diagram from Bureau of Indian Affairs handbook, illustrating how blood quantum may be conceptualized and calculated. (Source: Bureau of Indian Affairs, *Tribal Enrollment*, 82.)

the implication of racial admixture for tribal identity, using mayonnaise and ketchup to represent Caucasian and Indian genetics:

Donald G.: If you took mayonnaise and ketchup and mixed it equally, what is it? Mayonnaise or ketchup?

Author (laughing): Both.

Donald G.: Or if you took just a small portion . . . of ketchup and a larger portion of mayonnaise, then what do you have?

Author: Does it get to the point where you're not Indian any more, with all the intermarriage? Do you finally just end up with mayonnaise?

Donald G.: Well, see, that's it. That's the big question. Because I was going to say — at what point? At what point is it more ketchup or at what point is it more mayonnaise? That's a question that remains to be answered, I guess. . . . [But] obviously, if you put more of one, it's going to be more of that one. And that's how I feel about it.

Cornelia S., a full-blood Cherokee mother, offers similar sentiments: "My opinion is [that people should be] a quarter or a half [to be considered Indians]. . . . Because I think that the less Indian . . . blood that you have in you. . . . Well, [the non-Indian blood] is watering it [the Indian blood] down."

Hopi geneticist Frank D. draws explicitly on the language of biology to express concerns about racial mixing: "I don't know what 'blood' means. But I do know what 'genes' means. . . . I don't like the idea of the blood or the genes being deleted [through Indians' intermarriage with non-Indians]. I think it should go the other way, [so that Indian people] . . . increase their Indian population [by marrying each other, rather than] . . . marry[ing] some non-Indian."

Sociologist Eugeen Roosens summarizes such common conceptions about the importance of blood quantum for determining Indian identity:

There is . . . [a] principle about which the whites and the Indians are in agreement. . . . People with more Indian blood . . . also have more rights to inherit what their ancestors, the former Indians, have left behind. In addition, full blood Indians are more authentic than half-breeds. By *being* pure, they have more right to respect. They *are*, in all aspects of their being, more *integral*.[4]

Biological ancestry can take on such tremendous significance in tribal contexts that it overwhelms all other considerations of identity, especially when it is constructed as "pure." As Cherokee legal scholar G. William Rice points out, "Most [people] would recognize the full-blood Indian who was enrolled in a federally recognized tribe as an Indian, even if the individual was adopted at birth by a non-Indian family and had never set foot in Indian country nor met another Indian."[5] Mixed-race individuals, by contrast, find their identity claims considerably complicated. Even if such an individual can demonstrate conclusively that he has *some* Native ancestry, the question will still be raised: Is the *amount* of ancestry he possesses "enough"? Is his "Indian blood" sufficient to distinguish him from the mixed-blood individual spotlighted by an old quip: "If he got a nosebleed, he'd turn into a white man"?

Members of various tribes complain of factionalism between these two major groups — full bloods and mixed bloods — and they suggest that the division arose historically because of mixed bloods' greater access to the social resources of the dominant society and their enhanced ability to impose values and ideas upon others.[6] As Julie M., a citizen of the United Keetowah Band of Cherokee Indians, says: "For the Cherokee people, there's been this mixed blood/full blood kind of dynamic going

from before the removal [in 1838, also known as the Trail of Tears]. . . .
It's kind of like us-and-them. . . . It's almost been like a *war* in some
cases. . . . It's a 'who's-really-going-to-be-in-control-of-the-tribe?' kind of
thing." Many historians have similarly found it logical that political alle-
giances would tend to shift for those Indian people who formed
alliances, through intermarriage, with members of the dominant society,
and that this has made the division between full bloods and mixed
bloods politically important.[7]

Modern biological definitions of identity, however, are much more
complicated than this historical explanation can account for. This complexity did not originate in the ideas and experiences of Indian tribes.
Instead, they closely reflect nineteenth- and early-twentieth-century theories of race introduced by Euro-Americans. These theories (of which
there were a great many) viewed biology as definitive, but they did not
distinguish it from culture. Thus, blood became quite literally the vehicle for the transmission of cultural characteristics. "'Half-breeds' by this
logic could be expected to behave in 'half-civilized,' i.e., partially assimi-
lated, ways while retaining one half of their traditional culture, accounting for their marginal status in both societies."[8]

These turn-of-the-century theories of race found a very precise way to
talk about *amount* of ancestry in the idea of blood quantum, or degree of
blood. The notion of blood quantum as a standard of Indianness
emerged with force in the nineteenth century. Its most significant early
usage as a standard of identification was in the General Allotment
(Dawes) Act of 1887, which led to the creation of the Dawes Rolls that I
discussed in the last chapter. It has been part of the popular — and legal
and academic — lore about Indians ever since.

Given this standard of identification, full bloods tend to be seen as the
"really real," the quintessential Indians, while others are viewed as
Indians in diminishing degrees. The original, stated intention of blood
quantum distinctions was to determine the point at which the various
responsibilities of the dominant society to Indian peoples ended. The
ultimate and explicit federal intention was to use the blood quantum
standard as a means to liquidate tribal lands and to eliminate government
trust responsibility to tribes, along with entitlement programs, treaty
rights, and reservations. Through intermarriage and application of a biological definition of identity Indians would eventually become citizens
indistinguishable from all other citizens.[9]

Degree of blood is calculated, with reference to biological definitions,
on the basis of the immediacy of one's genetic relationship to those

whose bloodlines are (supposedly) unmixed. As in the case with legal definitions, the initial calculation for most tribes' biological definitions begins with a base roll, a listing of tribal membership and blood quanta in some particular year. These base rolls make possible very elaborate definitions of identity. For instance, they allow one to reckon that the offspring of, say, a full-blood Navajo mother and a white father is one-half Navajo. If that half-Navajo child, in turn, produces children with a Hopi person of one-quarter blood degree, those progeny will be judged one-quarter Navajo and one-eighth Hopi. Alternatively, they can be said to have three-eighths general Indian blood.

As even this rather simple example shows, over time such calculations can become infinitesimally precise, with people's ancestry being parsed into so many thirty-secondths, sixty-fourths, one-hundred-twenty-eighths, and so on. The Bureau of Indian Affairs uses the chart in table 1 as a means of calculating blood quanta. The chart constitutes a quick reference for dealing with such difficult cases as a child with one parent with a twenty-one thirty-seconds blood quantum and another with a thirteen-sixteenths blood quantum. (The answer in this example, the table informs us, would be forty-seven sixty-fourths.)

For those of us who have grown up and lived with the peculiar precision of calculating blood quantum, it sometimes requires a perspective less influenced by the vagaries of American history to remind us just how far from common sense the concepts underlying biological definitions of identity are. I recall responding to an inquiry from a Southeast Asian friend about what blood quantum was and how it was calculated. In mid-explanation, I noticed his expression of complete amazement. "That's the dumbest thing I ever heard," he burst out. "Who ever thought of *that*?"

The logic that underlies the biological definition of racial identity becomes even more curious and complicated when one considers the striking difference in the way that American definitions assign individuals to the racial category of "Indian," as opposed to the racial category "black." As a variety of researchers have observed, social attributions of black identity have focused (at least since the end of the Civil War) on the "one-drop rule," or rule of hypodescent.[10] In the movie *Raintree County*, Liz Taylor's character articulates this rule in crassly explicit terms. The worst thing that can happen to a person, she drawls, is "havin' a little Negra blood in ya' — just one little teensy drop and the person's all Negra." That the one-drop method of racial classification is fundamentally a matter of biological inheritance (rather than law, culture, or even

TABLE 1. Calculating the Quantum of Indian Blood

	Non-Indian	1/16	1/8	3/16	1/4	5/16	3/8	7/16	1/2
1/16	1/32	1/16	3/32	1/8	5/32	3/16	7/32	1/4	9/32
1/8	1/16	3/32	1/8	5/32	3/16	7/32	1/4	9/32	5/16
3/16	3/32	1/8	5/32	3/16	7/32	1/4	9/32	5/16	11/32
1/4	1/8	5/32	3/16	7/32	1/4	9/32	5/16	11/32	3/8
5/16	5/32	3/16	7/32	1/4	9/32	5/16	11/32	3/8	13/32
3/8	3/16	7/32	1/4	9/32	5/16	11/32	3/8	13/32	7/16
7/16	7/32	1/4	9/32	5/16	11/32	3/8	13/32	7/16	15/32
1/2	1/4	9/32	5/16	11/32	3/8	13/32	7/16	15/32	1/2
9/16	9/32	5/16	11/32	3/8	13/32	7/16	15/32	1/2	17/32
5/8	5/16	11/32	3/8	13/32	7/16	15/32	1/2	17/32	9/16
11/16	11/32	3/8	13/32	7/16	15/32	1/2	17/32	9/16	19/32
3/4	3/8	13/32	7/16	15/32	1/2	17/32	9/16	19/32	5/8
13/16	13/32	7/16	15/32	1/2	17/32	9/16	19/32	5/8	21/32
7/8	7/16	15/32	1/2	17/32	9/16	19/32	5/8	21/32	11/16
15/16	15/32	1/2	17/32	9/16	19/32	5/8	21/32	11/16	23/32
4/4	1/2	17/32	9/16	19/32	5/8	21/32	11/16	23/32	3/4
1/32	1/64	3/64	5/64	7/64	9/64	11/64	13/64	15/64	17/64
3/32	3/64	5/64	7/64	9/64	11/64	13/64	15/64	17/64	19/64
5/32	5/64	7/64	9/64	11/64	13/64	15/64	17/64	19/64	21/64
7/32	7/64	9/64	11/64	13/64	15/64	17/64	19/64	21/64	23/64
9/32	9/64	11/64	13/64	15/64	17/64	19/64	21/64	23/64	25/64
11/32	11/64	13/64	15/64	17/64	19/64	21/64	23/64	25/64	27/64
13/32	13/64	15/64	17/64	19/64	21/64	23/64	25/64	27/64	29/64
15/32	15/64	17/64	19/64	21/64	23/64	25/64	27/64	29/64	31/64
17/32	17/64	19/64	21/64	23/64	25/64	27/64	29/64	31/64	33/64
19/32	19/64	21/64	23/64	25/64	27/64	29/64	31/64	33/64	35/64
21/32	21/64	23/64	25/64	27/64	29/64	31/64	33/64	35/64	37/64
23/32	23/64	25/64	27/64	29/64	31/64	33/64	35/64	37/64	39/64
25/32	25/64	27/64	29/64	31/64	33/64	35/64	37/64	39/64	41/64
27/32	27/64	29/64	31/64	33/64	35/64	37/64	39/64	41/64	43/64
29/32	29/64	31/64	33/64	35/64	37/64	39/64	41/64	43/64	45/64
31/32	31/64	33/64	35/64	37/64	39/64	41/64	43/64	45/64	47/64

SOURCE: Bureau of Indian Affairs, Tribal Enrollment, app. H.

NOTE: To determine the degree of blood of a child, find the degree of one parent in the left-hand column and the degree of the other parent in the top row. Read horizontally to the right and vertically down to find the degree. Example: If one parent is 11/16 and the other is 5/8, the child is 21/32 degree.

TABLE I. *(continued)*

	9/16	5/8	11/16	3/4	13/16	7/8	15/16	4/4
1/16	5/16	11/32	3/8	13/32	7/16	15/32	1/2	17/32
1/8	11/32	3/8	13/32	7/16	15/32	1/2	17/32	9/16
3/16	3/8	13/32	7/16	15/32	1/2	17/32	9/16	19/32
1/4	13/32	7/16	15/32	1/2	17/32	9/16	19/32	5/8
5/16	7/16	15/32	1/2	17/32	9/16	19/32	5/8	21/32
3/8	15/32	1/2	17/32	9/16	19/32	5/8	21/32	11/16
7/16	1/2	17/32	9/16	19/32	5/8	21/32	11/16	23/32
1/2	17/32	9/16	19/32	5/8	21/32	11/16	23/32	3/4
9/16	9/16	19/32	5/8	21/32	11/16	23/32	3/4	25/32
5/8	19/32	5/8	21/32	11/16	23/32	3/4	25/32	13/16
11/16	5/8	21/32	11/16	23/32	3/4	25/32	13/16	27/32
3/4	21/32	11/16	23/32	3/4	25/32	13/16	27/32	7/8
13/16	11/16	23/32	3/4	25/32	13/16	27/32	7/8	29/32
7/8	23/32	3/4	25/32	13/16	27/32	7/8	29/32	15/16
15/16	3/4	25/32	13/16	27/32	7/8	29/32	15/16	31/32
4/4	25/32	13/16	27/32	7/8	29/32	15/16	31/32	4/4
1/32	19/64	21/64	23/64	25/64	27/64	29/64	31/64	33/64
3/32	21/64	23/64	25/64	27/64	29/64	31/64	33/64	35/64
5/32	23/64	25/64	27/64	29/64	31/64	33/64	35/64	37/64
7/32	25/64	27/64	29/64	31/64	33/64	35/64	37/64	39/64
9/32	27/64	29/64	31/64	33/64	35/64	37/64	39/64	41/64
11/32	29/64	31/64	33/64	35/64	37/64	39/64	41/64	43/64
13/32	31/64	33/64	35/64	37/64	39/64	41/64	43/64	45/64
15/32	33/64	35/64	37/64	39/64	41/64	43/64	45/64	47/64
17/32	35/64	37/64	39/64	41/64	43/64	45/64	47/64	49/64
19/32	37/64	39/64	41/64	43/64	45/64	47/64	49/64	51/64
21/32	39/64	41/64	43/64	45/64	47/64	49/64	51/64	53/64
23/32	41/64	43/64	45/64	47/64	49/64	51/64	53/64	55/64
25/32	43/64	45/64	47/64	49/64	51/64	53/64	55/64	57/64
27/32	45/64	47/64	49/64	51/64	53/64	55/64	57/64	59/64
29/32	47/64	49/64	51/64	53/64	55/64	57/64	59/64	61/64
31/32	49/64	51/64	53/64	55/64	57/64	59/64	61/64	63/64

self-identification) is clear from the 1948 Mississippi court case of a young man named Davis Knight. Knight, accused of violating antimiscegenation statutes, argued that he was quite unaware that he possessed any black ancestry, which in any case amounted to less than one-sixteenth. The courts convicted him anyway and sentenced him to five years in jail. "Blood" was "blood," whether anyone, including the accused himself, was aware of it or not.[11]

The same definition of identity held sway for blacks in America well past the 1940s. For instance, up until 1970, Louisiana state law defined as black anyone possessing "a trace of black ancestry." In an apparent seizure of racial liberalism, however, the legislature formally revised the definition of identity in that year. It decided that the amount of blood constituting a "trace" should be limited by declaring that only those possessing more than one-thirty-second-degree "Negro blood" would be considered black.[12]

A woman named Susie Guillory Phipps challenged this law in 1982–1983, when she discovered, at age forty-three, that she was a black woman. It happened this way: Susie Guillory was born in 1934 in Louisiana to a poor, French-speaking family. She married a tradesman, Mr. Phipps, who worked hard and did well — so well that, in 1977, the couple decided to take a trip to South America. Mrs. Phipps drove to New Orleans to apply for the first passport she had ever required. Upon arrival, she ran smack into one of the American definitions of racial identity.

There was a problem, the clerk at the records agency whispered, drawing Mrs. Phipps into a private office. She had declared on the application that her race was white. But, the clerk pointed out, Phipps's birth certificate described both her parents as "colored." Mrs. Phipps protested. She "looked" white, she said. She thought of herself as white. She lived as a white woman. She saw no reason why her personal documents should describe her otherwise. She felt so strongly about the matter, in fact, that she started a legal battle to have the racial identification on her birth certificate changed. It turned out to be a long road, but her perseverance illuminated some of the most interesting back alleys of America's biological definitions of racial identity.

The Division of Vital Records of New Orleans, it seemed, did not subscribe to Phipps's view of herself as white, and it was not about to change its mind. The *New Yorker*, reporting on Phipps's case in 1986, wrote: "At Vital Records, it was taken for granted that certain families were white and certain families had a traceable amount of black blood, and that it was up to the vital-records office to tell them apart. When it came to tracing traceable amounts, nobody ever accused the vital-records office of bureaucratic lethargy."[13]

Certainly in the case of Mrs. Phipps the office was on its toes. The office chief began by commissioning a genealogist to trace Mrs. Phipps' ancestry all the way back to the 1700s, and then he went in search of her living relatives and her childhood neighbors. (The similar ransacking of "Chief" Buffalo Child Long Lance's ancestral roots comes to mind.) By the time the case came to court, the office had gathered boxes of depositions and other records testifying to the Guillory bloodlines. And they could show that the Guillorys, indeed, had black ancestry: Mrs. Phipps's great-great-great-grandmother Margarita had been a slave in the 1700s. Margarita had borne children to her white master, and some of her descendants had married individuals of mixed race.

Confronted with the evidence, Susie Phipps consented to the argument that she might possess one-thirty-second-degree black ancestry — the amount that would bring her in just under the wire for establishing a white identity. Vital Records, however, by scraping together and adding up all the dribs and drabs of ancestral blood, argued that Mrs. Phipps was as much as five-thirty-secondths black. This was enough for the courts. They denied her petition to change the racial designation on her birth certificate to white, and in 1985 an appellate court upheld the decision. The complainant had failed to produce sufficient evidence to show that the document, as issued, was in error, and it would have to stand. Regardless of her self-perception, Mrs. Phipps had to bow to the biological definition of race, and its corollary, the one-drop rule. For legal purposes, she would forever be a black woman.[14]

Mrs. Phipps's story in and of itself is an interesting study of the way Americans link ideas about racial identity and biology. But it becomes far more intriguing when we contrast the logic underlying the definition of identity in operation there with the one that applies to Indian identity. Can the reader imagine a scenario in which an office of the American government legally *compels* a person professing anything more than one-thirty-second-degree Indian blood to accept identification as Indian? Can she imagine such a claim being widely *tolerated* as legitimate, even for the purposes of casual social interaction?

Far from being held to a one-drop rule, Indians are generally required — both by law and by popular opinion — to establish rather *high* blood quanta in order for their claims to racial identity to be accepted as meaningful, the individual's own opinion notwithstanding. Although people must have only the slightest trace of "black blood" to be *forced* into the category "African American," modern American Indians must (1) formally produce (2) strong evidence of (3) often rather substantial amounts of "Indian blood" to be *allowed* entry into the corresponding racial category. The regnant biological definitions applied to Indians are simply quite different than those that have applied (and continue to apply) to blacks. Modern Americans, as Native American Studies professor Jack Forbes (Powhatan/Lenape/Saponi) puts the matter, "are *always finding 'blacks'* (even if they look rather un-African), and . . . *are always losing 'Indians.'*"[15]

Biological Definitions: Contexts and Consequences

Biological definitions of Indian identity operate, in short, in some curious and inconsistent ways. They are nevertheless significant in a variety of contexts. And they have clear relationships, both direct and indirect, to legal definitions. The federal government has historically used a minimum blood quantum standard to determine who was eligible to receive treaty rights, or to sell property and manage his or her own financial affairs.[16] Blood quantum is *one* of the criteria that determines eligibility for citizenship in many tribes; it therefore indirectly influences the claimant's relationship to the same kinds of rights, privileges, and responsibilities that legal definitions allow.[17]

But biological definitions of identity affect personal interactions as well as governmental decisions. Indian people with high blood quanta frequently have recognizable physical characteristics. As Cherokee Nation principal tribal chief Chad Smith observes, some people are easily recognizable as Indians because they pass "a brown paper bag test," meaning that their skin is "darker than a #10 paper sack." It is these individuals who are often most closely associated with negative racial stereotypes in the larger society. Native American Studies professor Devon Mihesuah makes a point about Indian women that is really applicable to either gender: "Appearance is the most visible aspect of one's race; it determines how Indian women define themselves and how others define and treat them. Their appearance, whether Caucasian, Indian, African, or mixed, either limits or broadens Indian women's choices of ethnic identity and ability to interact with non-Indians and other Indians."[18]

Every day, identifiably Indian people are turned away from restaurants, refused the use of public rest rooms, ranked as unintelligent by the education system, and categorized by the personnel of medical, social service, and other vital public agencies as "problems" — all strictly on the basis of their appearance. As Keetoowah Band Cherokee full-blood Donald G. notes, a recognizably Indian appearance can be a serious detriment to one's professional and personal aspirations: "It seems the darker you are, the less important you are, in some ways, to the employer. . . . To some, it would be discouraging. But I am four-fourths [i.e., full-blood] Cherokee, and it doesn't matter what someone says about me. . . . I feel for the person who doesn't like my skin color, you know?"

There are circumstances, however, in which it is difficult for the victims of negative racial stereotyping to maintain an attitude as philosophical as this. In one interview, a Mohawk friend, June L., illustrated the potential consequences of public judgments based on skin color. She reminded me of a terrifying episode that had once unfolded while I was visiting at her house. Our conversation was interrupted by a phone call informing this mother of five that her college-student son, who had spent the summer day working on a roof, had suddenly become ill while driving home. Feeling faint, he had pulled up to a local convenience store and made his way inside, asking for a drink of water. The clerk refused. Dangerously dehydrated, the young man collapsed on the floor from sunstroke. "The worst thing about it," June recalled, "was that I have to keep wondering: What was the reason for that? Did that clerk refuse to help my son because she was just a mean person? Or was it because she saw him stumble into the store and thought, 'Well, it's just some drunken Indian'?" Anxiety about social judgments of this kind are a fact of daily life for parents of children whose physical appearance makes their Indian ancestry clearly evident.

At the same time, June's remarks showed the opposite side to the coin of physical appearance. In some contexts, not conforming to the usual notions of "what Indians look like" can also be a liability:

My aunt was assistant dean at a large Ivy League university. One day she called me on the phone. She had one scholarship to give out to an Indian student. One of the students being considered was blonde-haired and blue-eyed. The other one was black-haired and dark-skinned, and she looked Indian. The blonde girl's grades were a little better. My aunt didn't know what to do. She said to me, "Both these girls are tribal members. Both of them are qualified [for the scholarship]. They're sitting outside my office. What would *you* do?" I told her that, as an Indian person, there was only one thing I *could* say. Which was to give the money to the one with the dark skin. As Indian people, we *do* want to have Indian people that *look* like they're Indian to represent us.

Readers may be surprised by such a candid statement. But June's pragmatic reasoning takes account of certain historical realities. As she explained further, "We like people to *know* who's doing those accomplishments, like getting scholarships. We want them to know this is an Indian person doing this. Because I come from a background where if you looked Indian, you were put in special education because the schools said you couldn't learn. And it wasn't true. We need Indian people today who look Indian to show everyone the things we can do."

A physical appearance that is judged insufficiently "Indian" can also act as a barrier to participation in certain cultural activities. Bill T., a Wichita and Seneca minister in his midfifties, recalls that, in his youth, he witnessed light-skinned individuals who attempted to participate in powwow dances being evicted from the arena. "That kind of thing is still happening today," he added sadly, and other respondents readily confirmed this observation. A more unusual instance of the relevance of physical appearance to cultural participation was volunteered by Frank D., a Hopi respondent. His tribe's ceremonial dances feature the appearance of powerful spirit beings called kachinas, which are embodied by masked Hopi men. Ideally, the everyday, human identity of the dancers remains unknown to observers. Frank commented on the subject of tribal members whose skin tone is noticeably either lighter or darker than the norm:

Frank D.: Say, for instance, if a Hopi marries a black person . . . [and] you get a male child . . . it's gonna be darker skinned. It might even be black. A black kachina just wouldn't fit out here [at Hopi]. You see, everybody'd know who it is. He'd be very visible [in the ceremonial dances]. . . . It'd be very hard on that individual. Kids don't work the other way, too — if they're real light. . . . Kachinas gotta be *brown*.

Author: So there are certain ceremonial roles that people could not fill because of their appearance?

Frank D.: Well, they *could*, but it would be awful tough. A lot of these [ceremonial] things are done with secrecy. No one knows who the kachinas are. Or at least, the kids don't. And then, say you get somebody who really stands out, then everybody knows who that [dancer] is, and it's not good. For the ceremony — because everybody knows who that person is. And so the kids will start asking questions — "How come that kachina's so dark, so black?" or "How come that kachina's white?" They start asking questions and it's really hard. So I think, if you're thinking about kids, it's really better if kachinas are brown.

Finally, the physical appearance borne by mixed bloods may not only create barriers to tribal cultural participation; it may also offer an occasion for outrightly shaming them. Cornelia S. remembers her days at the Eufala Indian School:

You *had* to be Indian to be [allowed admission] there. . . . But . . . if [certain students] . . . didn't look as Indian as we did, or if they looked like they were white, they were kind of looked down upon, like treated differently because [people would say] "oh, that's just a white person." . . . They just [would] tease 'em and stuff. Say "oh, whatcha doin' white boy" or "white girl" — just stuff like that.

Nor is the social disapproval of light-skinned mixed bloods strictly the stuff of schoolyard teasing. The same respondent added that even adults confront questions of blood quantum with dead seriousness:

Us Indians, whenever we see someone else who is saying that they're Indian . . . or trying to be around us Indians, and act like us, and they don't look like they're Indian and we know that they're not as much Indian as *we* are, yeah, we look at them like they're not Indian and, ya know, don't really like why they're acting like that. . . . But you know, I'm not *that* far off . . . into judging other people and what color [they are].

The late author Michael Dorris, a member of the Modoc tribe (California), has written that humiliations related to his appearance were part of his daily experience. He describes (in his account of his family's struggle with his son's fetal alcohol syndrome, *The Broken Cord*) an encounter with a hospital admissions staff, to whom he had just identified himself and his son as Indians. "They surveyed my appearance with curiosity. It was an expression I recognized, a reaction, familiar to most people of mixed-blood ancestry, that said, 'You don't *look* like an Indian.' No matter how often it happened, no matter how frequently I was blamed by strangers for not resembling their image of some Hollywood Sitting Bull, I was still defensive and vulnerable. 'I'm part Indian,' I explained."[19]

Even his tragic death has not safeguarded Dorris from insinuations about inadequate blood quantum. Shortly after his 1997 suicide, a story on his life and death in *New York* magazine reported that the author's fair complexion had always caused some observers to wonder about his racial identity and archly repeated a rumor: "It is said he . . . [eventually] discovered tanning booths."[20]

In short, many Indian people, both individually and collectively, continue to embrace the assumption that close biological connections to other Indian people — and the distinctive physical appearance that may accompany those connections — imply a stronger claim on identity than do more distant ones. As Potawatomi scholar of Native American Studies Terry Wilson summarizes, "Few, if any, Native Americans, regardless of upbringing in rural, reservation, or urban setting, ignore their own and other Indians' blood quantum in everyday life. Those whose physical appearances render their Indian identities suspect are subject to suspicious scrutiny until precise cultural explanations, especially blood quantum, are offered or discovered."[21]

Negotiating Biological Identities

There are many reasons why people fail in their efforts to negotiate a meaningful identity as an Indian by reference to a specific biological definition. For one thing, many tribes today really do have large numbers of claimants to membership with relatively low blood quanta, due to intermarriage. However, difficulties in establishing an Indian identity by reference to blood do not stem solely from having a deficient corpuscle count. Many times, the problem lies with the way blood quanta are reckoned.

It would be an enormous understatement to say that the original assignments of blood quanta on the tribal base rolls that are still used to determine the blood quanta of Indians today were often not especially accurate. Modern observers may express disbelief at the decision of the Passamaquoddy tribe of Maine, which was recently recognized by the federal government. A highly intermarried tribe, they declared an intention in 1990 to constitute anyone appearing on the tribal census of that year as a full blood, automatically and by fiat.[22] But the arbitrariness of this decision is not unlike the methods employed in many historic records of blood quantum.

On some reservations, nineteenth-century Indian agents assigned and recorded blood quantum on the basis of the candidate's physical appearance, making darker people into full bloods and lighter ones into mixed bloods with a pen stroke, even when all the individuals involved were offspring of the same set of parents. In Oklahoma, the Dawes Commission dealt with people of mixed tribal ancestry by calculating blood degree based on the mother's tribe only. This could reduce an enrollee's total, recorded Indian blood quantum by as much as one-half. Applicants with discernible black ancestry were not assigned a blood quantum at all (even if they clearly had an Indian parent or grandparent), but were simply marked down in the census category for freedmen. As long as applicants did not appear to have black ancestry, some Indian agents simply took people's word about their racial heritage, but even then the results were not necessarily particularly reliable. The definition of blood quantum was not one familiar, historically, to Indian people of traditional upbringing, and not something they previously had reason to keep track of.[23] Moreover, by the time the U.S. government began collecting this information in the nineteenth century, Indian people had acquired incentives to creatively revise estimates of their blood quanta. They could not have been unaware of a widely prevailing sentiment in the larger society that "white blood makes good Indians." Given the social handicaps associated with Indian blood, it seems likely that people would frequently have admitted to as little of it as they reasonably could. Those decisions continue to affect their descendants' ability to demonstrate that they possess "enough" blood to satisfy particular biological definitions.[24]

The difficulties of negotiating a legitimate identity within biological definitions multiply as specific requirements shift, creating a whole new set of opportunities for, and constraints upon, identity claims. For instance, the Rosebud Sioux tribe (South Dakota) at one time dropped its blood quantum requirement for tribal enrollment, but then reinstated it a few years later (in 1966). This has created families in which the older children are enrolled tribal citizens, while the younger children of the same couple are not.[25] A similar situation occurs when a tribe "closes" its rolls and declines to accept further enrollments. In this case older people remain citizens while younger ones, no matter if they possess the same blood quanta as their elders, or even higher, can never be enrolled.

What all this means is that even though one's actual blood quantum obviously cannot change, the definition of identity that depends upon it can and does. Biological Indianness, just as much as legal Indianness, can wink in and out of existence, sometimes with remarkable rapidity.

Evaluating Biological Definitions

Like legal definitions, biological definitions of Indian identity have both advantages and disadvantages, when viewed from tribal perspectives. On the positive side of the ledger, biological definitions have their common usage to recommend them. They are drawn upon frequently for the purposes of both informal interaction and formal record keeping. Like legal definitions based upon documentary evidence, blood quantum definitions provide a relatively nonsubjective standard amenable to bureau-cratic needs.

Another virtue of biological definitions is that they allow for the expression of a justifiable pride of ancestry. For a family lineage to have survived for hundreds of years, with few or none of the benefits that accrued to those who attached themselves through marriage and other alliances to members of the dominant race, simply *is* an accomplishment. As Cornelia S. explains: "I know that both my parents are full-blood Cherokee, and I know that their parents are full-blood Cherokee, and [my ancestors] before them. I'm really proud that I am full-blood Cherokee in this . . . more modern society, . . . because I . . . know . . . it might be harder to be Indian, or just any minority."

Of course, all those who have maintained more or less unmixed blood-lines did not necessarily choose this course entirely out of a ferocious dedication to ethnic personhood. Cherokee sociologist C. Matthew Snipp remarks that, historically, "to be an American Indian often meant that one had not developed the requisite skills to avoid being identified as such."[26] Many more Indian people might have intermingled with and lost themselves in the larger, European population if they had had the opportunity to do so.

But acknowledging this fact should not diminish our appreciation of how bone-crushingly hard it has been for families simply to carry on in the absence of the resources that often came to those who merged their lives and fortunes with those of Europeans. Survival under such circum-stances is an extraordinary achievement, and the language of blood quan-tum gives people a well-deserved means to express it. Elder Martha S. has the right to her shy smile and the light that comes into her eyes when she says, in gentle tones, "I just feel real good about being full-blood Yuchi. I can trace my grandparents down to my great-grandparents, and they were *all Yuchis.*" Cornelia S. voices an equally justifiable pride in being a full-blood Cherokee: "I know *exactly* what I am. That's *it.* Like, you know, race horses that are purebred, . . . and they're the best ones. That's how I feel like about myself, because I'm a full blood of my tribe."

A related but more subtle benefit of a biological definition of identity is that it allows for a protest against a certain arrogance that Indians rather commonly encounter on the part of people who resemble, in all discernible ways, members of the dominant society. This arrogance is portrayed in an episode of Jamaica Kincaid's novel *Lucy.* Lucy is an indigenous woman from the West Indies, a Carib Indian, and she is aware of the price that this ancestry has exacted from her tribal people:

"My grandmother is a Carib Indian. . . . My grandmother is alive; the Indians she came from are all dead." Lucy works in a wealthy American household as a nanny, and one day her employer hesitantly announces that, like Lucy, she "has Indian blood in her." Lucy reacts with astonishment and bitterness: "There was nothing remotely like an Indian about her. Why claim a thing like that? . . . [U]nderneath everything I could swear she says it as if she were announcing her possession of a trophy. How do you get to be the sort of victor who can claim to be the vanquished also?"[27]

The claim "I have Indian blood in me" has many layers of implication that are difficult to tease out. Perhaps it is a compliment to the liberal attitudes of the speaker and her family: that her forebears did not shudder to conjoin themselves with others of a presumably "lesser" race. Or perhaps it is an effort to garner the prestige of exoticism without crossing over into disreputability. After all, "having Indian blood in you" is rather different than "being Indian."

These are only two possible analyses of a particular conversational foray, and perhaps they are overly cynical. However, when one observes the common reactions of Indian people to the statement "I have Indian blood in me," one suspects that it may often feel to them like the speaker is trying to lay claim to benefits that she did not earn. The definition of identity through biology and blood quantum, however, provides those most likely to have endured the life chances reserved for "the vanquished" with a way of thinking about the differences between themselves and those who, whatever remnant of racial admixture their genetics may admit, now openly enjoy the rewards of "the victor."

On the negative side of the evaluation of biological definitions of Indian identity: While some Indian people embrace the terminology and the logic of blood quantum, others find it offensive. Individuals of the latter persuasion may distance themselves from such definitions by means of humor. For example, Jimmie Durham, an artist whose self-identification as Cherokee has earned him a number of inquiries into his racial identity, has become well known for his comment: "The question of my 'identity' often comes up. I think I must be a mixed blood. I claim to be male, although only one of my parents is male."[28] Others express their displeasure more straightforwardly. An Anishnabe and Cree grandmother, Kathleen W., comments, "I don't like being talked about in a vocabulary usually reserved for dogs and horses." Her remark recalls Snipp's comment that, for Indians, the matter of "blood pedigree" assumes significance "in a manner bordering on flagrant racism."[29] A

Cherokee colleague expresses a similar annoyance with questions concerning whether or not he is "part Indian." "Indians," he writes dryly, "do not come in 'parts.'"[30] Lyrics from the song "Blood Quantum," by the Indigo Girls, capture some of the emotions suggested by the previous remarks:

> You're standing in the blood quantum line
> With a pitcher in your hand
> Poured from your heart into your veins
> You said I am, I am, I am
> Now measure me, measure me
> Tell me where I stand
> Allocate my very soul
> Like you have my land.[31]

Some commentators, in fact, object to the entire notion of mixed-bloodedness, which is central to biological definitions, because it is so frequently used to diminish a whole category of people. It more than hints that mixed bloods are some kind of degenerate representatives of a once-pure category. As Elizabeth Cook-Lynn, the Dakota Sioux (South Dakota) editor of the Native American Studies journal *Wicazo Sa Review,* argues, "To adopt this idea [of racial purity] in its fullest, most sophisticated sense makes hybridity a contaminant to the American Indian's right to authenticity."[32]

An emphasis on "pure" cultural expressions can encourage us to devalue the important role played by the "impure," the mixed blood. For centuries, mixed bloods have bridged the chasm between cultures — bridged it with their bodies, bridged it with their spirits, bridged it with their consciousnesses, bridged it often whether they were willing or unwilling. In the scholarly literature, researchers such as Terry Wilson, Clara Sue Kidwell, and Margaret Connell Szasz talk about mixed bloods as "cultural brokers," practical mediators of the relations between the different racial categories they simultaneously inhabit.[33] However, it is a fictional mixed-blood character created by Native novelists Michael Dorris and Louise Erdrich in *The Crown of Columbus* who states the intermediary role of mixed bloods most clearly:

We're parked on the bleachers looking into the arena, never the main players, but there are bonuses to peripheral vision. . . . We're jealous of innocence, I'll admit that, but as the hooks and eyes that connect one core to the other we have our roles to play. "Caught between two worlds," is the way it's often put in cliched prose, but I'd put it differently. We are the *catch.*[34]

This marginal, mediative role deserves to be honored alongside the roles played by full bloods, who are better able to accept the place of the unselfconscious insider in tribal communities. But biological definitions, with the fractionated Indians they create, work to the contrary effect.

Cook-Lynn finds still another reason to criticize these definitions. She argues that the American fascination with degree of biological connection to a given tribe finds its roots in, and encourages, a dismissive attitude toward the status of tribal nations. On the one hand, Americans regularly scrutinize the identity claims of well-known Indian authors. Yet, Cook-Lynn writes, "No one asks how much Egyptian Naguib Manfouz is, nor do they require that J. M. Coetzee provide proof that his citizenship and identity is embodied in tribal African nationhood." The reason for such differences, Cook-Lynn concludes, concerns differing levels of "mutual respect between nations."[35]

Observers are willing to defer, without question, to decisions that Egypt and other African countries make about citizenship, but obstinately believe that individuals, even those entirely unconnected to tribal affairs, should be able to second-guess similar decisions that Indian nations make. Cook-Lynn's analysis suggests that the embrace of a biological (or any other) definition of identity over whatever legal definitions a tribe elects to apply is an insult to tribal sovereignty. It suggests an underlying assumption that, regardless of tribes' formal status as separate nations that enjoy government-to-government relations with the United States, they are somehow less qualified to determine their own citizenship than are other nations.

Another negative product of determining identity by reference to biological characteristics is the issue of technical extinction, or "statistical extermination." Biological definitions have long been used to limit the numbers of Indians to whom the American government retains obligations, with the anticipation that those obligations would eventually cease altogether. In recent years, the long-awaited event has quickly drawn into view for a number of tribes. This is fairly unsurprising, given that Indians have the highest rate of intermarriage of any ethnic group, with slightly more than half of all Indian men and women marrying non-Indians.[36]

Under these circumstances, blood quantum requirements (used by about two-thirds of all tribes in the lower forty-eight states)[37] are clearly not well suited to the needs of groups too small to support endogamy, or marriage of members within their own group. Bill T. describes the circumstances of his own Wichita tribe: "We were decimated so low [as a result of European contact] that we can't intermarry. We're almost all related to each other now. . . . Now, in order to be on the [Wichita] tribal roll, you have to have one-eighth blood quantum. And after a period of years there will be no one [who meets this criterion]." As Native scholars Lenore Stiffarm and Phil Lane, Jr., put the matter, "To make genetics the defining criterion for continuation of [tribes with only small numbers of full blood members] . . . would be quite literally suicidal."[38] It projects, indeed, a scenario in which such tribes may find themselves redefined as technically "extinct," even when they continue to exist as functioning social, cultural, political, linguistic, or residential groupings.

A final concern that one might raise regarding biological definitions of identity is their inextricable entanglement with the notion of race. Biological definitions promote the notion that "race" constitutes an objective, genetically based difference between groups of people. Most Americans accept this assumption, unaware that it runs contrary to most current scientific knowledge, which tends to view racial distinctions as significant social, but not biological, realities.[39]

The most significant point here, however, is not the scientific "respectability" of the biological definition of race, or its lack thereof; more importantly, those definitions also have a dubious past, having been put to use in service of social goals that have been extremely oppressive to Indian populations. This becomes apparent if one looks, for instance, to the social science of the early to mid-twentieth century. Anthropologists of that period, operating from a conviction that "blood would tell" — and tell in all kinds of ways — assisted in defining membership for various tribal groups (including the Ojibwe, Lumbee, Creek, Choctaw, and others) on the basis of observable characteristics assumed to derive from biological inheritance.

Usually for the purpose of determining eligibility for legal rights, they ferreted out full-blood and mixed-blood Indians by such "scientific" methods as measuring feet (mixed bloods were supposed to have big ones), scrutinizing hair samples (full-blood hair was to be absolutely straight), and scarifying chests (mixed-blood chests knew enough to turn redder, when so assaulted, than their full-blood counterparts).[40] These procedures tended, as one might suspect, to yield rather variable results, even for members of the same immediate family: A study of the Lumbee tribe by physical anthropologist Carl Seltzer, for example, yielded at least one instance in which the same set of Indian parents found themselves with children of different racial statuses.[41] But reliable or not, the results of such tests were used to deny the Lumbee federal recognition on the grounds that, collectively, they did not possess enough "Indian blood."[42]

A more general goal of early-twentieth-century biological definitions of identity was to sort out the "superior" races from the "inferior" ones. "In this racial hierarchy, Indians were in competition with African Black Americans as the lowest race of mankind, in what was referred to as 'the great chain of being' by Eurocentric social scientists."[43] Biologists engaged in this lofty quest shipped countless Indian body parts to government institutions for research purposes. Some museum personnel or their agents stopped at almost nothing to acquire their grisly trophies. Indians who met with mortal misfortune on the battlefield (even those in the service of the United States) were frequently in danger of being snatched up by vigilant U.S. military personnel, decapitated, and their crania sent off to such institutions as the National Museum of Health and Medicine.[44]

Nineteenth-century army surgeons wrote of their resourcefulness in repeatedly plundering Indian cemeteries to secure the severed heads of those interred there, or filching the newly deceased from under the very noses of their comrades (who had developed the regrettable habit of "lurk[ing] about their dead").[45] But perhaps the most shocking single episode involving the theft of human remains in the interests of substantiating a biological definition of identity is the 1897 case of a group of Inuit (then called Eskimos). In that year, Arctic explorer Robert Peary visited Greenland and loaded his return vessel with an exotic cargo. It included the corpses of several Inuit, whom Peary had unearthed from their fresh graves, for delivery to the American Museum of Natural History. But it also included half a dozen living "specimens," among them a man named Qisuk and his son, Minik. These were to be put on display at the museum as a means of generating money to fund future Arctic expeditions.

Tragically, it soon became evident that the warm climate did not agree with the Inuit, and when Qisuk shortly died (along with four of the others), scientists dissected him. The remains of his physical body were then boiled and the flesh stripped away so that the skeleton could be placed in a museum collection. By way of a final indignity, the staff of the American Museum of Natural History then covered up what they had done by presenting the surviving Minik (then seven years of age) with a blanket-wrapped piece of wood, which they asserted was his father's corpse, and staging their own version of a traditional Inuit funeral for it, on the museum lawn. When, as a teenager, Minik learned the truth of his father's fate, he began a quest to retrieve and bury his father's body. Although he spent many years in the effort, he never succeeded.[46]

The point of this recitation of injuries to Native spiritual beliefs and practices regarding the dead is that it was a biological definition of Indian identity that motivated non-Native individuals and institutions to commit those injuries. It would seem that there is much to lose by embracing a definition of identity that encourages the fiction of race.

THREE

What If My Grandma Eats Big Macs?

Culture

Strange and perplexing legal cases have tried the sagacity of judges and juries throughout the history of the American judicial system. But in 1976, the country witnessed an unprecedented event. An entire tribe went on trial. Events began with the Indian community's efforts to bring a land claims case. But the point upon which the outcome quickly came to turn was whether or not that community had the right to a collective identity as an Indian tribe.

The trial involved a community of self-identified Indian residents of Cape Cod, Massachusetts, the Mashpee. They proposed to bring a land claims suit that had the potential to significantly reconfigure economic relations in the state.[1] The basis of their suit was the Indian Non-Intercourse Act of 1790, which stipulated that the federal government must approve all transfers of land from Indians to non-Indians.[2] In violation of this act, the Mashpee said, the Commonwealth of Massachusetts had allowed Indian land to be sold over a period of years without congressional approval. And the Mashpee wanted their land back — about 16,000 acres of it.

The non-Indian residents of the town of Mashpee had reason to be nervous about the threatened legal action, which involved approximately three-quarters of the land on which the town sat. The late 1960s and the 1970s had already seen a series of land claims cases based on violations of the Non-Intercourse Act, and some tribes — notably the Passamaquoddy and the Penobscot (both of Maine) — had received large settlements in consequence. Lawyers for the town of Mashpee, accordingly, decided to try a new strategy. They argued that the Mashpee were not real Indians — that they were not properly a tribe, and that they could not, therefore, bring suit under a law written to protect tribes. A judge ordered the Mashpee to prove otherwise. So it was that the Mashpee people found themselves defending their tribal identity to a jury. They presented such evidence as they could for their collective identity claims, and the (all-white) jury evaluated it.

Ethnohistorian James Clifford, who attended and analyzed the lengthy trial, records that "much, if not most, of the testimony at the trial concerned the status of Indian 'culture' in Mashpee."[3] Lawyers grilled Mashpee witnesses about their legends, their values, their spirituality, their language, their personal and family histories. The jury heard a great deal of testimony concerning whether the Indian residents of Mashpee had maintained lifeways and thoughtways that would distinguish them from other contemporary Americans. By fits and starts, the participants in this extraordinary legal process groped their way toward a definition of Indian identity grounded in culture.

In their statements individual Mashpee witnesses spoke of a long tradition of taking in outsiders and integrating them into their tribal community. In this process, the Mashpee said, they had crafted for themselves syncretic religions — a variety of expressions that often combined elements of the Christianity introduced by Europeans with important features of the traditional ways. In some historical periods, the Mashpee had been forced to nourish certain aspects of tradition secretly, and families had passed them along as best they could. But in the 1920s, the traditional ways had burst forth again. It was in that decade that the tribe underwent a cultural revival in which it reasserted its Indian heritage. Pride in their peoplehood had persisted to the present day, with young people eager to learn the language of their ancestors, along with their history, spirituality, and traditional art forms.

By way of further corroborating this account, and especially their present-day retention of cultural identity, the Mashpee presented their community's leader, Chief Flying Eagle, who related his work instructing young people in basketry, leather work, and beadwork. They brought forward, as well, local medicine man John Peters, who testified to his deep, traditional feelings regarding the sacredness of Mother Earth and his relation to it. All in all, the Mashpee suggested, theirs had been a difficult and often painful cultural history, but also one in which the spirit of a people proved unquenchable.

Lawyers for the defendants saw things differently. The "tribe," they argued, was little different from any other small-town community.

Intermarriage with both whites and blacks had occurred with such frequency over such a long period of time that bloodlines were hopelessly intertwined and Indianness had been erased. The Mashpee were mostly Baptists who also subscribed to generalized ecological values that the Sierra Club likewise endorsed. The supposed cultural revival of 1920, the defense continued, was a mishmash of borrowings from nonlocal tribes and from stereotyped images of Indians being promoted by the then-popular Wild West shows. The cultural knowledge and practices that the Mashpee presently possessed had not been passed down in families. The tribal language, for instance, was no longer being spoken in Mashpee homes, and the community members who had gained any mastery of it had done so through the instruction of one woman who had taken courses at a local university.

Nor were the lawyers satisfied with the testimony of Chief Flying Eagle — also known as Earl Mills. They complained that a witness could not specify the duties Mills performed in his chiefly role or describe how he had been chosen for this office. They likewise questioned the testimony of medicine man John Peters, wondering how a genuine medicine man could have followed the profession of real estate developer, ripping up his Mother Earth for profit. Fundamentally, the lawyers for the town accused, the Mashpee were an ordinary group of citizens who, while rather distantly descended from an Indian tribe, differed from their fellow Americans only in their ability to smell a potentially fruitful economic opportunity from a long way off.

During the course of the Mashpee trial, it became abundantly clear that tribal "culture" — its nature, its transformation, its endurance, its disappearance — was a slippery slope indeed. Who had it and who didn't? What should the jury even be looking for? If the Mashpee needed to be culturally distinctive in order to constitute a "real" Indian tribe, how distinctive was distinctive enough? What if the Mashpee had surrendered their traditional culture only under duress? Even after the endless testimonies of a parade of "experts," nobody seemed to know the answers to any of these questions. In the end, however, the jury found against the Mashpee, disallowing their land claims suit on the grounds that they were not a tribe and therefore did not have standing to sue.

Cultural definitions of Indianness are conceptually fuzzy, as the Mashpee trial highlights. But difficult to formulate and apply or not, cultural definitions have been used to determine Indian identity in a variety of times and places. A court case with striking similarities to the Mashpee trial was heard in Canada from 1987 to 1991 (*Delgamuukw v. the Queen*) to determine the rights of the Gitksan and Wet'suwet'en peoples to their traditional homelands. These tribes entered the arena of argumentation with more obvious resources than did the Mashpee. For instance, unlike the Mashpee, they had retained their tribal language and could use words, sacred stories, and songs in that language as part of court testimony to show their ongoing traditional relationships to the land they occupy. Lawyers for the Crown nevertheless challenged the plaintiffs' tribal identity on the grounds that they had abandoned their "real" traditional culture by making wills, working to improve reservation schools, driving cars, shopping at reservation stores, and eating in fast-food restaurants. Their aboriginal land rights, the lawyers concluded, should be judged "extinguished." Coauthor and illustrator of a book on the trial, Don Monet, satirizes such arguments in figure 3.1. The Canadian tribes, like the Mashpee, also failed to establish their identity on the basis of culture in a court of law.[4]

Efforts to create cultural definitions of Indian identity have a much longer history than the two contemporary examples reveal. Some of their more celebrated applications involved a series of decisions in the nineteenth century. In 1869, the Supreme Court of New Mexico Territory formulated a cultural definition of identity to decide the status of the Pueblo Indians, based upon their "habits, manners, and customs." Its deliberation took in evidence that the Pueblo were "a peaceful, quiet, and industrious people, residing in villages." Even more important, they "liv[ed] by the cultivation of the soil."[5] These cultural characteristics made them very different, in the court's opinion, from "the general class of Indians," who were "wild," "half naked," and "wandering savages." The court concluded that, given their admirable cultural characteristics, the Pueblos *could not* be treated as Indians for legal purposes.[6] In 1876, the U.S. Supreme Court agreed, citing the fact that the Pueblos had shown themselves to be "peaceable, industrious, intelligent, and honest and virtuous" — characteristics which it, too, considered definitively non-Indian.[7] In 1913, however, the Supreme Court, in *United States v. Sandoval,* rethought its initial judgment. It observed that the Pueblos were persistently "pagan," that they were "largely influenced by superstition and fetishism, and chiefly governed according to crude customs inherited from their ancestors." In addition, they were frequently unreceptive to the extension of railroads and unenthusiastic about "the benefits of schools and churches."[8] In light of the incorrigibility of the Pueblos' cultural habits, the court settled on the conclusion that they *were,* after all, Indians.

Given their experience with cultural definitions of this nature, one can understand the protests of many Indian people in regard to recent indications that cultural definitions of identity might be coming once again to

FIGURE 3.1. Ketchup. The land rights of some tribal groups in British Columbia have been extinguished because of their participation in modern culture. (Source: Drawn by Don Monet, a Canadian political cartoonist and author whose work appears in freelance publications around the world. Printed in Don Monet and Skanu'u, *Colonialism on Trial*, 66.)

legislative prominence. This is in relation to an important piece of recent legislation, the Indian Child Welfare Act of 1978 (ICWA). The ICWA requires that social service agencies make efforts to place Indian children in need of homes with other Indian families before seeking a non-Indian placement. In 1996, the House of Representatives passed the Adoption Promotion and Stability Act (H.R. 3286), which contained significant amendments to the ICWA. The amendments provided that the ICWA would apply *only* to Indian children born to at least one parent who "maintain[ed] significant cultural, social, or political affiliation" with a tribe.[9]

A number of tribal leaders and delegates were not eager to have Indian parents and children placed in the circumstance where the Mashpee tribe — as also the Pueblos, a century before — had found themselves. They protested that the bill placed the responsibility for judging the nature and degree of cultural affiliation in the hands of nontribal courts, the agents of which are typically non-Native, and not necessarily knowledgeable about Indian cultures. The protests were effective. Later in 1996 the Senate declined to pass the bill, and it failed to become law.

Nevertheless, the degree of controversy that the bill excited suggests that the outcome might well have been different. Senator John McCain (R-Arizona) reported that the final outcome was "a very hard-fought compromise."[10] Several related bills, moreover, have been introduced into Congress since the passage of the original in 1978, and they have similarly attempted to revise the ICWA with reference to the culture of Indian parents. All of this evidence suggests that — despite the courts' explicit and long-standing determination that "Indian" constitutes a strictly political/legal status independent of any other considerations — we might well expect further pressure to make cultural definitions more central to the way we think and speak about Indians in America.[11]

Negotiating Cultural Identities

A cultural definition, like the other available definitions of Indian identity, functions to exclude at least certain claimants to Indianness. There are a variety of reasons why people who can easily negotiate a legitimate Indian identity within a definition based on law or biology may fail to do so when measured against a cultural standard. Many of those reasons have more to do with the characteristics of the definition than with characteristics of the individuals and groups that are its objects.

After considering the Pueblo case, it is almost unnecessary to mention that many cultural definitions that emerge out of the dominant society feature some extremely odd requirements. For one thing, the cultural practices these definitions demand are frequently stereotyped to the point of absurdity. This point becomes painfully obvious to Indian people even in casual interaction, as suggested by the joke shown in figure 3.2, which circulated on an Indian listserv in 2002. This list of conversation starters illustrates the peculiarity of some commonly held assumptions about tribal cultures by inviting the reader to imagine the result if Indian people accepted the kinds of ideas about non-Indians that non-Indians frequently believe about them.

> ## Things Native Americans Can Say to a White Person upon First Meeting One
>
> 1. Where's your powdered wig?
>
> 2. Do you live in a covered wagon?
>
> 3. What's the meaning behind the square dance?
>
> 4. What's your feeling about riverboat casinos? Do they really help or are they just a short-term fix?
>
> 5. I learned all about your people's ways in the Boy Scouts.

FIGURE 3.2. Things Native Americans can say. What conversations would ensue if Indian people made the same kinds of assumptions about white people that white people make about Indians?

Even when cultural definitions have more grounding in fact, they sometimes impose a misleading and timeless homogeneity onto tribes. They do so by imagining a time in which all the ancestors of a particular tribe practiced a more or less identical set of traditions. This assumption tends to lead to the conclusion that only *one* group — the "real Indians" of that tribe — possesses the "true" tradition, and that distinct traditions are nothing but degenerate and inauthentic forms. In actuality, fairly distinct cultural practices have often characterized different bands, villages, families, clans, and other subdivisions within the same tribe. For instance, as Cherokee sociologist Russell Thornton points out, as far back in his tribe's history as any one knows, separate Cherokee towns spoke distinguishable dialects and practiced distinguishable lifeways. In later times, historic events impinged on the individual communities in different ways, creating even more differences among Cherokees. There have long been not one but "many different Cherokee populations."[12] Strict cultural definitions, however, can delegitimate the identity claims of people who are simply following what is, in fact, *their* tradition.

An even more obvious reason why those who are Indian by other definitions cannot always satisfy a cultural definition of identity is that Indian cultures, and people's practices and experiences within them, have changed a great deal over time; yet many of the most widely available cultural definitions of Indian identity are tied to stringent notions about ancientness that seldom, if ever, appear in the identity definitions related to other racial populations. By way of illustrating this point, anthropologist Jack Forbes compares commonly held assumptions about individuals of Indian ancestry with common assumptions about individuals of African ancestry. "Africans always remain African (or black) even when they speak Spanish or English and serve as cabinet secretaries in the United States government or as trumpet players in a Cuban *salsa* group." Indians, on the other hand, "must remain [culturally] unchanged in order to be considered Indian." This idea prevails in much popular, and even scholarly, thinking. Forbes continues, "I am reminded of a Dutch book on 'The Last Indians' featuring pictures only of South American people still living a way of life which is stereotypically 'Indian.'" By contrast, "Blacks . . . are not seen *only* as traditional villagers in Africa. No one would dare to write a book on 'The Last Blacks,' with pictures of 'tribesmen' in ceremonial costumes. So the category of 'black' has a different quality than has that of 'Indian.'"[13]

It is an undeniable historical fact that as Indian tribes encountered changing times and circumstances, they altered the way that they lived out their cultures. Yet evidence of cultural change frequently endangers a claimant's ability to establish a meaningful Indian identity within prevailing cultural definitions. Often, an Indian who is not an unreconstructible historical relic is no Indian at all.

A final element of many cultural definitions of Indian identity that likewise tends to severely circumscribe legitimate claims within them was articulated by federal district court judge Walter Skinner's instructions to the jury in the Mashpee trial. He explicitly required that the jurors consider whether or not the Mashpee had constituted a tribe at several specific historical dates, which together spanned three centuries. If the jury judged that the Mashpee had ceased to constitute a tribe at any time, then they must also conclude that the Mashpee had become non-Indians forever.

In other words, in the cultural definition that took shape in Judge Skinner's courtroom, the phenomenon familiar to anthropologists under the rubric of "cultural revival" was absolutely impossible.[14] Once a tribal community had disbanded or abandoned cultural expressions, it could never legitimately reconstitute itself or its practices. As trial chronicler James Clifford summarizes, "Life as an American meant death as an Indian. An identity could not die and come back to life. To recreate a culture that had been lost was, in the definition of the court, inauthentic."[15]

Judge Skinner's assumption that unbroken continuity forms the sine qua non of Indian cultural integrity is fundamental to many other cultural definitions of Indianness.[16] This premise, as historian James Clifford writes, reflects a Western, linear story about tribal existence in which culture is assumed to have an essentially straight and unbroken trajectory toward an end point of either survival and maintenance or disintegration and assimilation. This story makes no accommodation for "sharp contradictions, mutations, or emergencies" — the eventualities of which real life is, in fact, composed.[17] In other words, it is an unrealistic construct that reflects a great deal about the racial beliefs of those who formulated it and very little about the real world and the real people who inhabit it.

Cultural definitions of Indian identity applied to individuals rather than to whole tribes frequently make a parallel assumption: that the culture that confers legitimate Indian identity must be acquired at birth, or at least in the claimants' earliest years. This belief is instantiated in an 1846 court decision *(United States v. Rogers)*. Rogers, who was adopted as a Cherokee, asked that the court recognize him as an Indian. As his plea stated, he had not only married a Cherokee woman and taken up residence in the Cherokee Nation, where he continued to live even after her death, but he had also "incorporated himself with the said tribe of Indians, as one of them, and was and is so treated, recognized and adopted by said tribe and the proper authorities thereof, and . . . exercises all the rights and privileges of a Cherokee Indian." Rogers was denied, however, on the grounds that "a man who at *mature age* is adopted in an Indian tribe does not thereby become an Indian."[18] This legal view leaves room for the possibility that an adoptee who is raised in an Indian culture from his youth might be considered an Indian under law; however, it explicitly forecloses the possibility of changing one's identification to Indian in one's maturity.[19]

In short, the logic of cultural definitions commonly constructs culture as a mysterious something that only exists apart from intentional human activity. It can never *come into being;* it must forever *be preexistent.* It cannot be *chosen;* it can only be *given* — at the time of birth, or very close to it.

Oddly enough, although cultural definitions of identity based on such assumptions are frequently put forward by those who explicitly mock others who incline toward stereotyped ideas of "noble savages," these definitions create what must be the greatest mythical Indian of all. They create, that is, a remarkable being, unknown to social science, who can never be socialized except at a particular moment in time, his childhood. They then place this extraordinary creature into a community unlike any other in history: one that placidly carries on its lifeways unbeset by events that interrupt its cultural continuity and create lapses and disruptions that people must actively restore.

Cultural Definitions: Contexts and Consequences

Even when cultural definitions of identity are based upon stereotyped and unrealistic ideas about Indians, the consequences of being judged non-Indian by this standard can be very real. One such consequence is that many of those so judged become completely invisible to the larger society, along with their concerns. For instance, historian Alvin Josephy — then an editor at *Time* magazine — reports that, in the 1950s and 1960s, publisher Henry Luce refused any stories about Indians on the grounds that all such individuals were "phonies." "Whenever a correspondent in the field suggested a story on Indians, the query was simply crumpled up and thrown in the wastebasket. By edict, both *Time* and *Life* blacked out information about Indians."[20] The decision effectively barred Indian people from an important means by which their social and other concerns might have been brought to public attention in a period of great importance for minority civil rights.

Those who cannot establish meaningful identities within cultural definitions may lose not only their visibility but also their control over their cultural patrimony. That is, if it is concluded that certain tribes have changed so much from their authentic past that they are considered "extinct" — no longer "real Indians" — their cultural property becomes public. It becomes easy for pot hunters, scavengers, and cultural imitators of all kinds to help themselves to material objects, steal artistic designs, appropriate ceremonies, and even desecrate burial grounds. (I was once — briefly — in a family's home where, proudly displayed on the shelves overlooking the massive water bed, was a "collection" of dozens of Indian skulls the husband had unearthed.) If there are no more "real Indians," the conclusion that such behaviors are "not really hurting anyone" — and that anyone who complains is simply inventing grievances — readily follows.

A related dynamic affects tribes that invoke the Native American Graves Protection and Repatriation Act of 1990 (NAGPRA) in order to recover sacred objects from federally funded museums and similar institutions. NAGPRA provides for the restoration of objects needed for specific ceremonial observances to the tribes from which they were obtained (by, for instance, anthropologists, museum personnel, and private parties). If such objects are to be returned, the tribe must describe specific religious uses to which they will be put.

This requirement can weigh heavily upon tribes that have lost any part of their cultural knowledge and practice. Speaking at a 1999 Yale University conference, Ramona Peters of the Mashpee Wampanoag Repatriation Project regretted her tribe's inability to reclaim certain specific objects that are obviously Mashpee because knowledge of their ceremonial use is now lost.[21] Peters argued that the tribe's recovery of the objects might, in itself, stimulate cultural renewal. The objects were once known to have a power in themselves, she suggested, and if returned to the tribe, they might teach her people once again what her ancestors knew. NAGPRA, however, does not provide the Mashpee with an opportunity to explore their spiritual heritage through their material culture. Holding to the assumption that culture is strictly *invented*, not *discovered*, it demands the conclusion that specific practices are never subject to the kind of rediscovery Peters proposes. The outcome of that sternly secular assumption is, in certain instances, to deny the Mashpee a legal right which other tribes with a more fully intact body of cultural knowledge presently enjoy.

Finally, a tribe that does not satisfy certain cultural standards of identity can face serious consequences when petitioning to receive federal recognition. Interestingly, this is true even though the definition that the federal government now uses to define Indian tribes into formal existence makes particular efforts to avoid stereotyped assumptions about culture. It was formulated, that is, with an eye to escaping the assumption that the only real Indians are those who observe the cultural practices of the distant past. The identity definition relevant to federal recognition is embodied in a set of written criteria that guide the Federal Acknowledgment Process (FAP), created in the 1970s. Tribes that seek federal recognition must pass through the FAP by submitting a collection of documents to the Branch of Acknowledgment and Research (BAR), a subdivision within the Bureau of Indian Affairs.

The FAP's definition of identity attempts to incorporate cultural criteria without imposing stereotyped assumptions about Indian primitivism, such as those that arguably intruded into the Mashpee trial. That is, the FAP requires successful petitioners to show that their community is "in some way distinct from the wider society"; and cultural practice is probably the most obvious source of the required "distinctiveness."[22] But the BAR is at pains to show that it does not fall into the trap of denying Indians the right to cultural evolution. The BAR insists that it does *not* consider maintenance of any specific cultural practices, "traditional" or otherwise, a deciding factor in its evaluations. It does not subtract from the legitimacy of a tribe's claim, the BAR's regulations note, if members of a petitioning group display behaviors such as "conversion to Christianity, taking nine-to-five jobs, and eating Big Mac's." Indeed, the BAR announces itself content that "virtually all petitioners, like Indians throughout the country, have taken on characteristics of the dominant society and culture." It notes that it has recommended recognition, for instance, to groups held together as a distinct community by ties to decidedly Christian churches.[23]

It is not at all clear, however, that in its actual implementation the BAR's definition of identity avoids the same kind of prejudice enshrined in Forbes' example, which we saw earlier, of "the last Indians." If it does not require a tribal forswearing of the delights of McDonald's restaurant, it does require petitioners to show that their group has been "identified as an American Indian entity on a substantially continuous basis since 1900." The BAR then names the individuals whose opinions or actions can be pointed to in order to establish this identification: parish or government officials, anthropologists, historians, authors, and journalists, for example. Statements and actions of members of the petitioning group are specifically excluded.

In other words, groups seeking federal recognition must not only convince the BAR that they have been a "distinct" community over a long period; they must show as well that their differences have been observed and recognized as characteristically "Indian" — by *outsiders* — for an entire century. Given the long-standing linkage, in the minds of most Americans, between Indianness and ancient cultural practice, it seems likely that those who have been persistently recognized as Indians are, in fact, those whose cultural practices have conformed to stereotypes of exotic primitivism. As more than one petitioner has complained, "Tribes whose memberships exhibit the most cultural and physical attributes of the mythical, aboriginal 'Indian' will have the greatest likelihood of being acknowledged with federal recognition."[24]

Bud Shapard, former branch chief of the BAR, testifying in a federal hearing, observed a striking instance of just this kind of stereotyping on the part of government agents in the 1930s. These agents, he reports, judged a Michigan tribe culturally inauthentic on the grounds that most tribal members owned radios and were therefore "too civilized." Accordingly, the tribe was not invited to participate in the Indian Reorganization Act of 1934 and to create the formal political structures that have allowed many other tribes to receive federal recognition automatically, without passing through the FAP.[25] The FAP's dependence upon the testimony of historic outsiders to Indian communities suggests that the BAR may import, through a back door, a reliance upon a display of specific cultural attributes, particularly ones believed to be ancient, even where it attempts — and even appears — to avoid doing so. This tendency can effectively delegitimate the identity claims of entire groups of people simply because they have done what surviving groups always do: adapt themselves to changing circumstances.

Evaluating Cultural Definitions

How, then, can we evaluate the effects of cultural definitions upon Indian communities — their uses and the hazards they imply? First, cultural definitions turn our attention to people's behavior. For a number of observers, a definition centered on what people actually and ongoingly do makes more intuitive sense than do definitions of law or biology. As Melvin B., a Creek and Osage grandfather, remarks:

If I look at a person, and he's *actin'* and he's *doin'* and he's thinkin' in the direction of an Indian, then he's Indian, regardless [of his other characteristics]. My dad told me, he said, "I can tell you how to tell an Indian from a white person — is [to] get in a tepee, or a dark place at night and talk to 'em for fifteen minutes, and you can tell whether [he's] Indian or not. You don't *have* to see what color they are."

Julie M., a bilingual Cherokee who grew up in a Cherokee community, agrees:

A lot of times, I think [ordinary Cherokee] people don't even understand the nuances of this whole . . . debate . . . [about] the degrees to which someone is Cherokee. . . . Just like the people we see when we go to Stokes [Ceremonial Grounds]. You know, they're just too busy being Cherokee. . . . People who live in Cherokee homes, speak Cherokee, eat Cherokee dishes of food, and plant Cherokee gardens, and look at the world in a Cherokee way. Basically, that's what it really boils down to: who walks in that way and sees the world in that way. . . . Those of us who are Cherokee, who grew up in the Cherokee way, in the Cherokee tradition, in the Cherokee language — and just *being* Cherokee — we don't really *think* about it, you know? You just *live* it. You just *are*.

Some respondents found it distinctly odd that individuals without connections to tribal culture would nevertheless identify themselves as connected to the tribe. As Delaware tribal member Billy S. notes:

I have people who will come and say to me, "Yeah, I'm Delaware." Well, they may be. But . . . were they given a traditional name as a child? Do they go through the rites to receive an appropriate naming as an adult? Do they know anything *about* any of our ceremonies, any of our dances, any of the things that made us uniquely who we were? You can *be* that in name, but I frequently run across people who don't even know what the word *Lenape* [the word the Delaware people use for themselves, in their own language] *means,* and they turn around and tell me they're Delaware. Well [laughs], you know, I'm like — from *where*?!

Definitions based on culture seem, one might conclude, to accord better with a commonsense notion of peoplehood than the alternatives — with the idea that identity becomes genuinely meaningful when it is *lived out* in daily life, rather than merely professed or "certified" through one's documentary or genetic "credentials." Rather than grounding identity in what may be mere legal fictions, in distant and vaguely recalled genetic connections, or in simple assertion, cultural definitions hold out the promise of something observable and enduring which might underlie claims to identity.

Cultural definitions emphasize things that tribal peoples themselves have attended to as they made decisions about their community boundaries throughout history, and to which they still attend. Cherokee/Choctaw elder Joyce J. illustrates the importance of culture for Native peoples with an analogy. An Indian child without knowledge of his own cultural traditions, she says

is like a . . . a tree that, when it was young, did not have a lot of trees around it, to make it go straight up to the sun. . . . [On the other hand,] in a great forest, where you've got a lot of trees around this young tree, and that one tree grows straight up *between* those other trees to reach the sun, then it's going to be strong, and it's gonna be there for two and three hundred years. And that's the way it is with Indian children. . . . Without that foundation, or that . . . that *circle* of tradition, to raise that child in, it becomes weaker and weaker as its years go on.

One aspect of culture that often receives particular attention among Indian people in matters of identity is their relationship to land. Cherokee theologian Jace Weaver expresses that relationship by describing Indian people as more "spatially oriented rather than temporally oriented. Their cultures, spirituality, and identity are connected to land — and not simply land in a generalized sense, but *their* land. The act of creation [described in sacred stories] is not so much what happened *then* as it is what happened *here.*"[26]

Some Native peoples do not even make a firm distinction between their physical being and the land they occupy. Tewa author Gregory Cajete writes that, traditionally, Indian people often experienced Nature as a part of themselves and themselves as a part of it. They understood themselves literally as born of the Earth of their Place. That children are bestowed to a mother and her community through the direct participation of earth spirits, and that children came from springs, lakes, mountains, or caves embedded in the Earth where they existed as spirits before birth, were widespread Indian perceptions. This is the ultimate identification of being Indigenous to a place and forms the basis for a fully internalized bonding with that place.[27]

Cherokee-Chickasaw scholar of American Indian literature Geary Hobson points out linguistic evidence for sentiments such as Cajete and Weaver describe, which link tribal identity with relationships to land: "In many Native American languages the words 'people' and 'land' are indistinguishable and inseparable. In the name of 'Oklahoma,' for instance, that land of exile for great numbers of eastern tribes and people, the word taken from the Choctaw and Chickasaw tongues, we find the words enveloped in synonymity. . . . [The root word] means both people and land. There is no separation; they are one."[28]

Respondent Ramona P. also highlights this relationship between identity and land. When she describes herself as a Mashpee woman, she says: "I'm talking about the spirit and the collective consciousness of my people. And also about my connectedness to this *land*. We've been here for many thousands of years. Our experiences of joy have happened here, and our hardships as well. No matter where I've ever been in the world, my dreams and my spirit bring me back here [to Mashpee]. For nourishment. And I guess that's why we were planted here."

Yet relationships to land are not the only central identity-conferring aspect of culture for Indian people. When Billy S., an Eastern Delaware tribal citizen, is asked to consider the significance of the various aspects of culture to Indian identity, he says,

I think *language* is important. Because obviously, if you don't have some grasp of the language, how are you gonna understand the songs? How are you going to understand the true meaning of the ceremonies? And our ceremonies are part of what makes us uniquely who we *are*. If we don't have those, we've lost our identity.

Donald G., a lifelong speaker of the Cherokee language, makes a similar point, with simple elegance: "If . . . [Indian people] speak the [tribal] language, they know the *thoughts* of that group."

Some types of ceremonial participation are limited to those with fluency in the tribal language; and respondents tell of other, less formal community boundaries that also remind tribal members of language's importance. Cherokee elder Tom E. tells a story:

It used to be at Vian [a Cherokee ceremonial ground in Oklahoma] many years ago . . . that when they had [the annual dance honoring the birthday of historic leader Redbird Smith] . . . they killed a lot of hogs. They gave everyone who was going to camp for the whole weekend some of the meat, so they could fix it and eat it. It was called "the ration." This man said he wouldn't give a Cherokee any meat unless he could say it in Cherokee: say *siqua hawiya waduli* [I want some pork]. . . . You know, a lot of [people] camping [at the grounds] come up for meat. But if they couldn't say at least that much in Cherokee, they didn't get any meat.

Shared norms, values, and general patterns of thought are cultural characteristics that may also be taken seriously as determinants of identity. Retired educator Archie M., a citizen of the Osage Nation, illustrates this point when he says that

in general, when I say someone is an Indian . . . I [mean] they're like me. Not necessarily in appearance, but in spirit. They have a "Indian heart." Somebody is like me because somebody has taught them like my teachers have taught me, on how to live and how to look at other people. How to *feel* about other people. . . . I imagine myself sometimes if I was blind, and I couldn't see the color or the tones of someone's skin. But just by talking with them, [I] could feel that they — they thought, or they sensed, the same.

Even Donald G. — who previously likened racial mixing to a process that combines mayonnaise and ketchup and progressively dilutes tribal identity — is not always sure that genetics entirely determines Indianness. Although he thinks that blood quantum "seems to be a big deal" to many people, he also feels that "your attitude has a lot to do with who you are. And . . . being able to speak the language. . . . You can have those three [blood quantum, an appropriate attitude, and language ability] . . . or a combination of two without the others [and be Indian]. Because a person can be four-fourths [Indian] and their attitude may be 'well, I don't want to associate with those Indians. . . . They are below me.' And those kind of things. [In that case,] he's an outsider."

An individual's cultural characteristics may actually take precedence over anything else in the determinations of tribal belonging. Melvin B. voices his conviction:

I've seen some full-blooded Indians, that I *know* are full-blooded Indians, that are *not* Indians. They don't care about the Indian culture, they don't attend Indian functions. They don't care about 'em. . . . So I would say no, even though he's a full blood, he's not a real Indian. . . . I see a blonde-headed person, blue-eyed, that attends ceremonial things and goes to different tribal affairs and things like that. And they try to uphold the Indian tradition. To me, that's a real Indian. But that's again, that's *my* way of lookin' and seein'.

Joyce J. concurs:

It doesn't matter how much blood they are or how much this or that, but *if* they are of the old, of the spiritual, way; if their heart is Indian, . . . their *minds* and their thoughts are Indian, then they're . . . they're going to be enveloped in some family, in an Indian family that will *take* them and teach them even more. So I think what . . . what makes an Indian has nothing to do with amount of blood. . . . I think it's their thinking, their mind, their soul, and their heart.

History offers example after example that verifies and extends Joyce J.'s point. For instance, at one point in the nineteenth century, Indian Territory (later Oklahoma) boasted a whole population of African Americans who fully embraced, and were embraced by, tribal cultures, regardless of whether or not their genetics included any Indian ancestry. Adopting tribal languages, food, dress, and religions, these "black Indians" lived on tribal land and participated in tribal political and ceremonial life.[29] Some of these individuals had never been enslaved, but even those who had been owned by Indians and were freed after the Civil War might consider themselves and their families Indian in a cultural sense. For a time, at least some tribes (notably the Creeks and Seminoles) accepted the "black Indians" as fully participating members, even electing them to high tribal offices such as tribal judge and council member.

Today, as in the past, tribal people may show themselves flexible about inclusivity. Joyce J. has observed a dynamic of adoption across tribal boundaries during her more than seventy years of life among her people:

Some [Cherokee women] would take in babies from other tribes and raise them as theirs. . . . If there was a baby, no matter what . . . tribe it was, if its mother didn't want it, or its mother couldn't raise it, they would bring that baby to [my aunt Eliza], and she would raise it. And she would raise it *as* a Cherokee. Because that's all she knew. She couldn't raise it in whatever-it-was. But it didn't matter what that child was — it was *gonna* be *Cherokee*. And, I know she raised twenty-some-odd that way.[30]

In some cases, whole communities have collectively embraced particular individuals, even though they are not relatives by either law or blood, if they demonstrate cultural competence. Tom E. offers an example: "I know one [man] from around Tahlequah [Oklahoma], back south there. He's got long hair, and [he's] a good stomp dance leader. He's not Indian at all. The elders that know him say they brought him there [to a Cherokee community] when he was small. . . . They say he couldn't get no CDIB card. . . . [But] they taught him [to speak] good Cherokee, [and he's a] good stomp dance leader."[31]

Some tribes have even extended certain formal privileges of membership to those who are not tribal members by birth. This occurred in 1992, for instance, when the Yankton Nakota (Sioux) of South Dakota considered the case of a young man who had been adopted by a reservation family in his adolescence. He had learned to speak the tribal language and to practice the traditional culture, but as a non-Indian person biologically, he was forbidden by the Indian Arts and Craft Act of 1990 from marketing the artwork he created as "Indian produced." The tribe eventually found his exclusion intolerable and voted to certify him as a tribal artist, allowing him to market his work accordingly.[32]

All this is to say that, as both historical and contemporary Indian communities have thought about their membership, they have paid considerable attention to many of the same sorts of things that cultural definitions also illuminate: to aspects of thought and behavior. This reflection of traditional preferences can be considered another way that cultural definitions may recommend themselves to Indian communities. But the cultural definitions of Indian identity also create some profoundly infelicitous outcomes for tribes.[33] For instance, Dakota Sioux scholar Elizabeth Cook-Lynn suggests that cultural definitions tend to lead directly to an unwholesome fascination with tribal "authenticity." The notion, she suggests, that only a narrow range of practices, beliefs, objects, and the like represent "genuine" Indian culture eventually undermines a group's collective growth and vitality. She uses the example of storytelling to illustrate her point. When certain storytellers, stories, plots, characters, and themes are selected and labeled as culturally "authentic," these become the benchmark against which other cultural patterns must be measured. "Following this line of thought," she writes, "traditional storytelling must end. Almost everything outside of those patterns must be discarded. . . . There is no sense of an on-going literary and intellectual life. The new stories, should they somehow emerge, will always be lesser ones. There are no contemporary 'Homers,' as in Western Literature, no Shakespeares, no Isak Dinesens, no defenders of the faith, only pathetic imitators."[34] The logic of cultural "authenticity" may initially support the identity claims of individuals and tribes, only later to destroy them, along with the culture in which they arose.

There is also the question of whether cultural definitions of identity, even those that proceed from an informed grasp of the cultural practices characteristic of intact communities, adequately take into account the reality of the historical experiences of Indian people. We should not forget that European and American political, religious, and educational institutions have long sponsored relentless campaigns to destroy Indian cultures. The history of the Mashpee, whose late-twentieth-century legal battle was recounted at the opening of this chapter, is a case in point.

From its early days, the Massachusetts Bay Colony began interfering with Mashpee culture and attempting to transform it. To begin with, it is likely that European diseases, introduced by explorers, preceded European settlement, causing virulent epidemics, such that only a greatly diminished Mashpee population survived to see the Puritans arrive.[35] But once settlers did arrive, they passed legislation outlawing all traditional Indian religious practices. They also worked to bring the Indian under political control. They established "praying towns" — segregated and heavily regulated communities for those Mashpee they managed to convert. Upon entering such towns, the Mashpee Christians were forced to sever ties with family, friends, and tribe and to replace their economic, political, educational, religious, and other institutions with radically different forms. By the 1700s, European control had expanded even more, with overseers regulating the leasing and sale of Mashpee land, natural resources, and even children, whom they could hire out for labor at their discretion.[36]

The Mashpee story, in its general outlines, is far from unique, although the projects to extinguish the distinctive cultural characteristics of tribes took somewhat different forms in different parts of the country, and at different times. It would be very surprising if these efforts had *not* been widely effective in compromising or even destroying language, spirituality, family relationships, geographic ties, and other elements of Native cultures. Yet for many Indian people, feelings of shame attend cultural performance that they judge inadequate. One respondent (whose name I omit here) confides: "Sometimes, being a full blood . . . I feel like a stupid idiot for *not* speaking [my native language]. I just feel like a part of my identity is not perfect, 'cuz I don't talk [my language]."

The sad truth is that some Indian people have paid, and continue to pay, the economic, social, familial, personal, and other consequences of an Indian identity, but have little "culture" left to compensate them for it. Hopi-Miwok author and poet Wendy Rose provides an example when she discusses her own experience of cultural loss. Rose thinks of herself, she says, as an "Indian writer." Yet she is well aware that her biography is unlikely to satisfy the requirements of a cultural definition of identity. "It is not Indian," she writes, to be left so alone, to be alienated, to be friendless, to be forced to live on the street like a rat, to be unacquainted with your cousins. It would certainly be better for my image as an Indian poet to manufacture something, and let you believe in my traditional, loving, spiritual childhood where every winter evening was spent immersed in storytelling and ceremony, where the actions of every day continually told me I was valued.

In reality, she concludes, "there is nothing authentic about my past; I am sure that I would be a great disappointment to anthropologists."[37]

Can we read such words and still insist upon strict standards of cultural competence before we allow others to claim a meaningful identity as Indian people? Can we confront such pain and still enforce identity definitions that inevitably exclude precisely those who have already suffered the greatest degree of cultural loss and its profound consequences? Tom Hill and Richard W. Hill, Sr., write, in a book illustrating the collections of the National Museum of the American Indian, that Indian "children are born within circles of tradition that define the world views of their communities."[38] This is a beautiful thought. But many Indian people today acknowledge that such a description does not apply to them. And they do not know how to remedy what they feel as a profound loss.

Cheyenne-Arapahoe playwright Christina West, in her drama *Inner Circles,* shows that the insistence upon a cultural definition of identity not only excludes some individuals who feel their exclusion deeply; it can also actively discourage the very processes by which Indian people and communities might heal both themselves and others. West probes this painful wound by creating a character who is German on her father's side and Cheyenne on her mother's. This character says:

I remember one time, I went to an Oktoberfest with my Dad. . . . He didn't know that much about being German . . . but he seemed to fit right in. . . . He started talking to a vendor about lederhosen: "What are these made of?" . . . Then they started having this whole conversation about German immigration. I was amazed. . . . My father asked questions openly, and he got answers. No one ever questioned his German heritage. They didn't think any less of him for not knowing. . . . It would never happen like that in a Native community. You wouldn't give the sacred secret of lederhosen to just anyone.

Displaying ignorance, West's character concludes, "is like admitting that you don't know who you are. . . . If you are Native, then you should know your customs and all the rules about your tribe."[39]

So strict and unforgiving a linkage of culture and identity often leaves Indian people with a pervasive legacy of insecurity and pain. Admitting to such sentiments, moreover, may only create more "evidence" of one's insufficient Indianness for others to attack. Young people do not learn well when they are frightened — nor do adults or elders. The judgment that "he is not one of us" is a severe enough price that many people of Indian heritage with the potential to make significant contributions to Indian communities may choose not to participate in their traditional cultures at all, rather than risk the effort and be rejected for demonstrated lack of competence. There is probably no surer recipe for extinguishing a culture than this. This is not to say that Indian communities should abandon culture as a standard of identity. But perhaps they would do well to remember their histories — and their futures — as they think about how they use culture to define the boundaries of their communities in the present.[40]

In reviewing cultural definitions of identity, it sometimes appears that they present an insoluble dilemma. One the one hand, many Indian people agree that their identities are closely bound up with distinctive ways of being in the world. Yet this is a position that easily edges over into an unrealistic demand that "authentic" Indian lifeways must embody the farthest, most exotic extreme of otherness (such that no Indian person could ever satisfy the requirements). And there are good reasons why Indian communities might want to forgive themselves, and others, for the cultural losses they have suffered.

On the other hand, unless one is willing to surrender cultural definitions altogether, one must still ask: just how closely can Indian groups resemble their non-Indian neighbors and still embody a separate people, an *Indian* people? James Clifford, following his observations at the Mashpee trial, concluded that "all the critical elements of identity are in specific conditions replaceable: language, land, blood, leadership, religion. Recognized, viable tribes exist in which any one or even most of these elements are missing, replaced, or largely transformed."[41] If we agree that he is correct, the whole idea of culture seems to slip through our fingers. How could we ever know if it were present or absent? If all of its elements are replaceable, what is it, and where is it? If all the elements that compose a culture can disappear, while the cultural identity somehow remains, is there anyone who is *not* Indian? These are questions with no obvious answers, and to which we must return in a later chapter.

FOUR

If You're Indian and You Know It (but Others Don't)

Self-Identification

When Zug G. Standing Bear attends meetings of the Deer Clan of Georgia, he rubs shoulders with individuals with names such as Morning Star, Panther, Grey Wolf, and Wild Rose. The Deer Clan, in Standing Bear's description, is "a rather feisty unit of a larger Native American cultural association known as the Southeastern Cherokee Confederacy (SECC)."[1] Medicine men and a council of clan mothers assist in group leadership. Members share their interest in such cultural activities as powwows, Native American language study, genealogy workshops, tribal arts and crafts classes, and the like.[2]

As one might well suppose, Mr. Standing Bear and his comrades describe themselves as American Indians. They do so, however, within a distinctive definition: one based upon self-identification. The expression "self-identified Indian" is sometimes used to refer to anyone who does not satisfy the requirements specifically of legal definitions. This usage allows room for the possibility that the individual may nevertheless still ground his identity claim within definitions of biology or culture. My usage, however, is narrower.

Definitions of self-identification, for my purposes, describe systems of rules that systematically direct attention away from questions of law, blood, or culture. They concentrate, instead, upon the individual's understanding of herself as she expresses it in a personal profession of identity. Under these definitions, Indians are simply those who *say* that they are Indian. Cherokee demographer Russell Thornton provides an example of such a definition when he writes that "common to all

Cherokees is an identity as Cherokee. . . . All of the 232,344 individu-als described . . . [in the 1980 U.S. census] identified themselves as Cherokee. So they are."[3]

The Deer Clan is representative of a thriving popular movement cen-tered on interest in American Indian ancestry and heritage. The groups that constitute the movement, known as "Indian descendant recruitment organizations," have begun to spring up across the country, typically assembling through such means as newspaper advertising. The Deer Clan illustrates the self-identification definitions I have in mind, in that it minimizes claims about biological ancestry or legal status. Although most members profess Indian descent in one degree or another, their var-ious heritages derive from not one but a number of different tribes. Moreover, the group has typically consisted of individuals "who claimed Native American heritage but who could not prove a bloodline connec-tion to a federally recognized tribe."[4] Thus the biological characteristics of the Deer Clan's members are necessarily not central to definitions of identity because they are largely undocumentable. Legal definitions take a back seat for the same reason. (Although the group at one time partic-ipated in efforts to secure the status of a federally acknowledged tribe, the formal denial of recognition to its umbrella organization, the South-eastern Cherokee Confederacy, encouraged the Deer Clan to surrender this goal.)

The group even minimizes the definition of culture as the foundation of identity. It recognizes that its members, at least as they enter the group, typically do not have close associations with an intact Indian com-munity. Standing Bear, in fact, offers an interesting account of his own journey of "becoming a minority," as he puts it — or reclaiming an Indian identity after having lived in the white, cultural mainstream most of his life. One day, he says, at age forty, he simply put on his moccasins and walked into the office of his dissertation advisor — Standing Bear is a sociologist by professional training — announcing that he had changed his name and his racial identity along with it. From thenceforward, he intended to live as an American Indian, claiming an ancestry about which he had previously kept silent.

Standing Bear followed up his promise by helping to form the Deer Clan, an organization that would meet the needs and interests of others like himself — people who thought (or were beginning to think) of themselves as Indian, who were willing to proclaim themselves as such, but who might not satisfy the usual definitions of racial identity. A main purpose of the group is to explore and even *create* a new community: "to practice and promote traditional Native American customs, culture, and values for its members and the wider community."[5] The group has established its own version of Indian cultural practice from what members have been able to learn from their own research and discussion, and from observing various tribes. (Hence, for instance, the new names they have chosen for themselves.)

Personal Definitions: Contexts and Consequences

As with the other definitions of identity, there are certain benefits that accrue to those who assert by their own proclamation an Indian identity. For people who, for whatever reason, have been unable to successfully negotiate within the other definitions an Indian identity that others construe as legitimate, self-identification provides an important source of personal satisfaction. Standing Bear and many of his fellow Deer Clan members speak with great feeling about the personal significance of their self-proclaimed identity. It connects them to those they understand as "their people"; it allows them to express something central to their sense of self, even when other definitions of Indian identity close them out.

There can be other, more tangible rewards as well. For instance, some social service and philanthropic organizations — perhaps loath to impose a criterion upon Indians that is not imposed upon other minority groups — do not require any documentary proof of identity for those who apply. The same is true of minority scholarships offered by at least some universities. Literary and art organizations that reserve awards, special commissions, and other perquisites for Native artists also sometimes show themselves willing to simply accept an individual's word on her racial identity. There have even been occasional cases in which Indian descendant recruitment organizations have applied for and managed to receive federal funding intended for Indian tribes.[6]

Self-identification as Indian, moreover, is sometimes used as a sort of access card to American Indian spiritual and cultural practices, many of which have become objects of interest to a substantial proportion of the American population. This dynamic is particularly evident in some expressions of the New Age movement. The New Age is really a loose collection of vaguely "spiritual" groups interested in such diverse subjects as channeling, healing, psychic phenomena, crystals, goddess worship, and alternative medicine. New Age adherents frequently express an insatiable interest in all forms of American Indian culture, but especially spiritual and ceremonial practices. Some also claim identification as Indian and may parlay their assertion into attempts to enhance access to the cultural elements they desire — even when established American Indian communities object.

Finally, some individuals may use the definition of self-identification simply as a means to gain attention or admiration. As a recent expression goes, "it's in to be skin" ("skin" being a slang term by which Indians sometimes identify themselves). In other words, an Indian identity has recently become not only safer to assert than it once was; it has even become a source of pride and an object of envy in certain quarters, and a number of people have accordingly become eager to claim it. Consider, for instance, an organization named the Court of the Golden Eagle in Dallas, Texas. It is headed by an individual bearing the impressive title of "His Royal and Imperial Majesty, The Oukah, Emperor of Tsalagi (the Kingdom of Paradise), King of the Upper Cherokee, King of the Middle Cherokee, King of the Lower Cherokee, Keeper of the Ancient Traditions, and Supreme God of the Sun, The Cherokee Nation." His other name is Donald Robinson.[7]

Negotiating Self-Identification

Self-identification is the definition of identity that, in principle, offers the most opportunities for advancing an identity claim and the fewest constraints. However, the fact that anyone can assert an identity does not mean that all such identifications are accepted as meaningful. Perhaps the most effective way for others to delegitimate an individual's self-identification as Indian is to accuse him of "ethnic switching." This term conveys the suspicion that individuals who are now calling themselves Indian have not continuously sustained that identification, but have instead *jumped between* racial identities (a behavior to which Zug Standing Bear openly admits). "Ethnic switchers" have kept quiet about their Indianness for a long time, perhaps for generations, assimilating into the dominant culture and consistently "passing" as non-Indian. Perhaps for a time they were even unaware of their American Indian ancestry. Now, however, they have reclaimed this once-discarded or concealed identity.[8]

People who are accused of ethnic switching will at least come in for a great deal of ribbing. They will be labeled "new Indians" or — more irreverently — "born-again Indians." Cherokee novelist Betty Bell provides an example of the even more elaborate fun that may be poked at "new Indians" in her description of the Reverend Tim Cottonmouth. His commercial advertisements for his own Indian descendant recruitment organization run as follows:

This here's the Reverend Tim Cottonmouth. Speakin' to ya from the national I Wannabe a Cherokee network in Tulsa, Oklahoma. . . .

Ifn your having a little tribal uncertainty, ifn the drum is telling ya the Apache, the Choctaw, the Osage is not fer you, ifn ya say Iroquois and the white man thinks you're from the Middle East, then come on down to the Cherokee Meeting House.

Ifn y'all had bad credit, a turn a bad luck, think to yourselves, Indian brothers and sisters, maybe y'all need a new identity. An' ya can have it right here, no questions asked an' no references needed. Y'all had grandmommas, ain't no more needed than that. . . .

Send us your money now, Indian brothers and sisters. . . . Don't be left out of the new Cherokee Nation.

Cherokee. We mean Indian.[9]

Self-identifiers accused of ethnic switching also come in for far harsher criticism. Indian people who have maintained stable racial identifications within one or another definition — Indians who, as the expression goes, "were Indian before it was popular" — may harbor understandable resentments toward those who are perceived as not having "paid their dues." There are suspicions that new Indians only show themselves when rewards for doing so become available. As anthropologist Alfonso Ortiz, a Tewa from San Juan Pueblo, reproaches, "These [ethnic switchers] are people who have no business soaking up jobs and grants, people who have made no claims to being Indian up to their early adulthood, and then when there's something to be gained they're opportunists of the rankest stripe, of the worst order. . . . We resent these people who just come in when the going's good and skim the riches off the surface."[10] Many Indians — including those who might themselves be construed as ethnic switchers within certain definitions — will go to great lengths to rebuff, exclude, and demean "new Indians."

Evaluating Self-Identification

Like the other definitions of Indian identity we have explored, self-identification is a method of defining identity that raises a wide spectrum

of observations and concerns in Native communities. Indeed, the outcomes it can create are probably the subject of more heated debate than
are the benefits and hazards of any of the other definitions.

Some interview respondents note that Indians who excessively critique the identity claims of others often betray themselves as troubled
individuals who are anxious about their own place in a tribal community.
Principal chief of the Cherokee Nation Chad Smith suspects "the inade-
quacies and insecurities of those who want to argue" about identity,
while full-blood Wichita and Seneca clergyman Bill T. suggests that people accuse others of not being real Indians only "so that they can
draw . . . attention to themselves. . . . You know: 'Here *I* am Indian.' . . .
They [the accusers] are wanting to say they're more Indian than maybe
they really are."

Yet other Indian people also readily give sound, practical reasons for
their concerns about self-identification as a standard for establishing
racial identity. One woman describes her experience working for an
Indian service provider that followed a policy of self-identification
regarding recipients: "You really did have a lot of people showing up
claiming that one of their ancestors, seven steps removed, had been some
sort of 'Cherokee princess.' And we were obliged to accept that, and provide services. Hell, if all that was real, there are more Cherokees in the
world than there are Chinese."[11]

Complaints of this type suggest that there are simply too many tangible incentives motivating people to commit what is known as "ethnic
fraud." When tribal affiliation carries with it access to limited material
resources, their exploitation by illegitimate recipients occurs at the
expense of legitimate ones. A policy of self-definition does not allow for
regulating such access. June L., a Mohawk grandmother, phrases her
concern as a rhetorical question: "Federal law protects [Indian people's
rights to use] eagle feathers and [their right to market] Indian jewelry,
but does it protect from people that pretend to be Indians [and take] our
jobs or our scholarships? People that pose as Indian — this is the latest in
the Indian community." The Association of American Indian and Alaska
Native Professors has developed a formal Statement on Ethnic Fraud
that reflects similar sentiments and warns educational institutions about
applicants who inappropriately claim a tribal identity.[12]

Granted, informal standards of identification served earlier generations of Indians, who inhabited communities dominated by small family and clan groups in which members knew each other. Yet it is unclear
how these can function as the basis for the distribution of resources in

today's rationally ordered society, where people are processed by impersonal bureaucratic agencies — including tribal and other governments.[13]

Another serious objection to self-identification revolves around the
issue of tribal sovereignty. Sovereignty refers to the right of tribes, as
semi-autonomous "domestic dependent nations" existing within the
boundaries of the United States, to exercise governmental authority
over their internal affairs. "Tribal sovereignty," writes legal scholar
Charles Wilkinson, "is the lifeblood of an emerging Indian separatism
that permits tribes to decide in the matters that really count."[14] American
history reveals a long story of the erosion of tribal sovereignty, resulting
from both deliberate assault and simple neglect on the part of federal and
state governments. Tribes, accordingly, carefully guard their prerogatives
of sovereignty, most particularly the right to define citizenship. They
tend to view any interference in such matters as an intrusion of the thin
end of an infinitely expansible wedge against which they must exercise
constant vigilance.

A number of Indian people argue that a policy of self-definition, by
indulging the preferences of individuals over the formally expressed will
of the tribe that has declined to recognize them as citizens, constitutes
just such a wedge. Professor Emerita of English and Native American
Studies Elizabeth Cook-Lynn (Dakota) articulates this perspective. She
reminds her readers that, traditionally, American Indian tribes have
tended to place the authority of the group over the rights of the individual, and she takes to task those who suggest that their personal situations
warrant a reversal of those priorities. She contends that certain of her academic colleagues, lacking a firm grounding in the Indian identities they
profess, have taken advantage of the perquisites of academic positions to
embark on intellectualized quests to explore their individual selfhood. In
so doing, she asserts, "they [have] exploited the legacy of blood that
wrought cries into the night of personal agonies and private hells."[15]

Her point seems to be that Indian academics ought to be working for
their communities, not massaging individualistic ideas of self and racial
identity. Indianness, Cook-Lynn insists, is not simply a matter of personal decision or individual definition — and allowing endless debate
about various individuals' ideas of identity simply encourages them, and
the society in general, to believe that they have a right that they in no
wise enjoy: the right to determine who is a citizen of a tribal nation. In
general, arguments such as Cook-Lynn's emphasize that tribal sovereignty is such a delicate political prerogative that tribes cannot afford to

tolerate competition from definitions based upon self-identification, which only cloud the issue further.

Self-identification raises another threat to sovereignty: the cavalcade of self-identified people and groups who improperly present themselves as representing the views, values, commitments, or authority of entire Indian tribes. Certain Indian descendant recruitment organizations, for instance, have a disturbing habit of issuing documents "certified" by their own illegal copies of official seals belonging to federally recognized tribes and of making up "tribal enrollment cards" that may be indistinguishable from the real things. In such cases, tribes effectively lose control over what is said and done in their name. They lose it to people, moreover, who may be very hard to sanction because they are neither formal citizens of the tribe nor members of a tribal community. Individuals who display such behaviors may not understand them as threats to tribal sovereignty, but tribal officials are often hard pressed to see them in any other light.[16]

Perhaps more disturbing than threats to what is, for some, the rather abstract notion of tribal sovereignty are the large number of people who in recent years have used self-identification as an Indian in connection with acts of violent abuse. For instance, a few years ago *Indian Country Today* reported the conviction of one David Smith, a Pennsylvania man who called himself Two Wolves and claimed to be an Indian "shaman priest" although he was not enrolled in any federally recognized tribe. He had also gathered around himself an Indian recruitment organization. Reported charges against him include engaging in sexual misconduct with a little girl during what he called an Indian "cleansing ceremony." (He was at the time on probation from a conviction for similar assaults upon another little girl.) The charges, totaling forty-five, consisted of both felonies and misdemeanors, for which he received a prison sentence of up to forty years.[17]

Another example is found in the biography of Harley "Swiftdeer" Reagan. Reagan claims to be Cherokee and to occupy an invented, but supposedly traditional ceremonial office in the Cherokee tribe, which gives him the right and duty of "initiating" little girls into womanhood by teaching them how to give and receive sexual pleasure. With the help of his biographer, he extols the virtues of statutory rape, in the name of cultural continuity, for some hundreds of pages.[18]

Unfortunately, individuals who share the character and behavior of Smith and Reagan are anything but unheard of. The news article report-

ing Smith's actions and convictions notes that "many self-declared medicine men or spiritual leaders are found throughout the country, and they
appear to be part of a growing subculture."[19] In such a climate, tribes
must be able to repudiate those who make fraudulent claims of affiliation
with them the basis of criminal behavior. They must be able to do so,
first, in the interests of ensuring the physical safety of individuals, and
second, to protect their own cultures and spiritualities. When state or
federal courts encounter self-identified Indians who have used the context of religious ceremony to perpetrate sexual crimes, they may not
know that such behaviors are *not* part of any legitimate Indian ceremonial. They may therefore conclude that Indian religious practices in general are debased and dangerous. Such a conclusion already has a long tradition in American society: Many native ceremonial practices were
criminalized and otherwise circumscribed in the early twentieth century,
and some still are.[20] Widespread abuse of Indian spiritual practice by the
illegitimately self-identified could cause misinformed legislators to limit
once again the religious freedom of legitimate Indian worshippers.

Even when self-identified Indians' motivation for using Native ceremonies is not criminal, other Indians sometimes object. Of particular
concern here are the self-identified individuals who are part of the New
Age movement. New Age adherents have a prodigious interest in the cultures and spiritualities of other peoples, and American Indian peoples are
high on the menu of favorites. A number of New Age believers go so far,
in their enthusiasm for American Indian ways, as to identify themselves
as connected with one tribe or another.

Such a claim may be based on an ancestral connection with a more-or-
less distant relative. Given the history of intermarriage between Indians
and Europeans (not to mention the sexual assaults that the latter used as
part of their military strategy in the conquest of the Americas), it is certainly likely that many people do have some biological ancestry in an
American Indian tribe. But for some reason, one peculiar claim emerges
(and not only among New Age adherents) with a regularity so persistent
as to jar the sensibilities of many Indian people who hear it. It is even
included in a satirical list circulating on the Internet of experiences
definitive of "Indianness" (given to me by an interview respondent,
Nancy C.): "Being Indian is . . . having every third person you meet tell
you about his great-grandmother, who was a real Cherokee princess."

Although neither Cherokees nor any other tribe had traditionally
encountered, let alone institutionalized, the idea of royalty or monarchy,
Indian people are regularly approached by strangers with this same odd

announcement. As a staff member of *Indian Country Today* writes, the mysterious Cherokee princess who appears in the genealogies of so many white Americans really must have been "like the mythological Christmas fruitcake." That is, "there was just one, but she got around."[21] And it seems that many of her descendants decided, in the twentieth century, to take up New Age spirituality.

In some cases, New Age believers even refer to an Indian identity at the remove of one lifetime — which is to say that some individuals claim that they were Indian "in a past life," even if they presently exist in a non-Indian body. Other New Age adherents create new possibilities for self-identification by suggesting that they can or have essentially "become" Indian, even though they conform to none of the other definitions of identity. For instance, it is occasionally suggested that racial identities are available for purchase. A New Age magazine recently ran an advertisement headed by the remarkable announcement that "You can become a Native American . . . and how." The ad promises that "the Two Birds Society of Signal Hill, Calif., will give you your very own Indian name and authenticate it with a certificate stating that you are an honorary Native American." (All this for only $28.00.)[22]

Tribal objections to New Age theories and practices are less concerned with the way that believers come by their self-identifications and focus more on what those self-identifications motivate them to do. A common complaint is that the New Age faithful express unlimited eagerness to experience a variety of Indian sacred ceremonies, whether or not they have received the long and difficult training required to perform or participate in them properly. As Mashpee Wampanoag member Ramona P. notes, "Sometimes those who are making claims to [a tribal] identity are really using them to . . . get themselves into ceremonies and things that they should not be [in]." New Age believers frequently piece together their own versions of a ceremony from bits of tribal sacred practices. Sweat lodges are particularly popular, as are observances of the solstice, the creation of "medicine wheels," participation in plains-style "vision quests," and so on.[23] Others simply insert themselves into the ongoing ceremonial lives of Native communities to the extent that they are able.

Such activities suggest a conceptualization of Native cultures as a collection of consumable commodities that can be individually extracted from a larger complex of beliefs, practices, and daily life activities and put to use to serve whatever agenda the buyer conceives, much like a lucky rabbit's foot. Archie M. expresses the feelings that arise in him, as an Osage and Cherokee man, when outsiders simply appropriate traditional ceremonies for their own purposes, imposing their own meanings and values:

> I can relate personally, as a visitor to [a ceremonial dance at] the San Ildefonso Pueblo. . . . I saw some non-Indians there, who I call my "organic-type people," in their sandals and long dresses. And they were in the audience, but they were beginning to swing and sway, with their . . . eyes closed. . . . They were going through the motions like there was something really *affecting* them. . . . So I think that I've observed people who are searching for something and feel that they get it by attending our ceremonies. Whether they're invited or not. And that's the major difference. They don't have any ownership in it, or cultural history, or background that would allow them to be a part of this ceremony. But yet, they come and take it.

Such appropriation feels wrong to him, Archie continues. It even gives rise to a persistent resentment. "Because they don't know what they're getting. They *think* they know. And they think they may be 'balanced,' and that the universe is all in balance, and the four directions, and all this stuff. And perhaps they're well read about this. But they still don't have a clue what's really going on out there [in the ceremony]."

Worse yet, when individuals who are not subject to the control of a larger community of Indian people take hold of the idea that they can create their own versions of Indian traditions, they sometimes even presume to instruct individuals who have grown up in an Indian culture in their own ceremonial practice. Various respondents commented on this dynamic. As Cherokee/Choctaw great-grandmother Joyce J. remarks:

> What bothers me is the wannabee Indians that go around, and all they learned is from books. You'll see them even in *schools*. Setting up dressed like an Indian, ya know, telling stories and all. . . . Yeah, I do get irritated when I have these people correct *me*, and try to tell me that I'm wrong because they have read it in a book that a white man's written!

Delaware and Peoria respondent Billy S. offers another example of cultural appropriation:

> One of the real dilemmas we're up against today is that we have numerous authors out there who tout themselves as being Native American and have *no* lineal ancestry. . . . And unfortunately, they are basically writing about ceremonies and other things that they have no *authority* to. . . . I've had an ongoing controversy with an individual who has co-opted the last name that is my family's and went through and actually had her name legally changed to that. And [she] has written several books on Native American philosophy from a "female standpoint." . . . Short of filing a lawsuit, we've kind of been at a stand-off on the issue.

So I think there *has* to be some method of determining who is recognized as being Native and who isn't.

Philip Deloria (Dakota), in a fascinating book titled *Playing Indian,* gives a more elaborate example of religious appropriation when he describes the Hopi tribes' experience with a group calling itself the Smoki (a deliberate approximation of the Hopi tribe's self-designation, *Moki*). For decades the Smoki have insisted, over tribal protestations, that *they* need to preserve the Hopi Snake Dance in its "proper" form by performing it regularly. Hopi leader Don Nelson, unimpressed by this argument, eventually resorted to escorting some of the Smoki members to his village to show them that the Hopis themselves were "willing and able to carry on their own traditions without help from non-Indians."[24]

By way of comparison, one might wonder how a devout Catholic would feel upon hearing about a group of people who had read some books on that faith and then undertaken to celebrate High Mass in the back yard. ("Hang on a sec'; I'll just be turning the cheese doodles and Kool-Aid into the body and blood of Christ now.") Many Indians experience a similar queasiness at the thought of individuals with no specific qualifications carrying out, or inviting themselves into, the sacred ceremonial rituals belonging to their people.

Acceptance of self-identification as a standard of Indian identity blurs the boundary between legitimate, trained ceremonialists and knowledgeable participants, on the one hand, and on the other, outsiders who dredge the cultures of others in search of exotic trinkets. It can supply those New Age practitioners who self-identify as Indians with a means to argue for an apparently equal *moral right* to the cultural practices they covet. That is, it allows any number of people to claim that *they* are Indian, too, at least by their own lights. Why should they then be denied their proper "heritage"? And why should they be scolded if others judge their cultural performances as improperly orchestrated? As Indians, are they not equally capable of defining what the "real" practices are? Self-identification thus becomes a significant resource for argumentation among groups that each have their own stake in the use and preservation of Indian cultural practice.[25]

Many Native voices have joined the recitation of the dangers and difficulties of uncritically embracing self-identification as the standard of Indian identity. And many of the issues they raise are, indeed, serious concerns that must not be ignored. But other commentators point out the positive side. Some argue that the right to name one's own identity constitutes the most basic of personal and collective prerogatives, regard-less of how the speaker fares within other definitions. "We must come to recognize," writes scholar of Native American Studies Jack Forbes, "that *one of the fundamental human rights of individuals and of groups includes the right to self-identification and self-definition,* so long as one does not adopt an identity which has the effect of denying the same rights to others."[26]

Even so formidable a figure in Native American literature as N. Scott Momaday celebrates self-identification as a central component in American Indian identity. Of his mother, who was biologically one-eighth Cherokee, Momaday writes:

In 1929 my mother was a Southern belle; she was about to embark upon an extraordinary life. It was about this time that she began to see herself as an Indian. That dim heritage became a fascination and a cause for her, inasmuch, perhaps, as it enabled her to assume an attitude of defiance, an attitude which she assumed with particular style and satisfaction; it became her. She imagined who she was. This act of imagination was, I believe, among the most important events of my mother's early life, as later the same essential act was to be among the most important of my own.[27]

For individuals such as Momaday's mother, the uncontrollable cir-cumstances of their personal and ancestral biographies can make meth-ods of identification other than self-identification infeasible. Racial iden-tity is the locus of a great variety of associations and personal meanings that can be important to people (and groups) for reasons quite apart from the desire to discover — as the ever-vigilant critic of new Indians, historian James Clifton, puts it — "a key to the treasury."[28]

It is simply not the case that all self-identified Indians are "up to some-thing" — or are wishing they were. To at least some commentators, it seems cruel and unreasonable to discourage them from expressing their racial identity in the only definition left to them, namely, self-identification. As Melvin B., a Creek and Osage elder, sympathizes:

It's a hurtin' thing to find someone that can't find where they come from. Really. Because they're trying to find out how to go about — they *know* they're part Cherokee, or they *know* they're part Choctaw, or they *know* they're part Creek. But they can't *prove* it. They can't get their [tribal enrollment] card. And, it's a hurtin' thing. . . . It's a kind of a mental and a heart-breakin' thing to me, to see those people trying to find the lineage and so forth.

Thornton argues that a definition of self-identification represents not only a genuine respect for individual human rights, but also a proper submission to the constant reality of Native communities. By his logic, the simple observation that groups such as the Deer Clan, described at the outset of this chapter, may not resemble other Native communities does not *necessarily* render them not-real Indians: "American Indians have always had tremendous variation among themselves," he writes, "and the variations in many ways have been increased, not reduced by the events of history. . . . Allowing self-definition and the differences it encompasses is simply to allow American Indians to be American Indians, something done all too infrequently in the short history of the United States."[29]

Such a remark brings us back to the issue of tribal sovereignty. Whereas some speakers and authors name this principle as the basis of their strenuous objections to self-identification, others adopt a cautionary stance toward it. In particular, the Mohawk writer Taiaiake Alfred argues that framing arguments by reference to tribal sovereignty is inappropriate for indigenous communities. He grants that, "until now, [this concept] . . . has been an effective vehicle for indigenous critiques of the state's imposition of control."[30] But at the same time, he declares it dangerous.

It implies, for instance, that tribes can and should behave as bureaucratically organized nation-states, in which power is distributed hierarchically and the function of governance is segregated from other institutional spheres. It implies that tribes should exercise absolute authority over members and coercively enforce decisions. In such ways, "'sovereignty' implies a set of values and objectives in direct opposition to those found in traditional indigenous philosophies." Indeed, "traditional indigenous nationhood stands in sharp contrast to the dominant understanding of 'the state.'"[31] For Alfred, the concept of sovereignty introduces foreign values into tribal communities. These values may destroy those communities' original foundations, and they may lead to unnatural and divisive distinctions among tribal members who occupy different legal statuses.

A number of interview respondents expressed sentiments closely linked to Alfred's scholarly mistrust of tribal sovereignty as a concept. They viewed the idea of sovereignty not as dangerous, however, but as simply irrelevant to questions of tribal identity. Their comments show that living native communities frequently make a distinction between the tribe as political entity and the tribe as human community. The distinction is evident, for instance, when Cherokee respondent Donald G. suggests that "the *tribe* will recognize who an Indian *is*. I mean, not the government [aspect of the] tribe, but the individual members of the tribe."

Archie M. stated the same idea at greater length:

[Formal] tribal membership is linked into perks and fringe benefits, politically speaking. . . . But I'm more concerned personally with *people,* which is different than the tribe, the bureaucracy of tribal government. The tribe is *different* than that because the *people* out here — they're the ones who invite you to dinner, invite you to this, invite you to that. That invitation is *more* than an invitation from the tribe to come and sign a piece of paper saying that we're gonna let you be one of us. [It has to do] . . . with the people who, to me, are *The People.* They are the roots, the *root.* And the living part of Indian nations is The People. It's not the politics, or the politicians.

From this perspective, a tribe in the most meaningful sense is not the formal political structure to which words such as "sovereignty" and "citizenship" are attached but the community of interrelated individuals. The most important criterion of belonging to that community is not the formal citizenship bestowed by the tribal bureaucracy; it is that one is known and accepted by others like oneself.

To conclude this discussion of the ways that personal definitions of American Indian identity may be evaluated, I would like to take one more look at the question of ethnic switching. Not everyone agrees that this practice is always as reprehensible as its detractors proclaim it. Archie M. welcomes Indian people who genuinely return to the tribe, even after an extended period of living as non-Indians. He acknowledges that people sometimes revise their claims to racial identity in an exploitative fashion. But at the same time, there are

folks who are looking and searching, who *don't* have the opportunity [to learn their tribal cultures from childhood]. . . . I hope that we as Indian people can help one another in that aspect: [to] get people *back.* Because they have a blood right to that [culture]. They have a cultural heritage . . . that flows within their veins. They have a *right* to those things. If I could assist them to get there, to exercise that right, then — I'll help 'em.

Perhaps Archie M. would feel his sentiments validated by the example of Greg Sarris. Sarris is a much-published author of studies in Native American literature and culture who claimed his identity as an American Indian only as an adult. The explanation is not an uncommon one. Sarris was adopted as an infant by white parents and was, for many years, unaware that he was of common ancestry with the Miwok and Pomo Indians who shared his neighborhood. Yet, he says, he felt strongly and inexplicably drawn to them: "My experience was as an orphaned coyote at the edge of the camp where everyone else was eating."[32] It was only when Sarris undertook to research his birth records as an adult that he made a significant discovery. His birth mother had been Jewish — and his father part Filipino and part Miwok and Pomo Indian. With this information in hand, Sarris was allowed to claim formally the Indian identity that had been unavailable to him before. Today he serves as the elected chief of the Coast Miwok tribe.

Sociologist Joane Nagel suggests that there are, in fact, *many* new Indians who are serious about reclaiming an Indian identity and membership in an Indian community for their own sake, and who may be willing to make considerable sacrifices toward that end. In her study of individuals who reclaimed racial identities that they had earlier minimized, ignored, hidden, or been ignorant of, Nagel writes, "Many reported becoming Sun Dancers for the first time as adults, many spent time with tribal elders seeking instruction in tribal history and traditions, many learned more of their tribal language, many abandoned Christian religions and turned to native spiritual traditions, and some have returned to their home reservations."[33] The reality that Nagel describes suggests that the ethnic switching permitted by self-identification is not always motivated by the desire for illegitimate personal gain. And, at least sometimes, it allows for the introduction of new resources into tribal communities — resources ranging from the professional, intellectual, and financial, to the cultural, emotional, and spiritual.

Strictly self-identified individuals who are accepted into established tribal communities probably require a great deal of patient (even exhausting) retraining to help them to learn how to live there responsibly. (Greg Sarris tells stories about his own tribal resocialization in *Keeping Slug Woman Alive*.)[34] But sometimes the effort to keep communities open to the movement of human and other resources is worth it. At least some long-standing citizens of tribal communities explicitly acknowledge this. Anishnabe and Cree artist and poet Kathleen W. laments that excessive tribal exclusivity on the basis of such things as blood quantum, enrollment status, skin color, or cultural experience "is deteriorating our capacity to live in community, and to benefit from the incredible resources that come with the gift of each new life to those communities. [I believe] that we're actually turning down gifts from the Kind-Hearted Great Mystery when we deny tribal participation to one of our own." Such sentiments offer a strong rationale for including in tribal communities even those who start out with no claim on membership other than a self-identification as Indian and an interest in humbly learning how to make a contribution.

As with other definitions of identity, both the advantages and disadvantages of self-identification are compelling. On the one hand, the many potential difficulties discussed in this and foregoing chapters suggest that regulation of tribal boundaries is a heavy but a necessary task for tribes. Simply to abandon this duty and embrace a universal definition of self-identification would, for many purposes, be disastrous. "To try to grant *a priori* equal recognition to all identity claims . . . amounts to taking none seriously."[35] On the other hand, efforts at boundary maintenance easily become self-defeating. Is it possible to find a way out of the bitter disputes about identity which characterize a great deal of the interaction among Indian people today? Can tribes take identity issues seriously without being destroyed by them? What role can American Indian academics play in contributing to questions about racial identity? Those are questions that will require some more work, but they have profound implications — not only for tribal communities but also for the academy. It is such questions to which the following chapters are devoted.

FIVE

"Whaddaya Mean 'We,' White Man?"

Identity Conflicts and a Radical Indigenism

"Whaddaya mean 'we,' white man?" is the punch line to one of the more venerable Indian jokes. It purports to be the trusty sidekick's response to the Lone Ranger's shout of "What should we do, Tonto? We're completely surrounded by Indians!" But the same phrase, by a different construction, might well be considered the keynote of a mood that presently pervades Indian country. Whereas the previous four chapters of this book have sketched some of the many competing definitions of Indianness, and the positive and negative consequences of each as seen from various perspectives, they may not have communicated the level of pain that characterizes many discussions about identity among American Indians.

The angry mood that frequently surfaces in Indian country in relation to identity issues draws harshly enforced boundaries around communities. It encourages Indian people to distrust and attack many others who assert an Indian identity: to demand of them, in effect, "whaddaya mean, 'we,' white man?" This mood suggests that many of the people who identify as Indians are unauthentic by one definition or another, being "really" white (or black, or some other race). The identity conflicts that beset today's Indian communities are so severe that they are sometimes characterized as "race baiting" and "ethnic cleansing."[1]

A published letter to the newspaper *Indian Country Today,* in which one well-known activist for American Indian causes attacks another, illustrates the animosity that seethes through many discussions about real Indianness among those who claim to possess it. She is not an Indian, the writer suggests, but rather "a former redhead, a 'white' female radio personality in New York who made an abrupt transition to Lady Clairol black hair-dye and a career as a professional Washington Indian some fifteen years before she was ever enrolled in anything other than night school."[2] Yet the accuser in this instance has also been weathering serious assaults upon the legitimacy of *his* identity. And so it goes.

Such accusations often emerge in relation to highly charged tribal political issues, as suggested by a comment from Donald G., a Keetoo-wah Band Cherokee:

There is a lot of tension [about Indian identity]. I'll give you an example. We are in the middle of [a tribal] election. . . . [On] one of the web boards on the Internet [dedicated to election issues] there's a lot of discussion of who is and who is not Indian. There's a lot of name-calling. "You are so-and-so." "You are not." "You are not Indian: you don't speak the language." . . . And . . . even in person, a person may get into things like that. [But] I think [this kind of attack occurs] more so behind people's backs, you know.

But while special circumstances such as elections may exacerbate tensions, allegations of illegitimate identification have also become a feature of ordinary life in many Indian communities. As Hopi elder Frank D. summarizes, Indian communities

certainly talk about it [the identity issue] a lot. In closed circles [Indians get] . . . angry with maybe [non-Indian] people who want to try to identify with them. But there's also a lot of tension *within* the tribes. And this has gone on for a long time. There's a real thing about jealousy [in tribes]. Tear down, put down. Not constantly, but sure, it's out there. If you're Indian anywhere in this world, you're aware of it.

Anxieties about identity have stifled useful discussion on a variety of subjects by creating an aura of suspicion and even rage. They divert a great deal of energy and attention from other pressing issues. They can also deprive a community of potentially valuable resources. As Kathleen W., an Anishnabe and Cree grandmother, sadly reports:

I've heard it . . . said . . . that when a person . . . shows up at the lodge door, and *we* [other Indian people] make the judgment that they're not Native enough to come in, we're turning away our own ancestry. And we can't afford to do that. I myself have *plenty* of experience with people who've, all their lives, been told that they're not Native enough to spit on, so to speak, whose dreams and visions and life purpose is as formidable as any great leader or healer or visionary or namer or herbalist that our ancestry has ever produced. And so I understand what that elder said when he said we're turning away our own ancestry, and we can't afford to do that. Because that person is bringing with them the ancestry and the potential to flower in that community as a gift of healing, insight, guidance, resolution, closure, prophecy, and so on. Can't afford to turn *that* away!

In the first four chapters of this book I have shown how competing definitions of Indian identity complicate the process of defining tribal people and communities. I have shown that while each one is useful in certain ways — perhaps indispensable — each can also be harmful to Indian people in particular circumstances, provoking the hostilities to which the preceding respondents allude. I have shown that while Indian communities have good reasons to attend carefully to identity issues, no one of the dominant definitions provides them with an entirely satisfactory means of doing so.

Radical Indigenism: A Distinctively American Indian Scholarship

Is there any way for Indian people to move beyond the divisive animosity of intense conflicts over identity? I believe that there is. I also believe that there is a way to bring together the project of Indian people to live together in communities in a good way *with* the project of the academy to cultivate knowledge. To do so, however, requires that those of us with access to the academy make it a safe place for indigenous knowledge. This requires, in turn, an intellectual perspective dramatically different from any that is currently available within the academy. It requires us to develop new ideas about the very nature of scholarship and how it is done. It requires a distinctively *American Indian scholarship.*[3]

In the pages that follow, I consider what such a scholarship might look like, and I give it a name: Radical Indigenism. By this name, I do not imply a connection to Marxist theory (as sociological usage often does) or an excessively confrontational stance (as casual usage tends to do). Instead, my choice reflects the Latin derivation of the word "radical": *radix,* meaning "root." Radical Indigenism illuminates differences in assumptions about knowledge that are at the root of the dominant culture's misunderstanding and subordination of indigenous knowledge. It argues for the reassertion and rebuilding of traditional knowledge from its roots, its fundamental principles.[4] Although I pay particular consideration to the interest and role that American Indian scholars might have in contributing to the new perspective, this is not because I presume that non-Indians or nonacademics will have no interest in it or because I think they have no place in it. It is simply because I know that American Indian scholars experience the issues I will discuss with particular intensity. I believe it is their passion that can ignite the first flame — the flame that blazes up to illuminate a radically new vision of scholarship and new possibilities for Indian communities.

In crafting this new scholarship, we have much to learn from the work of the postcolonial theorists.[5] These thinkers have taught us that non-Western peoples all over the world had — and *have* — viable intellectual traditions. They have shown us how those intellectual traditions have, nevertheless, often been overwhelmed, deformed, and rendered invisible by what Walter Mignolo calls "academic colonialism" — the attempt of Amer-European thinkers to construe them through categories of thought that are foreign to them.[6] They have explored Antonio Gramsci's idea of "organic intellectuals" — individuals who mediate between the interest of a local community and the dominant societal group — as it applies to indigenous peoples.[7] And they have struggled with issues that must also be of concern to anyone who attempts to develop American Indian forms of scholarship.[8] In these projects, the postcolonial theorists have pointed the way to a rediscovery of "alternative ways of knowing which may impinge on our current conception of knowledge, understanding, and the politics of intellectual inquiry."[9]

It is such a way of knowing that a new, American Indian scholarship must also seek. But postcolonial theory may be limited in its ability to inform an American Indian scholarship. A persistent complaint directed at postcolonial theorists is that they have had difficulty really separating themselves from the categories of knowledge provided by the "academic colonialists."[10] The most serious criticism in this category concerns the postcolonialists' failure to grapple with very fundamental assumptions regulating the conduct of inquiry, and the difficulty is especially apparent when one considers indigenous philosophies of knowledge.

Kwame Anthony Appiah (drawing substantially on the work of anthropologist Robin Horton) observes that the models of inquiry that dominate the academy (which he calls "scientific," but are alternatively referred to as "modern" or "post-Renaissance") distinguish themselves from indigenous models in many ways: their pronounced experimental emphasis, their orientation toward narrowly defined sensory information, their value on the acquisition of new knowledge strictly for its own sake, their "adversarial" approach in which knowledge emerges from the competition of precisely articulated theories, their value on the universal dissemination of knowledge, their preference for explanations in terms of material forces rather than personal agents, and their willingness to eschew questions of ultimate meaning.[11] Many of these differences derive from the modern interest in creating a thoroughly secular means of seeking knowledge.

The cultural ascendancy of scientific models of inquiry means that indigenous knowledge can be integrated into scholarly discourses only if it is severely pared down, sanitized of the spiritual elements pervading the models that birthed them. The sanitizing process typically means one of two things: either indigenous knowledge is presented as a set of "primitive beliefs" that have been superseded by contemporary "factual knowledge," or it is reconstructed (without reference to the often contrary assertions of the indigenous carriers) as *symbolically* rather than *literally* truthful. The first strategy portrays indigenous claims as simply wrong (although possibly interesting), while the second strategy allows them to be right only by "deny[ing] that traditional people mean what they say."[12]

While postcolonialists have observed differences between conventional academic and indigenous models of inquiry, they have yet to work through their meaning for the practice of scholarship. What Appiah writes about indigenous African peoples is more broadly applicable. Their frequent conviction that the world cannot be approached with a model of inquiry that excludes assumptions about a spiritual reality, he observes,

means that most Africans cannot fully accept those scientific theories in the West that are inconsistent with [such assumptions]. I do not believe . . . that this is a reason for shame or embarrassment. But it *is* something to think about. If modernization is conceived of, in part, as the acceptance of science, we have to decide whether we think the evidence obliges us to give up the invisible ontology [that is, beliefs in spiritual agencies]. We can easily be misled here by the accommodation between science and religion that has occurred among educated people in the industrialized world, in general, and in the United States in particular. For this has involved a considerable limitation of the domains in which it is permissible for intellectuals to invoke spiritual agency. The question [of] how much of the world of spirits we intellectuals must give up (or transform into something ceremonial without the old literal ontology) is one we must face: and I do not think the answer is obvious.[13]

A central goal of a new, American Indian scholarship must be to confront exactly this latter question, and to formulate an answer. Radical Indigenism suggests resistance to the pressure upon indigenous scholars to participate in academic discourses that strip Native intellectual traditions of their spiritual and sacred elements. It takes this stand on the grounds that sacred elements are absolutely central to the coherence of our knowledge traditions and that if we surrender them, there is little left in our philosophies that makes any sense. Perhaps we should say that the postcolonial theorists have led us to a high plain from which we may glimpse the landscape of a radically different scholarship. But they have not yet led us into the new country. We American Indian scholars, it seems, must find our own way. With the help of our tribal communities and those others in the academy who will join with us, we must find perspectives that respect and reflect distinctly American Indian ways of knowing the world.[14]

New and Old Perspectives on American Indian Studies

A series of articles in the *Journal of the American Academy of Religion* illustrates the fundamental insight that grounds what I think of as Radical Indigenism. It also illustrates how this new perspective differs from the dominant academic view. These articles are therefore worth exploring in some detail. They are penned by Sam Gill (University of Colorado, Boulder) and Christopher Jocks (Dartmouth), both scholars of American Indian religious traditions.[15]

Gill presents a position likely to be endorsed by established scholars in the social sciences and other disciplines in which the pursuit of objective claims is a goal. Such disciplines conventionally include, for instance, history (as opposed to literature) or religious studies (as opposed to theology). Gill expresses concern that his discipline of religious studies is becoming populated with scholars who apply themselves to their subject matter "primarily because it has religious and political importance to their personal religious, racial, ethnic, or gender connection with it."[16] The problem, he warns, is that investigators who enter too deeply into the lives of the communities they research risk being drawn into political agendas. Their objectivity diminishes and their scholarship shifts into partisan advocacy, proselytization, or social activism.

The resultant work, Gill suggests, may be interesting and useful in its own way, but it tends to be narrow because the individuals doing it are so focused on goals prescribed by their faith or value commitments that they refuse to engage broader, theoretical issues of consequence to the discipline. Moreover, such work tends to become dangerously blinded by dogma. "Persuasion overshadows criticism. Academic freedom is replaced by the requirements of conformity. Inarguable results produced by relying on some religious givenness displace academic responsibility." Gill does not, he insists, suggest that "the religious study of religion" is intrinsically less valuable than its academic study; but he feels it is not proper scholarship within the discipline of religious studies.[17]

Another matter, which concerns Gill even more than the possible loss of academic detachment, is the possibility that the academy is responding to the new, activist scholars by compromising its intellectual standards. Gill complains that work by some new scholars in religious studies is coming to be "evaluated more on the authority granted by religion, race, gender, or ethnic identity than upon academic performance."[18] The "mature" discipline of religious studies, he says, must remain firmly grounded in the face of this challenge. It ought to acknowledge that "it is academic; it is Western; it is intellectual." It is therefore to be established strictly upon "discourse conducted on the authority of rational definition, hypothetical inference, and the application of scientific method," rejecting "the authority of vision, insight, or experience."[19]

Gill's complaints are hardly new ones. They address issues that have been discussed in the social sciences and related disciplines for decades, and that get dredged up and batted back and forth with great regularity. But this time the respondent, Gill's colleague Christopher Jocks, takes the discussion in a new direction. First, he insists on the importance of the view from inside Indian communities — far inside. "One simply cannot gain an accurate understanding of what goes on in Indian Country without living in and around an Indian community for a long period of time. . . . In fact, one really needs not just to reside but to reside *as a relative,* since there are vast dimensions of meaning that are only acted out in this way."[20] For Jocks, closeness to one's subject matter — a deeply personal commitment to it that exceeds even the engagement of, for instance, participant observation — allows for insights into things which may well be invisible to outsiders.

Second, and even more significantly, Jocks is not content with Gill's definition of "mature" scholarship. He is particularly dissatisfied with Gill's equation of the "Western," the "intellectual" and the "scientific" with "rational" discourse. Jocks, in fact, suggests that it is possible and legitimate to understand Native philosophies as embodying their own rationalities — their own coherent, complete, and functioning logics that are separate from, but no less useful than, those more frequently encountered within the academy. "I have no interest in promoting *irrational* discourse," he writes, "but the religious discourse of any community responds to its own rationality."[21]

Given this presupposition — that not *all* rationalities are Western or scientific — it is possible for work on Native religions (or other aspects of culture) to be "a conversation between rationalities, not wholly congruous but not wholly incongruous either."[22] Jocks concludes that this viewpoint allows Indian peoples and cultures to escape from their present intellectual ghetto for the first time. It gives them the opportunity to function in the academic economy as something more than "merely another 'subject,' another kind of specimen, for Amer-European intellectual frames, categories, and tools."[23]

So far I have presented the arguments offered by Jocks and Gill as representing opposite positions. Yet fairness demands that I not overdraw the differences between them. For his part, Gill clearly appreciates some of the problems that accompany the attempt to construe Native religious traditions by the imposition of foreign categories. In fact, he mounts a strong critique of religious studies for its historic tendency to apply fundamentally Christian concepts to those Native traditions, which he thinks only distorts the latter.[24] And for his part, Jocks acknowledges that Native scholars have yet fully to define a research agenda that is substantially different from the more conventional one that Gill advocates. As he notes, such an enterprise must be undergirded by a coherent theory:

To say that theory should "come out of" the cultural world being studied sounds great, but we [Native scholars] haven't really taken it seriously yet. If we are writing about the religious life of a single community, and trying to more accurately and sympathetically describe how members of the community understand the world and what they do in it, that is a very worthwhile thing to do, but it isn't really *theory*. It's ethnography. . . . As long as we confine ourselves to narrow, descriptive studies . . . we are doing religious ethnography, not religious theory, and we are buttressing Gill's critique.[25]

If Jocks and Gill sometimes find themselves with points of agreement, the differences that underlie their positions are nevertheless substantial. For me, the central point of their divergence is more implied than explicit; it concerns the status of American Indian religions as bodies of knowledge that might compare to those generated by professional scholars. That is, the kernel of a revolutionary American Indian scholarship, as I imagine it, would extend Jocks' contention that American Indian peoples possess distinctive and coherent rationalities. It would reject the academy's long-standing assumption that the main reason to examine Indian cultures is to learn something about the *people* who practice them — their beliefs and values, their worldviews, their psychological predispositions, the social structures they move within, their mental processes or abilities, and so on. This is the position that Gill's remarks suggest to me. By contrast, a new perspective — a Radical Indigenism — would dare to suggest that American Indian cultures contain tools of inquiry that create *knowledge*. By this construction of Native cultures, one would draw upon them as part of a process of learning about *the world,* and one would do so without leaving the proper domain of scholarship.

Radical Indigenism and American Indian Identity

Given this fundamental assumption, what kinds of questions would an American Indian scholarship that responds to the perspective of Radical Indigenism permit us to ask about Indian identity? In what directions would it lead us in the search for answers? It would allow us to go beyond describing the ways that meanings about identity are presently made and discussing the consequences of choosing one definition over another (as I have done in the foregoing chapters). It would allow us, instead, to think about the possibilities that Native communities might hold for making *new* meanings about identity. It would help us to consider, as well, what some of the new definitions of identity might look like, what purposes they could serve, who might contribute to them, and how.

Radical Indigenism has the potential to help us formulate definitions of identity that can contribute to the survival of Indian people, even as it teaches the academy about philosophies of knowledge it has failed to see and understand. But it will also require a great deal of those who choose to pursue it. First, it will require the researcher to *enter tribal philosophies.* Second, it will require him to *enter tribal relations.* Let us examine these ideas more closely.

By asking scholars to enter (rather than merely study) tribal philosophies, Radical Indigenism asks them to abandon any notion that mainstream academic philosophies, interpretations, and approaches based upon them are, in principle, superior. It asks them, instead, to accept tribal philosophies as containing articulable rationalities alternative to those of the conventional academic disciplines. It asks them to seek the assumptions upon which Native philosophies are grounded and to understand how such assumptions allow for coherent reasoning and defensible conclusions. To make such assertions is not to travel beyond what our colleagues in African and Latin American postcolonial theory (and some earlier scholars) have asked of us. Not yet.[26] But Radical Indigenism, as I imagine it, does transgress academic boundaries when it requires that researchers also honor the *methods* and the *goals of inquiry* toward which indigenous philosophical assumptions direct us.

This last stipulation implies that the new brand of scholarship for which I am advocating relies upon people who will genuinely give themselves to American Indian philosophies of knowledge. Unlike Galileo's contemporaries, who refused to look through his telescope, researchers within Radical Indigenism must be brave enough to stand inside what may be to them a foreign means of encountering the world. They must be willing to look through the lens of our traditional ways of knowing. They must be willing to look for answers where tribal philosophies direct them to look, and how those philosophies direct them to look. Thus, for instance, if those philosophies understand ceremony as a means of gaining knowledge of the world (and many of them do just that), then those who would learn through this means must surrender themselves to its requirements. It will not suffice to *read about* or *think about* such means of inquiry; one must trust them, practice them, live within them. This requires a level of devotion, and perhaps a level of intellectual flexibility, that many scholars may be unwilling to give. But those who are willing may learn to understand the world in ways never before available to them.

The demand that researchers enter tribal philosophies cannot stand by itself. If the adoption of those philosophies is to be something more than mere appropriation and exploitation of Native cultures, it must be accompanied by the second requirement of Radical Indigenism stated earlier — that researchers must enter tribal relations. Entering tribal relations implies maintaining respect for community values in the search for knowledge. This respect is much more than an attitude; it requires real commitments and real sacrifices on the part of those who practice it.

The values of Native communities in relation to the acquisition and dissemination of knowledge often differ from academic ones, and it is to these values that responsible academic researchers practicing Radical Indigenism must look. This probably means, for one thing, that the scholar should be willing to accept a considerably diminished measure of authority, compared with what most scholars are accustomed to. The philosophies of knowledge to which scholarship in the mold of Radical Indigenism must turn for guidance do not frequently operate on a top-down principle, whereby "experts" administer conclusions that are binding upon the remainder of the populace. Those philosophies are more likely to be inclusive, to understand knowledge as emerging out of collective deliberations that include contributions from a variety of perspectives and sources.

For another thing, even where Native philosophies lend greater weight to the contributions of those who have specialized information, they do not necessarily regard academicians as the most relevant experts on many or most of the questions that they take up. I think it is reasonable within the boundaries of Radical Indigenism that scholars may be able to raise topics for discussion, to contribute information and insights drawn from their particular perspectives, and to play a part in carrying forward the collective projects of acquiring knowledge that have been defined as useful and appropriate by Native communities. But Radical Indigenism is not a disguised mechanism by which scholars can impose their own conclusions upon tribal communities or become their self-appointed mouthpieces. As Osage literary scholar Robert Allen Warrior writes, American Indian scholars "are not simply the bearers of truth who will make everything right." In their own Native communities, they "can give voice to the voiceless, but . . . cannot speak for them."[27]

Another requirement of genuine respect for Native communities that may be even harder for scholars to agree to is to observe the community's values in deciding what is discussed publicly. The values of Native communities often regulate the circulation of certain kinds of knowledge outside the community. In practice, this means that communities may prohibit scholars from researching or writing about some subjects.

This proscription is, of course, anathema to researchers responsive to conventional social scientific values, which incline strongly in favor of the wide dissemination of all knowledge. It is one of the outcomes that Sam Gill fears most. He regards it as the strangulation of free inquiry, the death of scholarship. I would suggest, by contrast, that even such proscriptions still leave the scholar sufficient room to do her work in the academy. One who genuinely enters into tribal relations and philosophies, accepting the responsibilities and orientations that accompany these, will be able to write well and responsibly on a range of topics. If the price of this accomplishment is to forbear writing about certain other topics, the cost is justified.

The interview respondent who exemplified this value most clearly was Frank D., a Hopi scientist who has since tragically passed away. Frank had trained as a geneticist, and was, during his lifetime, one of only two American Indians in the world with a Ph.D. in his discipline. He offered the following story, which illustrates an attitude toward scholarly research that I believe Radical Indigenism would require.

Frank had, at one time, focused his studies on human genetics. However, when it became clear that his field was developing in directions that were (and are) generating intensely angry divisions in tribal communities, he arrived at a life-changing crossroads. He decided that if Indian people don't want it [genetic research], I respect that and I won't do it. And [I will] even sacrifice my career for it. Which is what I've done. I'm not doing genetic research any more. Because of all the controversy that's surrounding this issue. . . . I couldn't do the research and be scientifically "clean" with my own people. So I had to throw some [of my investments] away. I'm glad I did make [that decision]. . . . I'm not doing any laboratory or bench work [any more].

Having given up the work for which he had trained, Frank turned to writing on scientific ethics, trying to communicate to the academy the viewpoints about research that he had learned from elders. His commitment to put the values of the community even above his own career is an example for those who would practice Radical Indigenism.[28]

Radical Indigenism: What Is to Be Gained?

To my way of thinking, when scholars accept the twin requirements of Radical Indigenism — to enter tribal philosophies and to enter tribal relations — and begin doing intellectual work within an American Indian philosophy of knowledge, allowing themselves to be guided by its assumptions, values, and goals, they perform a significant service to the academy. Indigenous philosophies of knowledge lay out strategies for knowing the world that proceed from strikingly different assumptions and values than those with which Western inquirers are familiar. Consequently, scholars who attend to them may lead their colleagues into new ways of conceptualizing problems and finding solutions. By handling those philosophies of knowledge in a proper and respectful way, students of Radical Indigenism have the potential to show the modern world ideas that many or most of its citizens were unable to think before.

Finally, scholars — whether Native or non-Native — working within Radical Indigenism can build bridges between Native communities and the academy. At present, tribal peoples often perceive the work of scholarship as something remote from their interests and concerns as members of Native communities. This is because it so often *is* remote. For example, Linda Tuhiwai Smith, a New Zealand Maori woman, writes of the perception in the indigenous community of her upbringing: "Research was talked about both in terms of its absolute worthlessness to us, the indigenous world, and its absolute usefulness to those who wielded it as an instrument. It told us things already known, suggested things that would not work, and made careers for people who already had jobs."[29]

Faith Smith, the Ojibwe cofounder and president of Native American Education Services, likewise illustrates the divorce between the academy and Indian communities when she tells of hearing a scholar complain bitterly about an Indian "informant" who had misled him with invented stories, causing the scholar to waste his entire fellowship before he realized he was being duped. Not everyone heard the story the same way, Smith notes. "The Indians in the audience knew that the scholar would organize a theoretical construct about tribal life that might have nothing to do with reality. We knew that whatever he wrote, our lives would be the same."[30] Such views extend to the anxiety — vividly expressed in the cartoon in figure 5.1 — that scientific research not only ignores Indian people and perspectives, but also actively endangers Native cultures.

Similar sentiments are easily attached even to scholarship performed by researchers who are themselves Indian. This is illustrated in the following exchange with Joe B., a Lakota/Dakota elder.

> *Joe B.:* Education is another way of life. . . . Lot of people get educated, and they come back [to their Indian community] and they kind of *lose* it with their own people.
>
> *Author:* Do they kind of forget their families and things like that?
>
> *Joe B.:* Yeah. Yeah. I've seen *that* happen. And I say, "Well, he's *educated.*"

Another respondent, Cherokee elder Tom E., hesitated a moment when asked to express his feelings about Indian people who become highly educated. Then he offered a simple but poignant reply: "Well, that's good. We're proud of someone that does that. But we just don't want 'em to turn against us."

Scholarship guided by the values of Radical Indigenism need not turn community members against each other in the ways suggested by the foregoing remarks. Nor does it need to manipulate Indian communities for the exclusive benefit of those who do not belong to them. By insisting upon the legitimacy of tribal philosophies of knowledge, it puts in place fundamental principles that allow for actual *exchanges* between Indian people and the academy. This is different from the simple transfer of knowledge from communities to scholars, who then recast that knowledge and exploit it for their own purposes, in the processes critiqued by postcolonial theory. It is different because it makes indigenous communities that have retained distinctive philosophies of knowledge

FIGURE 5.1. Research. Indian people are often concerned about the effects of research on their culture. (Source: Drawn by W. Sommers Quistorf, a member of the Oneida Indian Nation of Wisconsin, whose cartoons are published in the newspaper *Indian Country Today*. Printed in *Indian Country Today*.)

the central reference group for scholars. This means that the self-defined needs of indigenous communities will generate questions for study, that *their* philosophies of knowledge will inform the conduct of research and judge the legitimacy of conclusions, and that *their* norms will regulate the dissemination of knowledge.

CHAPTER SIX

Allowing the Ancestors to Speak

Radical Indigenism and New/Old Definitions of Identity

Radical Indigenism is centered on the assumption that American Indian (and other indigenous) philosophies of knowledge are rational, articulable, coherent logics for ordering and knowing the world. It pushes beyond that assumption to argue that indigenous philosophies of knowledge, and the models of inquiry they imply, have a place in the academy. This position invites an understanding of these philosophies not merely as objects of curiosity (unusual things that people have believed) but as tools for the discovery and generation of knowledge.

In this chapter I develop these ideas by applying them to the issue of American Indian identity. I consider some assumptions that might frame such an inquiry, and I explore the implications of that framing: how and where these assumptions might direct us in the search for answers. Although it is not a task appropriate to an individual to assert claims about the identity definitions proper to tribal communities, I speculatively offer some ideas about the *sorts* of definitions that might emerge from collective deliberations framed in this manner. I consider the ways that the answers produced through such processes might differ from those typically produced in academic contexts and the implications for subsequent discussions about identity in both academic and indigenous communities.

What follows is not meant as a *prescription* for how tribes should think about identity issues; rather, it is a *suggestive exploration* of a place from which they might begin to work out their own definitions of identity with the participation of all their members. Nor is what follows intended as a definitive scholarly analysis; rather, it is an illustration of a different way to pose and pursue a question. Thus, I conceive this chapter as a means to encourage Native communities in their own conversations about identity: as a vehicle for reminding Indian people that they can proceed in those conversations confident that they have the resources to create — or recover — definitions of identity that serve them better, in certain ways, than those discussed earlier in this book. I conceive it, as well, as a way to encourage academics toward a conversation about the meaning of scholarship in a pluralistic world.

It is clear that researchers have, over time, changed some of the assumptions they bring with them to Native communities, and some of the ways that they interact there.[1] But Radical Indigenism will ask them to change even more. It is likewise clear that many Native communities are already thinking about identity issues by looking to their traditional knowledge. But as Indians we, like all people, sometimes forget our teachings, along with our responsibilities to them. In response to the present level of anger and argument over issues of tribal belonging, we can usefully remind ourselves that, in our various tribes, we *do* have traditional teachings concerning such questions — that we must continue to rediscover them and, in this way, bring them alive.

Radical Indigensim: Assumptions for an Inquiry

As we have seen, Radical Indigenism permits — indeed requires — that the researcher work within assumptions drawn from American Indian philosophies. For all the differences among these many philosophies, there are certain features that appear frequently, although not universally, across numerous tribes.[2] One such assumption is the emphasis on *practicality* in the pursuit of knowledge. In most Native American philosophies, one seeks knowledge because one is prepared to use it. As Mohawk scholar Christopher Jocks writes, "Knowledge requires a network of knowers, or more accurately, of actors. Knowledge is something you do; not a preexisting tool independent of the person holding it, nor of the uses to which it might be put."[3] A second assumption characteristic of American Indian philosophies is their attentiveness to the distinctly *spiritual* dimensions of inquiry. There is frequently an unwillingness to separate "the search for knowledge from sacred learning or 'religious' training."[4] This sacred knowledge is what makes us as Indian people most uniquely ourselves, and it rightly affects and is reflected in all that we do and discover.

These two assumptions, specifying both a practical and a spiritual orientation in the quest for knowledge, guide our inquiry in some specific directions. A search for a definition of identity that takes shape within these assumptions must, I think, take seriously the many pragmatic concerns fueling the identity debates. The new definition must neither invite nor ignore any of the abuses that community boundaries are intended to prevent. In particular, it must take care to protect against exploitation by those who would abuse communities, or use their resources without contributing any. This requires the new definition to be *robust,* allowing for sufficiently strong community boundaries. But it should be *flexible* as well, because flexibility allows for the embrace of those who truly belong to the community, even if they do not satisfy certain technical criteria of membership. Flexibility permits the community to remain open to the entry of new and valued resources.

At the same time, the search for new definitions of identity within the assumptions just described will recollect that many traditional Indian communities speak about themselves as having a specific spiritual role to play in the world: a particular place to occupy and a particular task to perform. The words of Julie M., a Keetoowah Cherokee grandmother, reflect this idea: "We [Cherokees] . . . have a *special* place in the world. God put us here." Members of many different tribes often express the unique purposefulness of their existence by using an English phrase invoked here by Mashpee cultural firekeeper Ramona P.: "As traditionalists, we have our *Original Instructions* from our Creator that are important to fulfill" (emphasis mine).

These "Original Instructions" (sometimes called "First Instructions," or a similar variant) usually concern coming into relationship with other beings — human and nonhuman — in the natural world in particular ways: "We are indigenous people because of our relationship to the earth and the understanding of the natural law."[5] Or, as Dakota scholar Vine Deloria, Jr., writes, "The task of tribal religion . . . is to determine the proper relationship that the people of the tribe must have with other living things and to develop the self-discipline within the tribal community so that man acts harmoniously with other creatures."[6] The Original Instructions by which many Native people still live have never been revoked, as my own elders frequently remind me. A definition of identity that acknowledges this spiritual heritage will recall each tribal community to its Original Instructions — to its specific teachings about the nature of the world and how its members are to live in it.

The orientation of tribal peoples toward Original Instructions suggests, in turn, a specific purpose for the definition of identity that I explore in this chapter. It is probably inadvisable to attempt to *replace* any of the extant definitions. The definitions of law, biology, culture, and self-identification function in particular contexts to meet specific needs, and in those contexts each may well be irreplaceable. But Indian people who remember themselves within the framework of their Original Instructions will be looking for a definition of identity that allows them to determine who they will invite to join them in their sacred work. Who will properly be part of their daily lives, their communities, as they go about the fulfillment of their Original Instructions? To whom will they teach the language, the stories, the nature of their relationships to land and to each other, the many meanings that inform their lives as Native peoples? Whom will they trust to carry them forward? With whom, in short, will Indian people share the burden and the joy of the work the Creator called them to do in this world?

This is not just a question about the thorny issue of who may properly enter into forms of explicitly spiritual practice, such as the sweat lodge and ceremonial dances. That issue may well be part of the discussion, but it is not all of it. In traditional American Indian societies, spirituality and ceremony are not usually separated from other domains of life. Government, the judiciary, education, the legal system, the family — all these institutions have been constructed in the light of the sacred. It is possible for them to continue to be so constructed today, and various tribal communities are making deliberate efforts to do this. In the process, it becomes important to consider who will be taught how to carry out the Original Instructions as they apply to each institutional sphere. Who will we ask to join us in responding to the demands of living *our whole lives* in a sacred way? If communities find a way to answer this question satisfactorily, they will have gone a great way toward resolving the more particular issue of ceremonial participation.

Radical Indigenism: Method for an Inquiry

Having framed our inquiry by reference to the values of practicality and spirituality, and having shaped a specific question — the question of identity — in accordance with them, we need to define a method by which to proceed. We need to indicate where we might look for answers and the kinds of evidence we might accept as the foundation for our conclusions. Here I turn to what my friends, elders, and colleagues have taught me about American Indian models of inquiry, and I take the risk of extending those ideas with my own. To repeat what my interview respondents said again and again: in what follows I speak only for myself. What I say may not be right for others, but it is how I understand and think about things.

A common assumption of American Indian knowledge pursuits is that the seeker always looks backward. As Pawnee/Otoe poet and author Anna Lee Walters writes, "It is in remembering that our power lies / and our future comes / This is the Indian way."[7] As Indian people, we look to our traditions for guidance. This is implicit in the idea that we have Original Instructions provided at the times of the beginning. But where, exactly, can an inquiry within the parameters of Radical Indigenism turn to discover the traditions?

The first place to look, I think, is pointed out in the straightforward advice of Yuchi elder Mose C. When asked how Indian tribes might go about addressing identity tensions, he urged Indian researchers to "use the elders as teachers about their own tribes." In the statements of elders, and others who know community lifeways from their own long experience, we can examine how Indian people today speak about their concerns.

Next, we will want to see how (and if) those statements of the elders are grounded in larger bodies of teachings. Anishnabe and Cree artist and teacher Kathleen W. urges that the new scholarship be shaped around a process of "returning to the creation stories and taking them very, very, very seriously." As part of the inquiry into tradition, we can ask if there are specific stories, teachings, oral narratives — not to mention songs, dances, and other such records — that support the contemporary statements of American Indian elders or help us to understand them more completely.

Finally, we might look to the ways that the ancestors created forms of community life that made flesh the teachings that the stories set forth. We can look to records of historic practice and forms of community life or social structure. This allows us to deduce traditional principles and ideas not only from what the ancestors *said,* as this is enshrined in stories and other oral forms, but also from what they actually *did.*

Once Indian people look to their traditions for the teachings that might help them build up a definition of tribal identity, what might they discover? The only way for a community to really arrive at an answer to this question is to seek, *as* a community, within its own knowledge traditions. But for the purposes of illustration, I will start the conversation down a specific pathway: I propose that a definition of identity that is available within many knowledge traditions is what I call a definition of *kinship*. In one way, this assertion will seem unsurprising: for well over a century, social scientists have recognized the centrality of kin relationships for organizing virtually every aspect of tribal life. In another way, an exploration of a kinship definition of identity will lead to conclusions very different from those social scientists have entertained.

As I see it, a definition of identity founded in kinship responds to at least two themes that one encounters across a range of tribal philosophies. One of these reflects a condition of *being*, which I call *relationship to ancestry*. The second involves a condition of *doing*, which I call *responsibility to reciprocity*. In what follows I examine each in turn, considering for illustration how it is expressed in the statements, stories, and histories of various tribal peoples.

A First Kinship Principle: Relationship to Ancestry

The significance of relationship to ancestry for determining inclusion in Native communities is readily apparent in the published remarks by and about Indian people. Ella Deloria, the early and monumental student of Lakota (Sioux) culture, wrote that the genealogical connections of her people were "assiduously traced and remembered, no matter how far back."[8] Scholar of Native American literature Elizabeth Cook-Lynn explains this genealogical preoccupation:

One cannot be a Lakota unless one is related by the lineage (blood) rules of the *tiospaye* [tribal community]. While it is true that the narrow definition of biology was not accepted by the Lakotas, since they are also related to the animal world, spirit world, and everything else in the world, biology is *never* dismissed categorically. On the contrary, it is the overriding concern of the people who assiduously trace their blood ties throughout the generations.[9]

Ray DeMallie has shown that the distinctiveness of relationship through birth lineage is enshrined at a linguistic level among the Sioux. Although it would be impolite to use such words as terms of personal address, "linguistic forms existed that differentiated between one's biological and other mothers and fathers, as well as between stepchildren and other children."[10] Similar linguistic distinctions characterize the languages of tribal peoples as diverse as the Cherokee, the Cheyenne, and the Inuit.[11]

Nor have ideas about the importance of ancestry disappeared among contemporary American Indians. Sentiments about the significance of communality of blood for determining identity, and for connecting tribal members to something beyond the individual, were frequently repeated by my interview respondents, as in the following statement by Oo-yost Oo-jil-dos, a full-blood Cherokee grandmother: "That [blood relationship]. Yeah. It's *real* important. 'Cuz it shows our *origination*." Offered an example of someone whose Indian identity was challenged because he had less than one-quarter tribal blood quantum, she responded: "That's not fair to say that [the person is not Indian]. His great-grandmother . . . was probably a full-blood Indian. So the same bloodline runs from her to him." Cornelia S., in discussing physical relatedness, similarly observed, "It shows, you know, who your people are and where you came from. It's *very important* to know your blood relationship to other people" (original emphasis).

Julie M. describes the significance of family relationship at greater length:

In Cherokee culture, it [relationship to a lineage] is *very* important. . . . It's *all*-important in Cherokee culture. Without it, it's like you're a person without a . . . country. It's actually even worse than that. . . . I think Cherokee culture operated on that [principle] from ancient times, and it still does to this day. Because of the clan system and because of the extended family. . . . It's part of being Cherokee. It's what we're *about*.

Some of the respondents added that relationship to a lineage provided not only an organizing principle recognized by tribal communities, but also a conviction of tribal belonging recognized by the individual. Creek and Osage elder Melvin B. suggests that if a person has tribal ancestry,

that [tribal] identity is *in* you from the day you're born. The *day* you're born. If you're an Indian, it's *there*. What . . . an Indian person has the hardest time [with] is *losin'* it, gettin' rid of it. Because it's *there*. Like a tiger or a lion has an instinct to kill to live. And that's *born* in them. Born in that tiger or the lion. The same way with a *human* being. The day you're born, if you're an Indian, whether you, you pet it [one's identity] and grow up with it [or not], it's there. . . . It's [present from] the day you was born. It's *in* you. It *comes* that way.

This respondent's statement is reminiscent of published remarks on the part of N. Scott Momaday, a Kiowa-Cherokee author. Momaday hints at the significance of the intimate, physical connection shared among tribal people in his repetitive and oft-quoted statements about "memory in the blood" and "a racial memory that leaps across generations" linking him to his ancestors.[12] "I think that each of us bears in his genes or in his blood or wherever a recollection of the past. Even the very distant past. I just think that's the way it is."[13] For Momaday, the people of a tribe share a powerful connection by virtue of their physical relatedness. It is something heritable, fundamental, and effectual.

Statements such as these, which highlight and privilege the importance of physical relationship as a means of determining tribal belonging, have received scornful treatment in the scholarly literature, where they are frequently discussed (and dismissed) under the rubric of "primordialism" or "essentialism." Some of the most prominent postcolonial theorists, for instance, argue that essentialist ideas are colonial impositions. Thus, Salman Rushdie describes them as "the respectable child of old-fashioned exoticism," and Edward Said suggests that their difficulties "have much to do . . . with the embattled imperial contexts out of which they came." Wole Soyinka's comment about the essentialism of negritude is similar: it "stayed within a pre-set system of Eurocentric intellectual analysis both of man and society," he asserts, "and tried to re-define the African and his society in those externalised terms."[14]

Other scholars are even less impressed with essentialist claims. In a representative critique, sociologists Jack David Eller and Reed M. Coughlan lament the "poverty of primordialism,"[15] while Eugeen Roosens, in his study of Native ethnicity in Canada, invests it with distinctly threatening associations:

The less critical can be led to believe that the "ethnic feeling" is a primordial, essential dimension of every human being, that it is inborn in the blood, that one can almost feel it physically, that one must fight to safeguard this "high value," that one is indebted to the ancestors from whom one has received life and "everything." Political leaders can create stereotypes that give almost religious exaltedness to ethnic identity and, via stereotypes, lead to economic and cultural wars with other groups and even to genocide.[16]

Scholar of Native American literature Arnold Krupat is more succinct in his critique. He angrily labels Momaday's claims to "memory in the blood" as "absurdly racist."[17]

In such assessments, as elsewhere, essentialist ideas — ideas presupposing a connection to ancestry rooted in the individual's fundamental nature — are displayed as the property of the intellectually deficient and the politically rabid. That leaves the American Indian speakers and authors who have articulated ideas about the centrality of genealogical relationship in determining tribal identity (many of my interview respondents included) in unfortunate company. But before rushing to the judgment that this is where they belong, let us proceed as a research program within the model of Radical Indigenism might direct us. Do these claims, offered by American Indian people themselves, have a foundation in coherent tribal philosophies of knowledge? Are there stories suggesting that American Indian peoples may have possessed, traditionally, understandings of essential relationships between tribal members? Are such claims part of larger bodies of traditional philosophy? And if so, can they be understood *there* in different ways than blanket criticisms of essentialist ideas propose?

Even a cursory examination reveals that sacred stories about the importance of kinship, defined in terms of genealogical descent, abound in tribal oral traditions. These stories tell of kin lost and found, kin newly discovered, kin physically transformed and recognized in different guises, and many other themes. But to suggest the distinctiveness of some American Indian ideas about kinship, let us examine only one type of story. These are the narratives, present in a number of tribes, that describe the birth and life of great mythological figures.

In these stories the hero is frequently born from a miraculous union of a spirit being and a human woman. His mother may not, herself, know the identity of his father, but the child knows, or sets out to discover it. Thus, when Water Jar Boy of the Tewa-speaking Pueblos (New Mexico) questioned his mother about his miraculous paternity, "somehow [he] . . . knew the answer to his own question. He announced to his mother, 'I know where my father is, and tomorrow I will go and find him!'" On his ensuing quest, Water Jar Boy discovered a man sitting near a spring (in which the man lived) and recognized him. The father joyfully led Water Jar Boy into the spring to meet his other paternal relatives. "Water Jar Boy stayed in the spring and lives there to this day." Although Water Jar Boy had not previously met those relatives, he shared a powerful and meaningful bond with them: a bond of common ancestry.[18]

In a thematically similar story told by the Cherokee, the offspring of the thunder being and a human woman seeks his unknown father and is restored to his paternal family after a series of ordeals. Through his journey, he is cured of physical affliction and discovers the powers that are his birthright: he learns that he is the lightning being, with the power to

rend the sky with his deadly bolts and strike down his opponents in battle. Lightning's journey is a journey in pursuit of wholeness. He is physically disfigured and does not even know *who he is* — does not realize that
he is a powerful spirit being. Healing and self-knowledge follow reunion
with those heretofore unknown others with whom he shares a relationship of ancestry and, with it, an essential nature.[19]

Still another story, this one from the Hopi (Arizona), features a child
conceived of the sun who seeks and finds his father. In the interactions
that follow, he discovers extraordinary abilities that belong to him as the
child of his father; he then returns to earth, transformed from an object
of village contempt into a radiantly attired teacher of how the people
should live. As in the Cherokee story, the child's genealogical relationship has real consequences for who he fundamentally is and for what he
becomes.[20]

My remarks here can only be suggestive. A proper interpretation of
sacred stories requires that they be considered in the context of tribal languages, cultures, and community life. These are tasks that belong to
those with very special competencies and, most of all, to tribal communities who take on such tasks *as* communities. But these examples of a
story theme found across various tribes show evidence — not only in
what contemporary elders say but in what sacred stories relate — for a
kind of traditionally grounded essentialism (or, more likely, essentialisms) among at least some American Indian peoples. In so doing, they
provide a context for remarks such as those of Momaday and other elders
about the importance, for tribal identity, of genealogical relationship in
and of itself. They invite tribal communities to explore these ideas further
by examining their own stories about tribal belonging.

The existence of essentialist themes in tribal sacred stories suggests
that their academic dismissal as racist incitements or as colonial arti-
facts must be inspected carefully. Do the versions of essentialism that
Native communities may discover in their traditional stories differ
from the essentialist claims that arise in academic contexts and have
been so roundly criticized there? Do all essentialist definitions of identity come from the same intellectual place? Do they all function in the
same way? Social scientific studies of kinship provide a context in
which to address such questions: to determine if there are indigenous
and nonindigenous essentialisms, and to consider the implications of
differences between them.

Whereas contemporary social scientists frequently and explicitly reject
essentialist assumptions, anthropologist David Schneider shows that

their work has often implicitly depended upon such assumptions. In his impressive analysis of nineteenth- and twentieth-century studies of kinship, he concludes:

There is an assumption that is . . . widely held and necessary to the study of kinship. . . . It is the assumption that Blood Is Thicker Than Water.

Without this assumption much that has been written [by social scientists] about kinship simply does not make sense. . . . [This assumption posits that] *kinship is a strong solidary bond that is largely innate, a quality of human nature, biologically determined, however much social or cultural overlay may also be present.*[21]

The consistent orientation of kinship studies, Schneider summarizes, has understood "true" kinship as founded exclusively on biological relationships. Such an assumption clearly implies a kind of essentialism, in that it posits a fundamental substance connecting relatives. This substance is conceived as a physical material — "blood" — that can, like other physical materials, be attenuated and eventually exhausted. The corollary of what Schneider calls this "biologistic" assumption is that the significance of kin relationship depends absolutely on the proximity of the ancestral connection:

Primary relatives are closer than secondary, secondary are closer than tertiary, and so on. Civil law, canon law, and genetics provide . . . [alternative] modes of calculating closeness and distance. . . . [Nevertheless,] all depend on the assumption that what has been called "genealogical distance" is a crucial variable in the strength of the bond of kinship, and genealogical distance is a measure of the magnitude of the biological component and hence the strength of the bond.[22]

It is precisely this belief about the importance of genealogical distance that gave birth to the notion of blood quantum as a measure of the exact degree to which the strictly physical kinship substance was depleted.

How do these prevalent social scientific ideas compare to the essentialisms that might be expected to emerge from indigenous communities' contemplation of their own philosophies of kinship? Certainly we have seen that some modern American Indian people embrace a similarly biologistic construction of identity and its corresponding measure, blood quantum. But others suggest the very different idea that Indian identity is a discrete, not a continuous, variable. Momaday, for instance, makes no indication that his tribal "memory in the blood" is in any way compromised by being mingled with his European ancestry, and several interview respondents went out of their way to reject the conclusion that diluted blood quantum implies an attenuated identity.

For instance, Melvin B., whose statements quoted earlier characterized Indianness as something instinctual and inborn, concluded his comments with the remark that "it doesn't make any difference if you're *one-
ninety-second* [degree of Indian blood]. You're still an Indian, whether
you're a full blood or not. So, I mean, that's the way that *I* look at it."
And Kathleen W. argued that in the teachings she has learned from her
elders the simple *fact* of physical relationship is significant in a way that
overwhelms any ideas about *degree* of relationship:

When a person says they're Native, it's very important to me that they *are*
Native. . . . It's *not* important to me what their blood quantum is. I really — honest to God — do believe that the teensiest, tinsiest — in order to use the language
of blood quantum — blood degree is nevertheless the most powerful presence of
ancestry. And I know that I'm not alone in that. I know that elders who I really,
really respect see it that way.

From the perspective that such sentiments imply, one either belongs to the
ancestors or one does not, and the notion of fractionating one's essential
substance, as the terminology of blood quantum presupposes, is untenable.

The historic social structures of some tribes suggest a similar assumption. Among the Cherokee, the most important organizing category of
tribal life was the clan. Children inherited their mother's clan and were
understood to share a literal bond with her and with all other members
of her clan.[23] As in biologistic theories of kinship, this bond was often
spoken of as a bond of blood, but it was understood to operate quite
differently. An important difference is illustrated in a document penned
in 1810 by Moravian missionaries to the Cherokee. The missionaries
observed that, in this tribe, the bond of maternal blood was understood
to be so powerful that it was not extinguished or compromised even
with repeated intermarriages to non-Indian men: "someone . . . descended from [Cherokee] Indians on his mother's side, no matter how
many years back" was considered a Cherokee. The same was true even for
one who had "lost himself among white people so that his Indian origin
is in doubt. . . . [If] such a one can indicate only that his grandmother or
his great-grandmother was an Indian woman or a half Indian or a quarter Indian, he belongs to the clan or family of his ancestress and is helped
by them if he is in need."[24]

A discussion offered by anthropologist Jack Forbes (Powhatan/
Lenape/Saponi) augments this example with an explanation that provides greater insights into the type of essentialism it implies. In many
tribes, Forbes writes,

persons are descended in the female line from a "first" ancestor, usually a being with an animal or plant name. If, for example, one is a member of the "turtle" matrilineal lineage, one might find this situation: 500 generations ago the first "turtle" woman lived, and in each subsequent generation her female descendants had to marry men who were non-turtles, i.e., with other lineages in their female lines. A modern-day "turtle" person, then, might well be, in quantitative terms, one-five-hundredth "turtle" and four-hundred-ninety-nine-five-hundredths non-"turtle," and yet, at the same time, be completely and totally a turtle person.[25]

This example elegantly demonstrates that the essentialism of tribal philosophies can be founded on a different logic than the one that has dominated social scientific thinking about kinship: a sacred logic to which notions of genealogical distance and blood quantum are foreign and even irrelevant.[26]

A second significant, and even more striking, difference in the way Native and non-Native philosophies construct essentialist ideas concerns assumptions about the way that the identity-conferring substance is transmitted. Biologistic theories assume that the essential substance is inherited strictly through birth. In a number of Native philosophies, however, it appears that essential nature is usually, but not necessarily, so transmitted. Alternatively, it can also be created ceremonially. We learn this, for instance, from an examination of social patterns related to the adoption practices of specific tribes.

Although some tribes, at certain points in history, were very bounded and closed societies (and some, to a significant degree, continue as such today), others had strong, incorporative traditions. In the wake of disruptions introduced by the arrival of Europeans, for instance, "interethnic cooperation and acceptance of new members into the group to achieve a numerical advantage over other groups became an important strategy. . . . Some groups added outsiders who were captives, slaves, orphans, outlaws, social outcasts, mixed-bloods, trading partners, or fictive kin."[27]

Various interview respondents gave examples of "outsiders" who were taken into the tribe in ways that caused them to take on relationships that are stated in essentialist terms, and that may even be spoken of as physical or "blood" relationships. Archie M., for instance, reported that, along with his Osage and Cherokee ancestry, he

can claim [to be] Ponca because of a relationship of two women long ago [in the nineteenth century]. A Ponca woman and an Osage woman, who was my relation, took each other as sisters. . . . It [the adoption ceremony] was a very *special* ceremony held on the Arkansas River, between the Osages and the Poncas, a very special, spiritual thing way back there. That was a heavy, heavy decision among two women who took each other as sisters. And when that happened, there was a . . . connection between families. And today, I have Ponca people who are my *family*. . . . [W]e recognize each other as *blood*. We're the *same*. . . . I know that and it affects *me*. I tell my children and my grandchildren these kinds of things. (original emphases)

Archie M.'s words suggest an understanding of ceremony as the vehicle for a powerful transformation by which the object of ceremony becomes a different kind of person — in his case, a person related to other Ponca people in fundamentally the same way that those born with Ponca ancestry are related.

There is a long tradition, at least in certain tribes, of the kinds of practices that this contemporary speaker suggests. The tribes of the Iroquois Confederacy, for example, were very active, in certain times and places, in adopting outsiders.[28] Evidence suggests that among the Iroquois adoption rituals did not merely alter the formal citizenship status of the person involved; rather, they ceremonially *re-created* the individual, changing her essential nature in accordance with what I am calling a definition of kinship. Frederick Webb Hodge, in his *Handbook of American Indians North of Mexico,* tells the story of two white sisters who were captured by the Seneca (a member tribe within the Iroquois Confederacy) and were prepared for tribal adoption. However, Hodge writes, "instead of both being adopted into one clan, one [sister] was adopted by the Deer clan and the other by the Heron clan, and thus the blood of the sisters was changed by the rite of adoption in such wise that their children could intermarry."[29]

Had these sisters been born Senecas, they would have belonged to the same clan. All their children — first cousins — would have belonged to that clan as well and thus would have been restrained from intermarriage by incest prohibitions. But the Seneca ceremonial procedures permanently transformed the sisters' fundamental nature and being. The choice of wording — that their very "blood . . . was changed" — may, of course, reflect an outside observer's interpretation, while the Senecas themselves might have spoken about it differently in their own language. Yet the consequences of the act are clear, regardless of the language used to describe it. The adoption ceremony made the sisters different from each other at a level that transcended their straightforward genealogical relationship. It caused a *sacred* transformation of the individual that brought into being what nature had originally wrought otherwise. It seems to have bestowed, in a quite literal sense, a connection of fundamental substance to other members of the tribal body.[30]

These new Seneca relatives are not properly described by the notion of "fictive kin" — the category to which anthropological studies of kinship since the nineteenth-century writings of Henry Maine would relegate them. They entered the ceremony as one kind of being, and they emerged as another. The kinship substance thus acquired is real and consequential, enabling new relationships — both social and physical. But it does not behave in its possible modes of transmission like the strictly material kinship substance assumed by social scientific theories because it can be created in ceremony. Given the limitations of the English language, and of the conceptual categories upon which social scientists depend, perhaps we can only say that this kinship substance has attributes of both the physical *and* the more-than-physical.

Such observations, like the themes explored in tribal sacred stories, challenge the postcolonialists' claim that any embrace of essentialism necessarily represents surrender to nonindigenous ideas and values. These examples suggest that there are indigenous essentialisms quite different from the biologistic, social scientific varieties. They also challenge the accusation that essentialist claims are necessarily racist: the essentialisms explored here have nothing to do with the idea of race, a concept rooted in the same biologistic assumptions that have driven social scientific studies of kinship. Instead, the identity definitions that I have explored emphasize the unique importance of genealogical relatedness to tribal communities while also allowing, at least in principle, for people of *any* race to be brought into kinship relations through the transformative mechanism of ceremony.[31]

A Second Kinship Principle: Responsibility to Reciprocity

As I stated earlier, the definition of kinship that I think may be recoverable in a number of American Indian philosophical traditions comprises not only the significance of genealogical relationship, but also the way that individuals behave toward others. As interview respondent Melvin B. commented: "To me, having a [CDIB] card doesn't necessarily make you an Indian. . . . As far as *acting* like one — a card don't make you do that. . . . If he's an Indian, he will help his brother."

For his part, Hopi elder Frank D. offered a list of what he thinks of as "those old Indian values" that function as evidence of membership in a tribal community. These include "sharing, helping, assisting, and then those other values of hard work, decency, honesty, and respect." Also important, he thinks, is "the spiritual part — how they [Indian people] treat themselves, how they treat each other, how they treat Mother Earth, from a spiritual perspective." For him, Indian identity is "not just the ceremonies, but daily living. How we get along, and how we treat each other. And of course, the ceremonies tie it all together."

Julie M. makes these statements more concrete when she describes the life of a small Cherokee community in Oklahoma:

I grew up in a . . . huge, extended family. And you never had to worry about anything. You always knew that you had help. If you needed food, that whole community helped you. You know, it was kind of like, [earlier in Cherokee history when] . . . the whole community went out to look for food, gather food, and bring it [back]. Nobody went hungry. And if there were widows or people [in need], the men that hunted would bring back their food, and they would share it with people in the community. And that's what I grew up in. . . . So I know what that kinship system does for you. . . . You [also] know that if you venture out into the [larger] world, you don't have to do it by yourself. . . . And that whole idea of individuality and competitiveness wasn't really in our [Cherokee] culture, in that kinship culture . . . because it was all about helping one another and sharing everything. . . . There are communities that still practice that [way of life] to this day.

Other Native peoples, separated from their communities of origin, express a sense of responsibility for finding new ways to contribute to tribal survival. For some, this means aligning themselves with tribes other than their own. Their actions may be quite ordinary, but they merit our notice because of the actors' expressed sense that these behaviors are part of the way they live as tribal people. For instance, Melissa Nelson, president of the Cultural Conservancy, a Native nonprofit organization working to preserve traditional cultures and lands, is of Ojibwe, Nordic, and French ancestry. Her mother was raised on the Turtle Mountain Chippewa reservation, but Nelson herself grew up in the San Francisco Bay area. She writes:

Because I live in central coastal California, which is primarily Ohlone territory, I support and work together with some Ohlone people and other California Indians who are working to protect the diversity and quality of all life in this region: endangered species, languages, habitats, songs, stories, and the free flow of rivers. Managing a native non-profit organization dedicated to these native land protection goals, I have spent many nights and weekends faxing letters to Congress, writing letters of support for tribes and communities, grant writing, compiling and sending out educational and technical information packets, and responding to various requests. This activism has been part of my commitment to my Native heritage.[32]

Such statements suggest a widespread conviction that The People — those who understand themselves as bound together in spiritually faithful community — are responsible for living with each other in particular ways. These ways of relationship constitute what I am calling a responsibility to reciprocity. It is likewise suggested by Christopher Jocks when he writes of the "ability to *participate* in kinship" (original emphasis). He regards kinship as an ongoing practice or skill, an active relationship that must be maintained and that is not invariably tied to one's genealogical connections: "In every Indian community I am aware of there are a few non-Indians who have gained [entry into kinship relations]. . . . Generosity of time and spirit, respect and politeness, willingness to help out, and openness to learn, are what our elders seem to value most; and all of us who pursue this work [in American Indian studies] know non-Indians who have succeeded in it." The same logic, he notes, also works in reverse: "There are full-blood Indians who have lost this ability to participate in kinship."[33]

The foregoing observations suggest an emphasis on behavior in defining tribal identity that is quite different than the ideas that have dominated social scientific studies of kinship. David Schneider's critique, discussed earlier in this chapter, argues that the biologistic preoccupation of such studies has long motivated social scientists to consider any kind of behavior as nothing more than a "social and cultural overlay" upon the fundamental fact of physical descendancy. Accordingly, it makes little sense within social scientific frameworks to speak of kinship as a venue of willful participation.

What can a consideration of tribal sacred stories and social structures show us that differs from the dismissal of behavior as an element of tribal identity? As in the preceding discussion of essentialist ideas, I propose to look at a single story theme that appears across many tribes and invite communities to consider its implications. All over North and South America, tribal traditions include a theme of humans who marry animals, sometimes going to live in the animal village. Often these animals are deer, buffalo, or bears, but they may also be turtles, butterflies, snakes, caribou, seals, or other creatures.[34]

One illustrative story expressing such a theme is found among the Thompson River Indians (British Columbia).[35] In it, a hunter takes a

deer woman for a wife and goes to live with her people in their under-
ground village. He learns to follow their way of life, and he and his new
relatives quickly take on their proper roles, each making an appropriate
gift to the other: whenever the people become hungry, one of the deer
people offers itself and the hunter kills it. Everyone eats, and the hunter
performs the appropriate ritual that allows the dead deer to return to life.
Thus there is a full circle of reciprocity: the deer people share their flesh,
each in turn for the others, while the hunter shares his skill with weapons
and his attentiveness to ceremonial requirements.

In this particular story, the hunter is fully and permanently transformed: "The hunter never returned to the people. He became a deer."
But stories of animal-human marriages do not always work out this way.
In many stories, even if the human spouse temporarily takes on animal
form, he or she may be unable or unwilling to entirely adapt to the
requirements of living with his new community. Ultimately there comes
a moment in which the person makes a choice, by his behavior, about the
community to which he truly belongs. Many times he ends up back with
his human relatives.

The children of human-animal unions may also have to decide their
proper place, and again their actions determine the answer. Thus, in the
Thompson River story, the hunter's son makes a choice that is the opposite of his father's. Although in his youth he is a deer who sacrifices his
flesh so that others may eat, when he grows older he decides to return to
his father's village, there to live as a human: "He became an Indian and a
great hunter."[36] Although this child's ancestry — partly human and partly
deer — gives him a potential claim on two communities of relatives, he
eventually chooses to bring the gift of hunting skills to the human village.
Thus, it is with humans that he belongs, and it is a human being that he
finally becomes. The story's theme about marriages that link human and
nonhuman communities provides a provocative starting point for a discussion of kinship conceived as an act of *doing* as well as an act of *being*.

Traditional social structures in a number of tribes likewise suggest an
explicit recognition that tribal belonging could manifest itself as a kind of
behavior, a relationship that was proven over time. The example of adoptions is once again instructive. As Hodge records, tribally adopted individuals might be invested with a fictitious age. Given that age was generally linked to rights, responsibilities, and social position, this practice
gave the adoptee time to mature into duties she would be expected to
assume: to explore the meaning of responsibility to reciprocity in her
new community.[37]

Thus, among the tribes of the Iroquois Confederacy, a trial period was required of adoptees, during which the new relatives (often prisoners captured to replace a deceased tribal member) proved themselves. After a ritual of initiation, "captives embarked on a period of probation — it might end months or years later or never — during which new relatives and fellow villagers judged whether they had truly become Iroquois."[38] Ultimate acceptance was contingent on what the adoptee did:

Captives became one people with the Iroquois by *acting* like Iroquois. . . . For some adoptees, especially potentially dangerous adult warriors, the behavioral test might entail such a dramatic act as participation in a raid against one's former people. For women and children, however, the requirements were more mundane: doing one's share of the work, fulfilling one's kinship obligations, marrying one's new relatives' choice of a spouse. Usually that was enough. . . . A newcomer could secure a permanent place in the family by adequately performing the duties of the person she replaced. Similarly, outside the family, adoptees won acceptance through appropriate behavior.[39]

Those who managed to assimilate were accepted as Iroquois in every sense. "There were 'no prisoners but Free and given over to them that receive them as there *[sic]* Children,' a Mohawk leader explained, of some Christian New England Algonquian adoptees. It would be 'very hard to deliver them back againe' to their former people, he continued, 'being it is Soe hard from *[sic]* any man to part from Flesh and blud.'"[40] On the other hand, some captives proved unwilling or unable to assimilate, and their fate could be unpleasant: those who did not choose to live as Iroquois could be treated as slaves or even killed.[41] The probationary principle fits comfortably with the idea that kinship is not exclusively about ancestral connections but also incorporates an emphasis on behavior that requires time to learn.

Other historic tribal social structures reveal an opposite reality: if some behaviors earned selected individuals a place in the tribal circle, certain acts could place one outside it. Sorcery, which manipulated others for an individual's gain, was such an offense in some tribes; so was the murder of another tribal member, which might well entail the perpetrator's giving up his own life. But seemingly lesser failures of reciprocity principles might cause others at least to question one's place in the tribal society. Ella Deloria devotes a great deal of effort to explaining the importance of generosity in traditional Lakota (Sioux) society. A significant part of tribal life, she writes, was to participate in reciprocal exchange: to share one's possessions unstintingly whenever possible and to accept help from others whenever necessary. Deloria also reports an expression characterizing people who seek to accumulate personal wealth rather than to share: "A man who showed that tendency was suspect, as if he were not quite human. *Tak-taninsni* they said of him; meaning 'what kind of thing (he may be) is not plain.' "[42] Those who did not participate in the kinship system through reciprocal behavior threatened their standing there, even to the point of bringing into question their place in the classification of humans. Although the relatives of such an individual might still try to protect him, their task would not be easy. He did not act like a Lakota.[43]

What might one learn about tribal identity by taking an emphasis on reciprocal behavior more seriously than social scientific studies of kinship have done? What might such perspectives allow academics to see that they have previously overlooked? One limitation of any strictly biologistic model of kinship becomes clear when one considers the extended nature of the reciprocating community typically presupposed in indigenous philosophies. That is, social scientific analyses have concerned themselves primarily with the relationships of humans to one another, presenting elaborate diagrams and analyses of kinship terminology and similarly detailed discussions of the specific behaviors that parents, children, siblings, cousins, and others expect from, and render to, particular categories of relatives.[44]

By contrast, in tribal philosophies people take their place, or find their identity, within a kinship network that includes not only other humans but also animals, plants, minerals, geographic features, the earth itself, celestial bodies, and spirit beings. They both owe certain things to, and expect certain things from, all of these entities. Acts of reciprocity in this extended community are not solely — perhaps not even *primarily* — for the benefit of humans. As is richly illustrated in the story of the hunter who became a deer, reciprocity serves humans no better — and no worse — than any other member of the natural world. Humans are simply one set of participants in the vast cycles of giving and receiving, of covenant and celebration, that constitute relationship to a tribal kinship community.

Indigenous perspectives on tribal belonging not only draw attention to more actors than conventional academic scholarship has recognized; they also reveal a different way to think about the behaviors by which humans establish and maintain kinship relations. Especially in the case of nonhuman relatives, these activities are likely to include behaviors that social scientists classify as ritual action. Although they have not included this type of action in their analyses of kinship, they have nevertheless studied it extensively.

Twentieth-century literature in the social scientific study of ritual activity — work by such disciplinary founders as Malinowski, Radcliffe-Brown, Homans, Parsons, Kluckohn, Geertz, and others — centrally concerns itself with the *functions* of ritual, particularly its role in reducing or channeling anxiety. A frequent claim is that humans resort to ritual where rational contemplation and utilitarian technological intervention fail to produce a certain outcome — as in the hunting of game animals that may or may not show themselves. Ritual, as Bronislaw Malinowski writes, "is . . . generally to be found whenever man comes to an unbridgeable gap . . . in his knowledge or in his powers of practical control, and yet has to continue in his pursuit."[45]

This construction of the ritual reciprocation characterizing the relationships between human and nonhuman kin differs substantially from understandings that are more likely to emerge from tribal philosophies. While relationships with nonhuman kin may be characterized, in indigenous philosophies, by awe and respect, they may also be characterized by emotions much more positive than the social scientific concentration on anxiety. In particular, many indigenous people speak of ritual reciprocation as a means of enjoying and expressing loving communion. Thus Herbert John Benally, writing from within Navajo philosophy, refers to "establishing an intimate relationship with nature."[46] Elsewhere the same author characterizes this relationship as one rooted in a sense of thanksgiving: "gratitude is directed to the water, the trees, the plants and animals that nourish and shelter, and especially to the creators, that their blessings would never diminish."[47]

Julio Valladolid and Frédérique Apffel-Marglin likewise describe the understanding among the Andean indigenous people of ritual as a means of establishing profound emotional relationships. In preparing the fields for planting, the Aymara (Conima, Peru) offer coca leaves and deep reverence: "'Pachamamma, Holy Earth, please pardon us, please excuse us. . . . Thus saying, we kiss her on our knees.'"[48] The relationship continues as new life emerges and matures:

The plants . . . that [the Andean indigenous people] nurture with dedication and love are members of their families. When the small shoots emerge in the *chacra* [small field], they are their children; when they flower, they are companions with whom they dance and to whom they sing; and when they give fruit at the time of harvest, they are their mothers. Andean peasant agriculture is this nurturance, full of feelings as for their own family.[49]

The sentiments described here can only be spoken of as love. They suggest the possibility of ritual relationships as a vehicle enabling people to experience the sheer joy of connectedness, the pleasure that comes from making and having relatives, the satisfaction of acting like a relative oneself. It is a perspective that makes the social scientific reduction of ritual behavior to a means to channel anxiety feel considerably less satisfying, or at least less complete.

The foregoing observations about the importance for tribal identity of a responsibility to reciprocity, and the distinctive ways that this idea may be developed within indigenous philosophies, add another dimension to our understanding of what I am calling a definition of tribal identity founded in kinship. They show us that even strongly essentialist definitions of identity do not necessarily reduce to determinations of one's fundamentally given nature: the ideas about tribal belonging just suggested imply that one must literally *be* a relative, and that one must also *act* like one.

Evaluating Kinship Definitions

This very preliminary investigation, framed and guided by principles of Radical Indigenism, not only suggests an understanding of tribal identity that differs markedly from conventional scholarly constructions; it also contrasts with the definitions explored in the preceding chapters of this book: the legal, biological, cultural, and personal definitions that are currently invoked in modern Indian communities, often to the exclusion of some who argue passionately against this judgment. Based on the preceding observations, I propose the following view about American Indian identity, which might be discussed in Native communities: individuals belong to those communities because they carry the essential nature that binds them to The People *and* because they are willing to behave in ways that the communities define as responsible.

To return the discussion to practical issues, we must ask how such a definition might function. I cannot possibly determine the best definition of identity for any tribal community. Each community must come to its own understanding of this issue, and its conclusion will probably differ from that of other communities. It is probably fair to say, however, that any definition founded on the general understandings of kinship discussed in the preceding sections is likely to maximize the benefits and minimize the disadvantages of the reigning definitions explored earlier in this book.

First, like definitions based on law, a definition of identity based on kinship as I have construed it respects the primacy of the collective, the tribal "we," without becoming entangled in legal fictions; for it reminds members that they enjoy their place in the community only by the community's collective pleasure. They must understand that should they offend the community or choose to act in ways that harm it, the community can renounce and remove them — individual claims to rights of belonging based on law, blood, culture, or self-definition notwithstanding.

Second, like definitions based on biology, a definition of identity based on kinship honors a person's essential connection to the ancestors; yet it does so without shaming or diminishing either mixed bloods or individuals who enter the life of a tribal community through a pathway other than birth.

Third, like identity definitions based on culture, one based on kinship presupposes a commitment to traditional tribal values; yet it does so without forcing the dilemma discussed in chapter 4. It does not demand that we see Native culture as either as a static, unchanging relic or as whatever anyone chooses to label Indian. Instead, it suggests that cultures *both* change *and* stay the same — that they include both specific practices, which may shift and change as circumstances demand, and stable underlying principles (such as the principle of reciprocity), which may properly be lived out at different times in different ways.

Finally, like definitions based on self-identification, identity founded on kinship respects the dignity and personhood of the individual. It does not ask communities to heedlessly spread out their economic, spiritual, cultural, and other resources for the rampant delectation of all comers. But it does encourage them to see even those who are on the margins of other definitions of identity — the nonenrolled, those of low blood quantum, the culturally dispossessed, and even the "new Indians" — as individuals who carry in their very bodies a powerful and important connection to the ancestors, and thus as potential relatives who possess personal worth and unique talents. And it allows these people to become relatives in the fullest sense, as they are taught to turn their talents to the benefit of Native communities and learn to live in reciprocity.

In short, a definition of identity founded on traditional notions of kinship sets the conditions for the potential, compassionate incorporation into the tribal community of Indian persons whom other definitions can exclude. Thus, it is a flexible definition. At the same time, it is a robust definition. Being grounded in the traditional value of reciprocity, it provides for protection of Indian communities from the abuse that can result from loosened boundaries. This is true because the themes of the sacred stories provide models of community life in which all members are instructed in and held to a rigorous standard of responsible participation. More than anything, this definition may let Indian people choose to be more gentle with one another than they frequently are in discussions about tribal belonging. It is a definition that might make it possible, as Indian communities, to grieve our losses and to come together in a new beginning to restore them.

Prerequisites for a Radical Indigenism

The particular ideas about tribal identity that I have explored in this volume are less important than the model of inquiry by which I generated them. This process might be labeled a first, tentative exercise in exploring the meaning and promise of the perspective I have called Radical Indigenism. It is such an exercise because it does not try to draw firm or universalizable conclusions based on examples from different tribes. Instead, it proposes a particular way to frame a question and then explores some implications of that framing. This effort responds to a common principle of traditional tribal philosophies by orienting itself to a practical goal. It tries to help tribal communities along in their own conversations on identity, inviting them to their own work of creating new definitions by displaying themes about tribal belonging found in particular indigenous contexts. Moreover, it moves beyond the practical to the spiritual. It is oriented toward Original Instructions, looking to elders, sacred stories, and historic practices for its support. It draws upon these sources — ones that have been neglected or used differently by the academy — to generate ideas about a question that is important to Indian peoples today. It proposes a place in the conversations for those who live and move in Indian communities, in scholarly communities, or in both.

Of course, I anticipate an urgent protest from my academic colleagues. The foregoing discussions urge an exploration and recovery of "traditional" ideas about tribal belonging — an endeavor that will generate little academic enthusiasm: Edward Said echoes a common sentiment when he asserts that "it is completely fallacious to suppose that there is such a thing as a pure, unalloyed tradition from which to draw. The only people who believe this are religious extremists."[50] Other scholars will certainly ask me what I can possibly mean by "tradition" — a word so difficult to define that most scholars have abandoned it. Happily, the answer to this question elucidates the central premise of Radical Indigenism.

I am glad to agree that "tradition" does not equate to some petrified pattern of life: to what The People have always, unchangingly done. American Indian communities have found so many and such varied solutions to the problems of survival that individuals living in different historic periods might have difficulty even recognizing their ancestors. It is likely, as anthropologist Ray Fogelson observes, that for many tribes, "the 'ancient ones' would seem like aliens."[51] Even in relatively recent times, Indian people have continued to adapt and change, and their practices in relation to kinship are no exception.[52]

Nor does "tradition," by my understanding, equate to ancient practice: to whatever The People did at the most distant historical moment of which we have knowledge. Certainly, as Indian people we must take seriously our ancestors' struggles and solutions, and we can usefully study the ways that they made their lives together. But that does not mean that we choose a single moment in time and enshrine it as the enduring touchstone. As an old family friend, a Navajo ceremonialist, once said to me with a grin, "Don't forget — not *everything* people did a long time ago was 'traditional.'"

What then *is* tradition? Respondent Joyce J. makes a significant distinction:

Nowadays we [Indian people] have "culture" and we have "tradition," and they can be separate. . . . Culture has to do with outward things that let other people see that you are Indian: what we eat, what we wear, the things we make. Those can be *part* of our teachings from the past; some parts of culture come from spiritual teachings. But some things that have become a part of culture might even be bad.

By contrast, she says,

tradition is what is passed on orally, and it tells you the way you are *supposed* to be. It has to give us *good*. It has to give us *growth*. It is the lessons that were taught us by the ancient ones and the elders to help [each of] us be a better person, and closer to the Creator. And we have to use it in the way it is intended. . . . It's spiritual.

My approach to defining "tradition" is consistent with the goal of Radical Indigenism: to respect the tenets of indigenous philosophies of knowledge. This approach accepts that tradition is fundamentally a *sacred* concept. As such, it is inextricably bound up with the idea of Original

Instructions: it designates the modes of thinking and acting that correspond to the fundamental principles of those teachings.

This definition of tradition has several implications. One is that we Indian people should not assume that our ancestors always chose (any more than we do) to live in the light of their sacred teachings, and time cannot transform behavior into tradition if it departs from those teachings. Another implication is that many different ways of organizing tribal life may be equally traditional — though to the extent that our ancestors responded to their Original Instructions, we may expect to find certain threads of continuity that reflect similar principles. We can expect, in other words, that what Gerald Alfred writes, in his study of political life among the Kahnawake Mohawks (Quebec) is generalizable beyond that sphere:

> There is no simple answer to the question: "Do ideologies/peoples/nations/cultures change or not?" They of course change — and they do not. . . . In Native cultures at least there exists a stable core which forms the basis of the political culture and nationalist ideology. There are also peripheral elements within the culture which are malleable and which do not shift and transform, rise and fall in importance and relevance according to shifts in the political context and according to the exigencies of the general political and economic climate.[53]

A third implication of the foregoing definition of "tradition" is that claims about it are ultimately validated through processes of inquiry that include a spiritual dimension, including such activities as dancing, singing, praying, dreaming, joining in ritual, and interacting with the natural world. Tradition, by my understanding, was first received in these ways, and indigenous philosophies of knowledge allow for knowledge to continue to be so received. This means that when communities seek knowledge in the context of their traditional philosophies, there is one more place to look, in addition to those I have discussed. Tribal communities can validate what they learn from elders, stories, and their own histories by comparing their conclusions to what they learn through individual and collective ceremonial participation.

My definition of tradition is, of course, completely indefensible from the perspective of the social sciences, or any other science. So are all of its implications. And that is the point. The point of Radical Indigenism is to respect the definitions and assumptions that characterize the philosophies of knowledge carried by tribal peoples. The rules of conventional academic inquiry relegate the types of explorations I describe here to the realm of faith and belief, rather than the realm of scholarship and knowledge. But the price for excluding information derived from inquiries that include (or are infused by) spiritual elements is that the academy also will never *really* encounter Indian people. Certainly it will not encounter them as equal participants in a common enterprise. It is simply not possible to split off or ignore the spiritual aspects of tribal philosophies and still make any sense of them or the people who carry them.

If Radical Indigenism is to advance, it will require the participation of scholars who find ways to embed themselves in communities as contributing members, who can look to the traditional knowledge of those communities from a position of personal commitment, who can profoundly encounter the sacred stories in the language that generated them, and who contribute to conversations that the communities themselves understand to be important. One of the very few scholars who has applied postcolonial theory to American Indian issues writes that "to enter into actual relationship with a traditional community . . . is already to initiate a decolonization process that ultimately subverts the old categories of 'self' and 'other' and generates a new and mutually respectful discourse. Such a discourse may rightly be called postcolonial discourse."[54] Such relationships are, indeed, a beginning. But for those relationships to yield a genuinely "postcolonial discourse" the academic participants in the conversation will have to broaden some of their assumptions about what it means to do scholarship.

I have provided an example of the way a particular inquiry — an investigation of American Indian identity — might be framed within certain values and assumptions common to Native cultures. Now it is up to individual American Indian communities to determine what they will do with these ideas. It is up to them to decide whether their own traditions reflect themes similar to those articulated in this chapter, and to confirm their conclusions by means appropriate to them. More importantly, it is up to communities to consider whether they would like to make use of those members who have commitments not only to their community but to academic communities to open a different kind of discussion with the academy — on this or any other subject. It is up to the academy to decide how it will respond to the invitation to engage with American Indian people from a position of real respect for their philosophies of knowledge. And it is up to individuals who have a place in both academic and Indian communities to decide if they are willing to encourage and shape such conversations as may emerge.

Long Lance's Ghost and the Spirit of Future Scholarship

One of the many conclusions one might draw from the foregoing discussions is that neither Indian communities nor scholarly ones have so far succeeded in sending the ghost of Chief Buffalo Child Long Lance to its proper rest. Long Lance, with whom we began our exploration of Indian identity, took both Hollywood and New York by storm in the 1920s. America in that era was greedy for Indians — but only for the "right" kind, and Long Lance comprehended this with great clarity. Indians whose tribes showed too clearly the brutal effects of European invasion because they had borne the first brunt of it; Indians whose tribes had been decimated, enslaved, and physically and culturally mutilated; racially intermingled and remnant peoples who had been later dispersed, in the wake of the great removals, to cities and settlements — Indians such as Sylvester Long represented to perfection — were not "interesting." In the view of most Americans, they were probably not even "real Indians," their authenticity having presumably trickled away from them somewhere along the desperate circuit of survival. So Long Lance invented himself within the parameters of the identity definitions available to him. While he was at it, he did so with the boldest possible strokes, making himself a noble Blackfoot, a full blood, a chief, and the son of a great chief.

As Long Lance entered his middle years, his fabrications and fantasies — perhaps eventually even he could not tell the difference — had brought him fame, admiration, money, and women. Yet he found himself strangely alone. The Indianness he had chosen for himself meant a life of irremediable isolation, and in the end, the tale unraveled around him anyhow. He could not go backward to recover the affection and tenderness of the family that had loved and raised him; he could not become, again, Sylvester Long. That would have meant abandoning career, professional accomplishments, social life, friends, romantic relationships, and indeed his future — the entire life he had created for himself. But he could not go forward in search of the bonds of community and family, either — for Chief Buffalo Child did not truly exist. He was a cardboard silhouette whose insubstantiality would soon be discovered by anyone whom he allowed genuine intimacy.

The stories hinting at Long Lance's partial African ancestry began to circulate, and his friends began to draw warily back. At last, when all of the carefully constructed artifice had dropped away, Long Lance stood before his former society companions revealed — in the words of one of them — as nothing more complicated than "a half breed nigger."[1] Long Lance confronted the reversal of his fortunes with the stoic resolve his fellow Americans had been pleased to think was characteristic of the "real Indian" they had demanded that he enact for their amusement. A servant discovered him early one morning, sprawled in a friend's library, with a pistol in his hand and a bullet in his brain. He was forty-one years old.

The Lessons of Long Lance for Understanding Racial Identity

Long Lance's attempts to negotiate a legitimate identity as an American Indian ultimately came to grief. His life, however, suggests certain lessons for scholars and other citizens who want to understand the meaning of race and racial identity; for it is a particularly powerful illustration of the fact that racial identities are, as sociologist Joane Nagel states, "*both* optional and mandatory."[2] It shows us that while individuals certainly formulate ideas about their race, it is the larger society that ultimately invests their assertions with legitimacy — or refuses to do so. This is a reality that is underscored in every chapter in this book. But my focus upon identity negotiations with particular reference to American Indians is more generally instructive.

While Americans are intensely interested in the legitimacy of racial identity claims among American Indians, the formal and informal rules by which they assign racial identities *in general* are changing. This is nowhere more clear than in the state and federal governments' decisions to finally acknowledge the reality of multiraciality and invest it with meaning by allowing people to classify themselves on official documents as belonging to more than one racial group. The change is a triumph for those individuals who, like Long Lance, were unsatisfied with the possibilities for racial identification formerly available to them. But it also promises to provoke some very heated societal debates about who can properly claim membership in the various racial categories observed by American law and institutional practice.

It is too soon to tell how American society will choose to deal with its burgeoning recognition of the complexity of racial identity and classification. But careful contemplation, such as I have undertaken here, of the various bases of racial assignment among American Indians — law, biology, culture, and self-identification — allows us to bring to the inevitable discussions of racial identity some understanding of where different choices might lead us. It teaches us the interests that may be served by the various definitions of identity as they each draw the boundaries of inclusion and exclusion differently, and it shows us the trade-offs that sometimes become necessary when one chooses one definition over another. It shows us the paradoxes of choosing different definitions in different contexts, and the dilemmas of refusing to choose at all. Not least, it shows us the pain that often accompanies conflicts about legitimate identity. Such lessons make all of us more sophisticated participants in the many debates about racial identity that America currently confronts, and in those that it will confront in the years to come.

This book also contributes to the academic debates on racial identity. By encouraging a turn to American Indian philosophies of knowledge as resources for responding to questions about tribal identity, it challenges both strictly "instrumentalist" and strictly "primordialist" views on racial identification. It observes (as do instrumentalists) instances in which racial identification has been subject to cynical manipulation on the part of individuals or groups, but it nevertheless proposes a basis for arguing that identification is not entirely reducible to rational calculation. It entertains essentialist ideas (characteristic of primordialist arguments) but suggests that such ideas that appear in American Indian philosophies may differ from the biologistic essentialisms more familiar in the academy. Most of all, this book encourages researchers and American Indian communities who may choose to align with each other in the pursuit of knowledge to believe that they can take up ideas about identity that are grounded in indigenous philosophies of knowledge, even if these do not correspond to regnant academic assumptions.

The Lessons of Long Lance for Indian Communities

The dramatic life and death of Chief Buffalo Child Long Lance remind us that when we attack and demean the identity claims of others, we can cause great injury. My interview respondents frequently expressed deep concern about the way that necessary attempts to protect Indian communities from exploitation often tip over into divisive and counterproductive racial vigilance. Cherokee respondent Julie M. assessed the battles over legitimate identity this way:

Any kind of tensions or conflict or strife among people creates spiritual wounds in the community, in the people of the community. And whether it erupts into violence or not, people carry these [wounds]. . . . What that [unhealed wound] does is — that *stops* your development, your growth. As a person . . . as a community. Right there. It *keeps* it there. And you can't move beyond that and grow beyond that. And that's what we [Indian people] were meant to do is overcome these things and then grow beyond that. . . . [If there is a] community that has those wounds, you have to come to grips with that.

Respondents who shared similar concerns often had suggestions for how communities might respond. Julie M. continued: "I really think the answer [to struggles about identity] is *there*, in our own culture, among us. It's just a matter of people taking it seriously and actually doing it." Hopi elder Frank D. also believed that resolution would come from Indian people "getting back to more practicing their culture. By accepting people. And if they are really practicing their culture, they would be more kind to each other."

One reason for writing this book is to urge Indian people and communities to remember that they all have cultural traditions that address the question of who The People are. In our communities we *already possess* the resources to meet the challenges of identity that confront us, and to do so without damaging those communities. We can only access those resources, however, when we come together to think through what our Original Instructions tell us — when community members of diverse talents bring their gifts to the process of working with the teachings, the stories, the histories. As I listened to my respondents, and as I wrote, I came to a greater understanding of these ideas. My understanding encouraged me to think about my own part in healing the American Indian communities with which I identify. What does it mean for me and other Indian scholars to live out our responsibilities to our cultures and our people in the academy? Can we craft a scholarship that allows us —

or even other colleagues who are not Indian but want to forge life-promoting alliances with Indian communities — to contribute to questions that are important to those communities while simultaneously fulfilling our academic commitments well?

Radical Indigenism: The Spirit of Future Scholarship

In response to the questions just stated I have proposed that the academy make room for a new kind of scholarship, a uniquely American Indian scholarship, grounded in the perspective I call "Radical Indigenism." It is intended not as a scholarship performed strictly by Indians, but as one in which Native peoples can see themselves and in which Natives — scholars and nonscholars alike — can participate. It is a scholarship in which questions are allowed to unfold within values, goals, categories of thought, and models of inquiry that are embedded in the philosophies of knowledge generated by Indian people, rather than in ones imposed upon them.

Here and there, researchers are beginning to pursue scholarly work that explores and responds to American Indian philosophies of knowledge in the way I describe — work that follows the path laid down in the models of inquiry traditional to their tribal community or to a tribe with which they have established a relationship. A few examples of the kind of work that seems consistent with the principles of Radical Indigenism include:

- the efforts of Gregory Cajete (Tewa) or Herbert John Benally (Navajo) to create innovative models of pedagogy. In their work, teaching and learning are positioned within an explicitly moral and spiritual framework that includes sacred stories, teachings, and ceremonial principles. "Just as Western science uses physical tools to extend the range of its exploitation of Nature, Indigenous traditions rely on the preparation of the mind and heart as well as physical tools. . . . If there is to be a true exchange of knowledge and mutual support the foundations of both systems must be appreciated as complementary ways of teaching, knowing, explaining and exploring the natural world."[3]

- the endeavors by members of the Peruvian-based nongovernmental organization PRATEC (Andean Project of Peasant Technologies). Many of the project's principals had earlier careers in international development, but have chosen to re-embed themselves in their Andean communities of origin and to subordinate their activities to local ceremonial cycles and knowledge. "They speak of the Andean world, not as judging outsiders, but as ones bonded to that world. They write books and articles like professional knowledge makers do, not with the intent to add to the fund of knowledge of their professions, but as their chosen field of action. They write of the Andean world, not primarily as a world to *know*, but as a world to live in, to participate in, to be a part of, and to collectively make."[4]

· the Storyscape project of the Cultural Conservancy (executive director, Melissa Nelson, Turtle Mountain Band of Chippewa Indians). The project approaches ecological restoration by first reestablishing sacred relationships with land through recovery and documentation of tribal songs and stories in culturally appropriate ways, with the participation of tribal wisdom keepers. "From a native perspective, restoring the spiritual relationship with a specific place is the first critical step in restoring the land itself. Song assists in connecting people to place, place to ancestors, ancestors to the living ecosystem and to future generations. Songs ensure that the spirit of the soils, plants, birds and animals have been respected. Only after thanking 'all our relations' and listening to the song of the land can protection in a Western sense — establishment of parks and preserves, biodiversity restoration, habitat enhancement — occur."[5]

Such work does not ask researchers to forsake interactions with the academy. Indeed, advanced academic training is part of what has enabled these individuals in their accomplishments. But these examples consistently suggest that researchers must align themselves with indigenous communities in ways that are often unusual from the perspective of the academy, and often costly in terms of individual advancement there. For instance, writings by the researchers just named are not published by mainstream academic journals or publishing houses; their outlets are limited to small, highly specialized journals, anthologies, or out-of-the-way presses.

Radical Indigenism suggests different activities in service of research and different goals for research. It encourages the approach to knowledge that Cherokee theologian Jace Weaver calls "communitist," in which "community is not only a tool or a framework . . . but also its ultimate goal."[6] Moreover, it explicitly recognizes that part of the prioritization of community is respect for its traditions of knowledge creation.

To accept Radical Indigenism will require the academy to make itself open to entirely new models of inquiry. I have argued that explorations within this perspective can properly be based upon the teachings of tribal elders, upon sacred stories, and upon knowledge of the ways that healthy Native communities functioned historically. In so doing I hope that I have offered some suggestions that tribal communities might investigate further. But Radical Indigenism will ask the academy to accept a great deal more than this.

A fully developed Radical Indigenism presupposes that Indian peoples possess complete philosophies of knowledge and models of inquiry that include not only the sources just named but also knowledge that is received through ceremonial means: through dreams, through communication with the nonhuman relatives that inhabit the universe, through collective ritualized seeking of spiritually faithful communities, and through interactions with land and language for which the conventionally defined academic disciplines have no name and no place. It will likely ask the academy to allow for different constructions of the "observable," of the relationship between mind and body, of the nature and powers of language, of the meaning and utility of "subjective" knowledge and of unique (nonrepeatable) events — and much more.[7] It will require, in other words, not discarding or replacing conventional scholarly models of inquiry, but a willingness to allow other, very different models to stand alongside them. These models of inquiry posit a very different order in the world than the one that academic disciplines generally assume, but one that is nevertheless not *dis*orderly. Radical Indigenism will ask the academy to allow scholars to demonstrate that the diverse philosophies of knowledge carried by many different tribal peoples can be the basis for genuine, worthwhile scholarship.

These are truly monumental requests. Even though some conventional scholars may be intrigued by the possibilities of an American Indian scholarship, they are certain to experience serious qualms about encouraging it. The most central concern likely to arise is that the acceptance of American Indian models of inquiry, and their underlying philosophies of knowledge, may leave the academy with no means to defend its intellectual boundaries. Wouldn't this encourage *everyone* who possesses some "system" of thought to claim the prerogatives and prestige of scholarship, leaving no means to distinguish between the work of the academy and any other claims, however nonsensical?

John Whittaker, a professor of anthropology and archaeology at Grinnell College, exemplifies this concern. He is not impressed with the observation common to many American Indian peoples that their own sacred stories do not support the Bering Strait land bridge theory by which archaeologists explain the arrival of American Indian peoples on this continent. If the academy allows American Indians to speak from within tribal traditions to issues that have conventionally been reserved for archaeologists and other scientists, Whittaker complains, "what is to prevent other crackpots from claiming that Columbus brought all the Indians over with him in 1492, or that they are really Jews who fled the tower of Babel?"[8]

Such reservations are understandable. But I do not think that acceptance of an American Indian scholarship implies embracing all the many others who clamor for recognition by the academy: creation scientists, UFO devotees, champions of the Loch Ness monster, spoon benders, and all their kin. The majority of these claimants purport to adhere to the same philosophies of knowledge and inquiry as do the conventional academic disciplines, especially the sciences. Essentially, they assert that they do better and more skillful science — archaeology, physics, exobiology, or what have you — than the mainstream scholars. Yet in the end they are unable to fulfill the standards of empiricism, intersubjective verification, replicability, and the like to the satisfaction of the scientists.

There is a difference, however, between "bad science" and "non-science." The genuinely American Indian scholarship I propose has no need to squeeze its distinctive claims and values into the frameworks provided by the sciences — an attempt that, I am convinced, is always doomed to failure. An Indian scholarship grounded in Radical Indigenism is, by definition, to proceed according to models of inquiry that are *genuinely separate* from those the academy customarily embraces. These indigenous models begin from fundamentally different assumptions about the fundamental nature of the world and how it is to be known. The accuracy of these assumptions is undemonstrable — but in this the American Indian models and philosophies do not differ from scientific ones, which have never been able to demonstrate, say, such a central and elemental concept as causality.[9]

Agreeing that there is a place in the university for indigenous models of inquiry is not to say that everyone who claims to do physics (for instance) does it equally well. It is only to make room for the possibility that conventional academic models of inquiry do not exhaust all the possibilities for knowing the world. It is to gamble on the chance that American Indian philosophies of knowledge enshrining principles, ideas, and values that have been tested and developed over thousands of years may have *something* worthwhile to teach the modern world.

It seems to me, moreover, that this gamble is not such a long shot. American Indian models of inquiry distinguish themselves from the products of those whom Whittaker calls "crackpots" in that the Indian models have already proven themselves. Technological accomplishments are certainly not the only measure of the adequacy of a philosophy of knowledge, but they are one, and the indigenous peoples of both North and South America have a long list of them to their credit, all of which they achieved without the benefit of the modern world's thoroughly secularized philosophies and methodologies. For instance, they built suspension bridges, enormous earthquake-proof buildings, water transportation systems, and thousands of miles of paved roads. (Significant portions of those roads are still in use, most notably in Ecuador and Peru; and the cities of Phoenix and Tucson, Arizona, have incorporated the preexisting engineering of the ancient Anasazi into their modern municipal water systems.)[10] A technique used by Mayan peoples to produce obsidian blades has been reconstructed from archaeological evidence, and the process is now employed to create surgical instruments that are more than a thousand times sharper than the modern surgical scalpel.[11] All over the Americas, Indian peoples made impressive discoveries in plant genetics, which allowed them to domesticate many food crops and develop innumerable strains of plants adapted to particular environments. They capably managed the biodiversity of large regions, and they were sophisticated astronomers. At the time of European contact, the medical and surgical knowledge of particular tribes far exceeded that of the newcomers.[12]

The construction frequently placed upon such facts is either that American Indian peoples somehow stumbled their way to their practical accomplishments by means of uninstructed trial and error, or that they were "really," in some sense, "primitive" or "early" scientists. The first interpretation openly insults Indian peoples in its assumption that (being ignorant savages) they could not possibly have had a developed philosophy of knowledge or method of exploring the world. The second interpretation is little better. It posits the ethnocentric assumption that there is *only one* workable model that underlies all successful attempts to approach the world and discover its secrets, and that Amer-Europeans have it; if American Indian peoples discovered anything about the real world, they must have used a variation of the methods and philosophies developed by Amer-Europeans. It ignores the enormous differences between American Indian and modern, secular models of inquiry, and presumes that the accomplishments of the indigenous peoples of the Americas occurred somehow *in spite of* many misguided and ignorant beliefs about the sacred elements of the cosmos.

American Indian Communities and Radical Indigenism

There is a great deal that the academy might learn not just *about* but also *from* American Indian peoples. Native communities have great traditions of knowledge that have not been appreciated or respected, and Radical Indigenism insists that this situation change. But it is not only the academy that could benefit from the development of a Radical Indigenism; modern Indian communities have an investment in it, as well. Part of the process of making American Indian communities whole and fully functional again is to re-create our institutions, including the institutions of scholarship and learning. As Mohawk scholar Taiaiake Alfred writes:

At first, the notion of an indigenous "intelligentsia" may seen counterintuitive, conjuring up visions of the privileged, educated elites in Western societies. But in the context of a unified, holistic approach to decolonization, writers, philosophers, teachers, and artists are essential. . . . The idea of an intelligentsia made up of teachers and wisdom-keepers is actually very traditional.[13]

Native communities are too often divided, and even torn apart, by bitter struggles such as the conflicts about identity explored in this book. The perspective of Radical Indigenism, by insisting that the academy and Indian communities can interact in ways that are inclusive of tribal philosophies and values, brings more personnel, more resources, more perspectives, to the collective project of maintaining and restoring the intellectual and spiritual heritage of tribal peoples. We should add, with Alfred, that "to propose an indigenous intelligentsia should by no means be seen as an attempt to supplant the traditional elders and healers."[14] It can be seen, rather, as an attempt to bring another set of hands, minds, and institutional commitments to the project of American Indian survival.

More importantly, Radical Indigenism allows for an approach to indigenous knowledge that goes beyond an aspiration to "preserve" cultures. Preservation is, of course, a worthy goal, but it is also one's response to knowledge that is agreed to be dead; it suggests a mad dash to save and keep cultural elements before their producers disappear forever. A Radical Indigenism that brings together the diverse concerns and contributions of Indians, of scholars, and of Indian scholars may hope not only to maintain, but to *extend* American Indian philosophical traditions. A comment by Melvin B., the Creek Nation's honorary chief, on this subject, contains one of the most powerful turns of phrase that I heard from my respondents: even when tribal traditions and customs are lost, "you can learn over again on cultural things like that, as far as going to ceremony or anything like that. You can re– . . . I guess you'd call it re-*inhabit* . . . the different forms of culture." The notion of culture reinhabited suggests that culture is not something people merely "practice" or "preserve" but something within which they properly *dwell.* To restore one's culture, then, implies that one lives differently in the world. As I see it, this is ultimately the goal of Radical Indigenism.

Finally, Radical Indigenism allows Indian people to settle their claims upon the academy, and even the larger society, on a different foundation. For many years we Indian people and our allies have asked universities to invest in the study and teaching of Indian languages, to recognize our histories and cultures, to divest themselves of stock holdings in corporations that are destroying the ecology of Indian homelands, to refuse funding for scientific research projects that entail the desecration of tribal sacred sites, and so on. Indian people have had very limited success in pressing such agendas because, to date, we have been unable to frame them as anything but *political* goals. They are subsequently relegated to the wish list dedicated to all the other campus "special interest" groups — the disabled, gays, lesbians, bisexuals, foreign students, women faculty, Italian-American students, college Republicans, and so on. The minimal resources universities dedicate to claimants on this list are divided among them all.

But from the perspective of Radical Indigenism, arguments that universities must protect American Indian land, languages, history, and cultures are not political claims at all, or even religious or legal ones; they are *epistemological* claims. Radical Indigenism supports the assumption held by tribal philosophies throughout the Americas: that relationships with all these things are rich sources of knowledge. Thus when we Native American scholars who are pursuing Radical Indigenism ask universities to protect sacred lands and our ability to be in relationship with them, when we ask them to support the teaching of our history, when we ask them to invest in the cultivation of our languages and cultures, we will be asking them to preserve the conditions under which we carry out our scholarship. We will ask for these things for the same reason that scholars ask for laboratory equipment, or books, or the protection of tenure: because they are basic to our ability to do our work in the academy. They are the wellspring of what we scholars pursuing Radical Indigenism can *know* and *discover* through the means laid out in traditional philosophies of knowledge and of inquiry. Radical Indigenism offers Indian people a means to help the academy understand what we need in order to pursue a new kind of scholarship.

Radical Indigenism: Final Thoughts

I close with a final bow to the question of *why* the academy should be motivated to expand its boundaries in such a way as to include Radical Indigenism under the rubric of scholarship. One reason is simple self-consistency. Including a genuinely American Indian scholarship within the academy is consistent with the ideal of university education in America. This ideal posits a setting in which many perspectives on reality can be discussed, where genuine intellectual freedom is achievable because students understand that there are alternatives to all the ideas they encounter. Scholarship based in Radical Indigenism will provide intellectual alternatives, without demanding that students choose them.

Perhaps even more compelling, by accepting indigenous perspectives on knowledge conventional scholars might discover things that they presently do not know, and have no means to know, because of the limitations of the intellectual frameworks within which they operate. American Indian philosophies present whole new ways of thinking about the world and the relationships within it. And new frameworks do not come along very often. Karl Marx gave the social sciences one such framework. Sigmund Freud provided another. The academy never saw the world in the same way again after the work of these scholars. This is why even those who do not think they were *right* still think they were *brilliant*. I submit that Radical Indigenism, properly pursued, has the potential to elucidate ways of thinking that would reorder our understanding of the world and everything in it even more substantially than these two modern "Western" thinkers did. It allows for the formulation of intellectual visions that are at once new and old. They belong to the modern world, yet tribal ancestors entertained them generations before us.

There are already pioneers who are working out the ways they can be in productive relationships with tribal *and* research communities. I believe that others will follow them who will address a range of issues well beyond the example of tribal identity that I have considered. I hope that this book, in its argument for a Radical Indigenism, will encourage the academy to attend to what such scholars are saying and to activities that will create a safe place for them to say it.

Appendix

In writing this book I drew on the usual sources of scholarship — books and journal articles in the disciplines of sociology, anthropology, religion, and Native American Studies; historic records; census data — for framing ideas and arguments related to racial identity. To illustrate how identity issues become real in the lives of people, however, I brought in information from other sources, both published and nonpublished.

Published sources include autobiographies, newspaper articles, and sometimes even fiction and poetry written by or about Indian people. Such literature, I contend, is a large part of the conversation about American Indian identity. Choctaw historian Devon Mihesuah has, in fact, criticized scholars for their failure to use literature as a research source: "Because many Indian . . . writers possess empirical data that cannot find acceptance in historical or anthropological works, literature is one effective outlet for their stories."[1] One can make the same point about autobiographies, or articles in Indian newspapers.

My unpublished sources include in-depth interviews with Indian and non-Indian people who find themselves caught up in conversations, controversies, and sometimes conflicts about tribal identity. I conducted these interviews, mainly in person, between the summers of 1999 and 2000. Three interviews, however, were conducted by telephone, and one respondent answered interview questions in writing.

The interviews were of two types, which I have labeled (somewhat arbitrarily) "professional" and "personal." The four professional interviews were conducted with the chief of the Cherokee Nation and with representatives of the Bureau of Indian Affairs, Branch of Acknowledgment and Research. This is the governmental organization most centrally involved in decisions about which claimants are formally invested with the status of federally acknowledged tribes. Although three of these respondents were themselves American Indians, they answered questions mainly in their capacity as governmental representatives, and that is why I classified their interviews as "professional." These interview respondents are identified in the text by their full names, similar to the way that published sources would be identified. The interviews were conducted at the Cherokee Nation complex in Tahlequah, Oklahoma, and at the BIA offices in Washington, D.C.

The "personal" interviews, which numbered eighteen, were conducted with members of American Indian communities. Although some of these people do occupy positions of authority with tribes or other entities, they spoke more as individuals than as representatives of an office, and it is for this reason that I classified their interviews as personal. These interviews were conducted in homes, restaurants, offices, and other comfortable places chosen by the respondents themselves.

Many of the individuals who offered a personal interview are people I know from living in the intertribal community of Tulsa, Oklahoma. Tulsa boasts the second largest American Indian population in the world, embracing members of many different Oklahoma tribes as well as tribes headquartered in other states. Other respondents are part of the network of relationships that I have formed through my academic interests and pursuits. They are Indian people who work in the sciences and in Native American Studies — another sort of "Indian community" in which I participate.

The varied personal characteristics of the respondents who generously agreed to help me suggest the diversity of opinion that I deliberately sought when I selected them. Some are well-known outside the immediate tribal community where they reside, and others are not. Some are leaders of one sort or another — religious, political, or ceremonial — in their communities, while others are not. Some have particular traditional training or life experiences that have shaped their ideas, while others have specialized and relevant academic training. Some have both. Some are full bloods, and some are mixed bloods. Some have lived on reservations, and some have not. Some speak from the perspective of those who are enrolled members of federally recognized tribes, and some speak from the perspective of those who are not. The respondents are united, nevertheless, in their personal knowledge of tribes and tribal cultures, even if many of them would modestly disclaim such a statement.

The kind and amount of data I have collected is clearly not large enough or random enough for statistical manipulations. Nor can the opinions encountered here be generalized to other groups of Indian people. My respondents did not intend their remarks in this fashion. ("I can speak only for myself, not for my tribe," is a statement commonly heard in Indian country.) And such generalizations would not be methodologically defensible. But especially when combined with the considerable data I have drawn from published sources, the interview data accomplishes its intended purpose: to illustrate some of the many ways Indian people today think and talk about their identity and the identity claims of others.

Because my respondents added so much to information drawn from published sources, I encouraged them to do what respondents are almost never invited to do — to attach their real names to their interview comments, if they wished to do so. I felt that they deserve credit for their ideas, without which the book would be much impoverished. Accordingly, personal interview respondents are typically identified in the text by their first name and last initial, which may be matched to a full name and a biography below. One respondent who preferred some degree of anonymity chose to be identified only by her Cherokee name, and a few others asked to be identified by an English pseudonym. All other respondents are fully identified.

The brief biographies that follow contain information about aspects of respondents' lives that they told me were important to them (either professionally or personally). Accordingly, some are very short, while others are more detailed. In part, these biographies are intended to inform the reader about the various perspectives that the respondents bring to this book. Above all, however, they are intended to honor and thank the respondents for their contributions. They are all magnificently knowledgeable people for whom I have the greatest admiration and gratitude. However, many of them, I should add, would not willingly compliment themselves by a public recitation of the accomplishments I attribute to them in what follows. The following remarks are my own description and recognition of the many gifts these remarkable individuals have brought to their various communities. Respondents appear in alphabetical order.

Professional Interview Respondents

R. Lee Fleming is the former tribal registrar (1987–1995) for the Cherokee Nation of Oklahoma, the tribe in which he is enrolled. He is now the branch chief of the Branch of Acknowledgment and Research, Bureau of Indian Affairs.

At the time of the interview, *Dr. Valerie Lambert* was employed as an anthropologist by the Branch of Acknowledgment and Research. She has since accepted a position in the Department of Anthropology at the University of North Carolina, Chapel Hill. Dr. Lambert is a Choctaw tribal member.

Dr. George Roth is a cultural anthropologist for the Branch of Acknowledgment and Research. He was instrumental in the drafting of the regulations governing the Federal Acknowledgment Process, the rules under which groups seek to become formally recognized as tribes by the federal government.

Chad Smith, born in 1950, is a Cherokee citizen. He is an attorney who has worked both in private practice and in the employment of the Cherokee Nation. In the spring of 1996, he enjoyed a visiting professorship at Dartmouth College, teaching Cherokee legal history and American Indian law. He was elected principal chief of the Cherokee Nation in 1999, a capacity in which he had just begun to serve at the time of his interview. In his inaugural speech he quoted his great-grandfather, a revered Cherokee leader: "Redbird Smith said one hundred years ago . . . 'Our pride in our ancestral heritage is our great incentive for handing something worthwhile to our posterity. It is this pride in ancestry that make men strong and loyal for their principle in life. It is this same pride that makes men give up their all for their government.'" Chad and his wife, Bobbie Gail, live in Tahlequah, Oklahoma, with their children.

Personal Interview Respondents

Melvin Bevenue, Sr., of both Creek and Osage heritage, was born in 1925 into a Creek-speaking household. "My mother did not even speak English until I was nine years old." He grew up in Tulsa, Oklahoma, attending the Creek Green Corn ceremonial dances and learning about the traditional uses of plants from his father. Melvin signed up for military service at age sixteen. Having retired from working as a heavy-equipment operator, he is now a musician. As a young man he learned silversmithing at Chilocco Indian School, and he continues to practice this skill as a hobby; those who attend powwows in northeastern Oklahoma are likely to be fortunate enough to find his work for sale. Melvin is honorary chief of the Creek Nation and holds a commission as federal marshal through the Creek Nation. He is a thirty-second-degree Mason and also belongs to the Indian Unit of the Akdar Shrine Temple in Tulsa because he is impressed with that group's work on behalf of crippled children. He has been an active member of the Intertribal Indian Club of Tulsa since its founding over twenty years ago. He and his wife, Billa Dean, live in Tulsa.

Joe B. describes himself as a Lower Brule and Santee Sioux. His traditional name is Ihunkiya Najin, or "Stands to the Last." He was born in 1917 on the Santee Reservation in Nebraska and grew up in Nebraska, North Dakota, and Oklahoma. Because his mother was Dakota and his father Lakota, he is a first-language speaker of both dialects. However, because of his attendance at Indian schools where tribal languages were suppressed, he feels he is no longer fluent. He can, however, understand the Sioux language and can "get by" speaking it. "They [fluent speakers] can understand me. And I haven't missed any meals. That's the main thing." Retired from working as warehouseman and supervisor for North American Van Lines, he works for the nutrition center operated by the Native American Coalition of Tulsa — in the capacity, he solemnly informs the inquirer, of "bouncer." Since the coalition's building also houses a Head Start, Joe is a familiar figure to the program's small students, who frequently refer to him affectionately as "grandfather." Joe makes his home in Tulsa.

Mose Cahwee, a Yuchi elder born in 1918, grew up in Kellyville, Oklahoma, and passed away in January of 2001, before the publication of this book. He was raised speaking Yuchi by his grandparents, and in his later years he was one of a handful of fluent speakers. As such, he was in great demand as a language teacher. He created books and tapes for use in language classes and with other elders authored a book on Yuchi and Creek culture for use in Oklahoma public schools. Mose was extremely knowledgeable about Yuchi history and culture, especially the traditional uses of plant medicines. He gave classroom and fieldtrip instruction to students and faculty at the University of Tulsa (including the author) on these subjects. He also served as an elected representative to the Creek Nation, as a soldier in World War II, and as a leader in the Pickett Chapel, a historic Yuchi congregation. He volunteered in his local commodity distribution center and wrote many Title IV grants that benefited local schools and the larger Indian community in northeastern Oklahoma. At the time of his death Mose resided in Sapulpa, Oklahoma, with his wife, Thelma.

Nancy Cahwee, a full-blood Dene (Navajo), grew up in Phoenix, Arizona. She graduated from Haskell Junior College and the University of Kansas, where she majored in design, with specializations in pottery and weaving. Nancy now works in the accounting department at International Chemical in Tulsa. She also researches and designs powwow regalia and contemporary Indian clothing by special order. In her free time, she enjoys attending powwows, where she sings southern style at the drum. She also studies local tribal languages, including Kiowa (in order to sing gourd songs) and Yuchi. She is a member of the All Tribes Community Church in Tulsa and has lived in Glenpool, Oklahoma, for the past twenty-three years.

A full-blood American Indian of Hopi and Laguna heritage, *Frank C. Dukepoo* was born 1943 and grew up in Phoenix, Arizona. At the time of the interview, he was living in Flagstaff, Arizona, and teaching in the Department of Biological Sciences at Northern Arizona University. A geneticist, he was a founding member of the American Indian Science and Engineering Society and the Society for the Advancement of Chicanos and Native Americans in Science. He was also founder and director of the Native American Honor Society, an organization that encourages scholarship and respect for traditional, Native American values. "I'm just thankful for all that's been given to me. I respect the gifts that the Creator gave me, and I want to use those for the benefit of my people. All people — just anybody. Including non-Indians." Sadly, Dr. Dukepoo passed away in October of 1999, before the publication of this book. In addition to his many professional accomplishments, he was an amateur magician who provided motivational programs for Indian young people. He was much admired and appreciated by the many younger American Indian scholars (such as the author) whom he encouraged with his warm good humor and kindly professional interest.

Tom E., who was raised in a traditional tribal community, chose not to be identified. The name used here is a pseudonym. In his seventies at the time of the interview, Tom is a first-language speaker of his Oklahoma tribal language.

Born in 1946, *Donald G.* is a United Keetoowah Band Cherokee who grew up in northeastern Oklahoma. Cherokee is his first language, and he has spent many years studying, preserving, and teaching it. In addition to the language, other aspects of Cherokee culture are also close to his heart. Reminiscing about his childhood, he says, "I remember [Cherokee] stories being told to me. In my own home. [Or] we would go visit some other family. Stay late into the night. Just kind of sit around. They'd sit around and tell stories. Build a fire and snuff it out a little bit and make smoke and chase the mosquitos away and things like that. While they were talking. We'd do that."

Born 1928 in Tulsa, *Joyce Johnson* is a mother, grandmother, and great-grandmother. She is Cherokee and Choctaw, her citizenship being in the Cherokee Nation. "I was brought up in the old traditions. And the old traditions is that each person, when they're here on this earth, if they're to do what the Creator wants them to do, then they must know who they are and what they are. And to know *who* you are, then you must know who the ancient ones and the ancestors that went before us are. We have to be a part of *them,* and to know *about* them." Over the years, Joyce has served her community as a board member for the Claremore Indian Hospital, as commissioner of Indian Affairs for the Greater Tulsa Area, as president of the Tsalagiya Club of Tulsa, as secretary of Cherokees for Responsible Government, and as elected secretary and council member for the Council of the Keetoowahs. Some of my fondest memories are of the many nights at her kitchen table, where elders worked at teaching me to speak the Cherokee language, and I taught them to read and write the Cherokee syllabary. (All in all, I had better students than they did.)

June Leach, born in 1941, is a full-blood Mohawk from the Six Nations Reserve, Ontario, Canada. She spent her earliest years on the reservation and later moved to an urban area. Nevertheless, she still feels strongly connected to her heritage. "When you were raised and entwined in your early childhood with your culture, things are ingrained into you. . . . Even when you leave the reservation. That experience makes you what you are as a person." She now lives with her husband in Albuquerque, New Mexico, where she has served on the Board of Directors for the Indian Center for eight years. She also supports her husband's work with the Cherokees of New Mexico, a charter organization of the Cherokee Nation that provides cultural programming and social activities to tribal members, their families, and friends. June is mother of five and grandmother of eight.

Born in 1944, *Archie Mason* is an Osage and Cherokee businessman and retired educator who grew up in Pawhuska, Oklahoma, and now lives in Tulsa. He is active in many American Indian organizations around the state and is an energetic supporter and participant at the Greyhorse Ceremonial Grounds in Greyhorse, Oklahoma. The Native American Student Association and the American Indian Cultural Association at the University of Tulsa have been particular beneficiaries, over many years, of advice and support from him and from his wife,

Ramona. As university alumni and the traditional advisors of those organizations, they have always opened their hearts and their home to Native students. Archie has served as commissioner of Indian Affairs for the Greater Tulsa Area and currently serves on the Advisory Council to the Indian Affairs Commission for the state of Oklahoma. He is in great demand as head man dancer and master of ceremonies at powwows.

Julie Moss is a full-blood, bilingual Cherokee. She was born and raised in Oklahoma. She holds citizenship in the United Keetoowah Band of Cherokee Indians headquartered in Tahlequah, Oklahoma. (The UKB is one of three federally recognized Cherokee tribes.) As UKB Federal Programs director, Julie works to direct resources to isolated, disadvantaged, tribal communities. Julie is a technical writer with a master's degree in community development. "The important thing to know about me is that I love my people. . . . I've grown up among them. One of my life-long missions has been to show the world . . . that we have beauty in our midst. Beauty is in our culture, our arts, our language, our stories, and in our ceremonies. . . . There is dignity, respect and honor in our culture. . . . I want to celebrate that." At the time of the interview, Julie was preparing to enter a doctoral program in American Indian Studies at the Union Institute (Cincinnati, Ohio). Julie lives with husband, Pat, and son, Nakwsi, at Eldon Valley near Tahlequah.

Oo-yost Oo-jil-dos wishes to be identified only by her Cherokee name, which she translates as "Blossom." Born in 1944, in Locust Grove, she is a full-blood Cherokee who now lives in Tulsa. She is a first-language speaker: "Cherokee is close to my heart. English is my second language." She has three children, of whom she is very proud. She also says, "I am proud of my health, my happiness, and my peace of mind on this earth. That's what I believe in." Oo-yost Oo-jil-dos was one of the two respondents with whom I had no acquaintance prior to the interview. Accordingly, her willingness to participate in this project deserves special recognition.

Ramona Peters, or Nosapocket, is a Mashpee Wampanoag of the Bear clan. She was born in 1952 in Mashpee, Massachusetts, and continues to reside in that community. She spent many years as a boat and house builder and now serves as a consultant on Wampanoag culture. She is also an artist who works in clay. During his lifetime her father, John Peters, was the medicine man for the entire Wampanoag nation. Ramona acts as cultural firekeeper for the tribe and conducts weddings, funerals, and other ceremonies for tribal members. "As [Wampanoag] traditionalists, we have our Original Instructions from our Creator that are important to fulfill. We are to live in a constant state of thanksgiving." Ramona is particularly thankful to have been blessed with a daughter, Majel.

Cornelia Vann Sago was born in 1967 and grew up in Pryor, Oklahoma. A full-blood Cherokee, she has two sons and one daughter and is married to Donovan Sago, a Kiowa and Mescalero Apache. Cornelia is active in the PTA at her daughter's school and in a women's support group at the Indian clinic. Her Cherokee name is Cedar Tree. Cornelia is the second respondent who was a stranger to me before the interview. I appreciate her generosity with her time, on behalf of a stranger. Cornelia resides in Tulsa.

Born in 1958, *Billy Longbone Skye* is of the Eastern Delaware and Peoria tribes. He is a behavioral health therapist who grew up north of Dewey, Oklahoma. He speaks the Delaware language and spends one weekend each month teaching traditional knowledge to those who make a commitment to learning. He himself knows the burden of that commitment: "[In] some of the ceremonies that I conduct, I'm using songs that have been in my own family for four and five generations. . . . And I didn't learn that by just showing up one evening and deciding I was gonna do it. I learned it by sitting, listening to these elders." Billy lives in Muskogee, Oklahoma.

Martha Squire was born in 1924. She is a full-blood Yuchi, raised in the community of Pickett Prairie, near Sapulpa, Oklahoma. Martha raised two daughters and one son. She has three granddaughters and one grandson, three great-granddaughters and one great-grandson. She and her husband, Charlie, are founding, active members of the All Tribes Community Church in Tulsa. She is the past president and treasurer of the Indian Community Center in Coweta and now works there in the kitchen and the office. She is proud that one of her granddaughters has earned a college degree and hopes that other young people in her family may do the same. The author is pleased to report, from considerable personal experience, that Martha makes the best potato salad known to humankind. Martha lives in Coweta, Oklahoma.

William (Bill) Addison Thompson was born in 1942 and grew up in Anadarko, Oklahoma. At the time of the interview he was pastoring All Tribes Community Church, a primarily Indian congregation in Tulsa, Oklahoma. His mother's people come from the Wind Society of the Wichita, the people who, traditionally, could influence the natural element from which they take their name. His father's people are of the Snipe Clan of the Seneca. The Seneca are known for their oratory, and it is from this ancestry that Bill feels he has received some of the abilities he uses as a minister of the gospel. Bill graduated from Central Baptist Theological Seminary in Kansas City, Kansas, and is a church planter who founded the All Tribes church. In addition, he has met the criteria set by his tribe to conduct the ceremony of the sweat lodge. He has served as president of the Greater Tulsa Indian Affairs Commission, and senator-at-large for the executive committee of the American Baptist Minister's Council. He has also served on the Interfaith Council on Prison Ministry for the state of Oklahoma, representing all Native incarcerated people. The council established the right of Native prisoners to practice the sweat lodge. At the time of the interview Bill was residing, with his wife, Virgi, and their two daughters, Connie and Faith, in Tulsa.

Kathleen Delores Westcott was born in 1946 and, at the time of the interview, was living in Brimson, Minnesota. She is Anishnabe and Cree, enrolled at the White Earth Reservation, Mississippi Band. Kathleen is Turtle Clan. She describes her occupations as healer, teacher, and creator of handwork. Kathleen has developed a curriculum employing a Native American creative process (as perceived in ceremony) to teach indigenous methods of inquiry. I owe her a particular intellectual and personal debt for the time and attention she invested in me as her student at the Institute of American Indian Arts in 1992, and for a friendship and working relationship that has continued to this day. Kathleen has one son, one daughter, and one grandson.

Notes

Preface

1. There is currently debate over the most useful term for designating the group that is the focus of this book. Of the alternatives, I usually use "American Indian," "Indian," or "Native." This is a personal choice; these happen to be the ways that I most often refer to myself, if I am called upon to invoke a broader label than my preferred designation as simply Cherokee. In some instances throughout this book, I also use "Native American" or "The People," which is an English translation of the word by which many different tribes call themselves. By all these terms I refer to the indigenous residents of the coterminous United States. On noted occasions, I also refer to Canadian Native, Alaska Native, and South American indigenous populations.

Introduction

1. Buffalo Child Long Lance, *Chief Buffalo Child Long Lance* (Jackson: University Press of Mississippi, [1928] 1995), 1.

2. Donald B. Smith, *Long Lance: The True Story of an Imposter* (Lincoln: University of Nebraska, 1983), 1.

3. Donald B. Smith quoting *Screenland* (October 1930) in his introduction to *Chief Buffalo Child Long Lance*, by B. C. Long Lance, xxx.

4. Smith, *Long Lance*, 8.

5. Irvin S. Cobb, quoted in Smith, *Long Lance*, 196. Earlier, Cobb had written the foreword to Long's "autobiography," in which he introduced Long as his friend and enumerated his many extraordinary personal qualities.

6. Smith, *Long Lance*, 189; emphasis mine.

7. James A. Clifton, "Alternate Identities and Cultural Frontiers," in *Being and Becoming Indian: Biographical Studies of North American Frontiers,* ed. James A. Clifton (Chicago: Dorsey, 1989), 30; James A. Clifton, "Presenting Buffalo Child Long Lance (1890–1932)," in Clifton, *Being and Becoming an Indian,* 184; Clifton, "Alternate Identities," 32.

8. Smith, *Long Lance,* xi, 6.

9. Smith, *Long Lance.*

10. Smith, *Long Lance.*

11. See Joane Nagel's wonderfully comprehensive and stimulating *American Indian Ethnic Renewal: Red Power and the Resurgence of Identity and Culture* (New York: Oxford University Press, 1996) for a discussion of the historic and social elements that together have helped produce an upsurge of interest in American Indian heritage and ethnicity.

12. The trend toward revised racial identification is most obvious is the U.S. decennial census. The first year in which census respondents were allowed to identify their own race (as opposed to being classified according to the enumerator's judgment) was 1960. Ever since that time, large increases in the American Indian population have been apparent in every decade. Particularly large gains appeared between 1970 and 1980 (a surge of more than 72 percent) and between 1990 and 2000 (a swell of more than 100 percent). Although the new method of racial classification on the 2000 census (which allowed respondents to choose more than one race) makes comparisons with earlier data problematic, the increases are so large that demographers argue that they are probably not the result of an increase in birthrates or a decline in death rates, but rather the result of individuals who once identified themselves as white, black, or Hispanic changing their reported identity to American Indian. Nagel, *American Indian Ethnic Renewal;* C. Matthew Snipp, "Who Are American Indians? Some Observations about the Perils and Pitfalls of Data for Race and Ethnicity," *Population Research and Policy Review* 5 (1986): 247–52; Russell Thornton, "Tribal Membership Requirements and the Demography of 'Old' and 'New' Native Americans," *Population Research and Policy Review* 16, nos. 1–2 (April 1997): 33–42.

Not all individuals who attempt to assert racial re-identification face identical societal reactions. The cases of individuals (like Sylvester Long) who specifically combine black ancestry with Indian heritage are particularly interesting. As I discuss in chapter 2, American norms of racialization may imbue this scenario with especially sharp controversies.

13. The American government formally confers "federal acknowledgment" on certain collectivities of Indian people. The process by which acknowledgment is conferred is a subject for discussion in a later chapter. Nevertheless, a note about my use of the expressions "Indian tribe," "Indian group," and "tribal community" may be useful here. Although the federal government distinguishes between Indian tribes, bands, pueblos, villages, and communities (different designations bearing somewhat different legal implications), I rely upon a simpler distinction: I generally reserve the word "tribe" to refer to groups that enjoy formal federal or state recognition. When I speak of collectivities of individuals who

meet the criteria of one or more of the identity definitions examined in this book, but do *not* enjoy governmental acknowledgment, I use the expression "Indian group." To refer to some self-defined *subset* of an Indian tribe or group, I use "tribal community," implying an entity that understands itself as a bounded group with shared interests and values. A tribal community may or may not include the entire tribe.

14. In August 2000, soon after the book's release, the online bookstore Amazon.com showed it as the number one best-seller in ten towns in Connecticut and Rhode Island. Reports of brisk sales continued in 2001 and 2002. Jeff Benedict, *Without Reservation: The Making of America's Most Powerful Indian Tribe and Foxwoods, the World's Largest Casino* (New York: Harper Collins, 2000).

15. Clifton, "Alternate Identities," 16; James A. Clifton, ed., *The Invented Indian: Cultural Fictions and Government Policies* (New Brunswick: Transaction, 1990), 6.

16. James A. Clifton, "Cultural Fictions," *Society* 27, no. 4 (1990): 26.

17. William W. Quinn, Jr., "The Southeast Syndrome: Notes on Indian Descendant Recruitment Organizations and Their Perceptions of Native American Culture," *American Indian Quarterly* 14, no. 2 (spring 1990): 147–54.

The writings of both Quinn and Clifton may be classed with a new body of social scientific work known as the "invention of tradition" literature, which intends to show how indigenous groups manipulate and even manhandle their oral traditions to support dubious claims to a tribal identity. Researchers within this school claim to document what David Henige, an Africanist who has also written on American Indians, refers to as "the disconcerting alacrity with which oral societies can assimilate newly-acquired information or speculation, particularly if it should be of obvious and immediate practical value." Henige argues that putatively Indian peoples invent, at will, "congenial 'traditions' of origin" whenever it suits them to do so. These newly born "traditions," he says, are calculatingly crafted and recrafted to support claims about identity or other important issues that the speaker wishes to make, but they are placed in the mouths of supposed tribal elders and ancestors. As another scholar in the invention of tradition school, anthropologist Allan Hanson, states, "Tradition [in indigenous groups] is now understood quite literally to be an invention designed to serve contemporary purposes." David Henige, "Origin Traditions of American Racial Isolates: A Case of Something Borrowed," *Appalachian Journal* 11 (1984): 209–10; Allan Hanson, "The Making of the Maori: Culture Invention and Its Logic," *American Anthropologist* 91 (1989): 890.

18. Angela Gonzales, "The (Re)Articulation of American Indian Identity: Maintaining Boundaries and Regulating Access to Ethnically-Tied Resources," *American Indian Culture and Research Journal* 22, no. 4 (1998): 199–225.

19. Maria P. P. Root, "Within, Between and Beyond Race," in *Racially Mixed People in America,* ed. Maria P. P. Root (Newbury Park, Calif.: Sage, 1992), 9.

20. U.S. Office of Management and Budget, "Revisions to the Standards for the Classification of Federal Data," *Federal Register* 62, no. 210 (30 October 1997): 58781–90.

21. Joan Ferrante and Prince Browne, Jr., "Toward a New Paradigm: Transcending Categories," in *The Social Construction of Race and Ethnicity in the United States,* 2d ed., ed. Joan Ferrante and Prince Browne, Jr. (Upper Saddle River, N.J.: Prentice Hall), 360.

22. For a list of the many purposes for which federal agencies use census data on race, see Ferrante and Browne, "Federal and Program Uses of the Data Derived from Race and Ethnicity Questions — The US Bureau of the Census (1990)," appendix B in Ferrante and Browne, *Social Construction of Race,* 493–96. For a more recent and more technical discussion, see the Tabulation Working Group of the Interagency Committee for the Review of Standards for Federal Data on Race and Ethnicity, "Provisional Guidance on the Implementation of the 1997 Standards for Federal Data on Race and Ethnicity," 15 December 2001. Available online at http://www.whitehouse.gov/omb/inforeg/.

23. Tabulation Working Group, "Provisional Guidance," 67–70, 62.

24. Such questions have, in fact, already been raised in formal deliberations over possible changes to the census. For instance, in a 1993 federal hearing on the census categories, Henry Der (representative for the National Coalition for an Accurate Count of Asians and Pacific Islanders) argued against automatically extending minority protections to mixed-race people. From his perspective, mixed-race individuals "have the burden to document" that they have experienced barriers to opportunity before they are properly covered by those protections. Material entered into the *Congressional Record* by Henry Der; House Committee on the Post Office and Civil Service, Review of Federal Measurements of Race and Ethnicity: Hearings before the Subcommittee on Census, Statistics, and Postal Personnel, 103d Cong., 1st sess., 14 April 1993, 96.

25. Racial allocation of respondents who select two minority races is more complicated. See "OMB Bulletin No. 00–02. March 9, 2000." Available online at http://www.whitehouse.gov/OMB/bulletins/b00–02.html.

26. One of many official suggestions for allocating people into racial categories for other purposes is to count mixed-race people as white, or to count them as fractions (half black and half white, for instance). Still another official proposal is to classify a person into the same single race as his or her nearest neighbor. For details, see "The Bridge Report: Tabulation Options for Trend Analysis." Appendix C to Tabulation Working Group, "Provisional Guidance," 5–7. Public discussion has suggested taking such things as physical appearance into account, or substituting measures of ethnicity (such as language) for measures of race. See, for instance, a flurry of articles in the *Chicago Tribune,* including Clarence Page, "When Old Labels Don't Apply," *Chicago Tribune,* 17 January 2001; Evan Osnos and David Mendell, "New Racial Choices in Census Pose Tricky Issue," *Chicago Tribune,* 5 February 2001; Clarence Page, "Piecing It All Together: What the Census Should Be Asking about Race, Ethnicity," *Chicago Tribune,* 14 March 2001.

27. Osnos and Mendell, "New Racial Choices."

28. For sociologists who study racial and ethnic identity, the issues I discuss

here have evident relevance to debates between two major perspectives: instrumentalism and primordialism.

Instrumentalism highlights the degree to which social actors rationally (even cynically) choose the identities that serve them best. Central to instrumentalist perspectives is the work of Nathan Glazer and Daniel Moynihan (racial-ethnic groups are "connected . . . by ties of family and friendship" but also by "ties of *interest*" [original emphasis]). It is further associated with the work of theorists such as Eugeen Roosens (North American ethnic groups are "pressure groups with a noble face" that "emerged so strongly because ethnicity brought people strategic advantages") and Daniel Bell ("ethnicity . . . is best understood . . . as a strategic choice by individuals who, in other circumstances, would choose other group memberships as a means of gaining some power and privilege"). Nathan Glazer and Daniel P. Moynihan, *Beyond the Melting Pot: The Negroes, Puerto Ricans, Jews, Italians, and Irish of New York City*, 2d ed. (Cambridge, Mass.: MIT Press, 1963), 17. Eugeen E. Roosens, *Creating Ethnicity: The Process of Ethnogenesis* (Newbury Park, Calif: Sage, 1989), 14; Daniel Bell, *The Winding Passage* (Cambridge, Mass.: Abt Books, 1980), 207. The reader may also consult Frederick Barth, ed., *Ethnic Groups and Boundaries: The Social Organization of Cultural Difference* (Boston: Little-Brown, 1969); Michael Banton, *Racial and Ethnic Competition* (Cambridge: Cambridge University Press, 1983); and Michael Hechter, *Principles of Group Solidarity* (Berkeley: University of California Press, 1987) for related discussions of ethnic identity as a strategic choice with material or political accompaniments.

Primordialist perspectives, by contrast, attend primarily to beliefs and emotions relating to collective identity — to social actors' powerful convictions of ethnic belonging that may exist apart from rational calculation. A few primordialists argue that these convictions are genuinely *given*, as in sociobiological theories, which propose that people are driven to preserve their genetic material by aligning themselves with those who share larger amounts of it. Less deterministic versions of primordial perspectives are associated with Edward Shils (attachments to members of one's ancestral group originate in "a certain ineffable significance [that] is attributed to the tie of blood") and Clifford Geertz ("some attachments seem to flow more from a sense of natural — some would say spiritual — affinity than from social interaction"). Edward Shils, *Center and Periphery: Essays in Macrosociology* (Chicago: University of Chicago Press, 1975), 122; Clifford Geertz, *The Interpretation of Cultures* (New York: Basic Books, 1973), 260. For additional discussions, the reader may also wish to consult Stephen Grosby, "The Verdict of History: The Inexpungeable Tie of Primordiality — A Response to Eller and Coughlan," *Ethnic and Racial Studies* 17, no. 2 (1994): 164–171; or Walker Connor, *Ethno-Nationalism: The Quest for Understanding* (Princeton: Princeton University Press, 1994).

A third perspective, something of a compromise between the two major ones, is distinguished by some scholars. This is the circumstantialist, or optionalist, view. Researchers pursuing this perspective suggest that *many* influences may impinge upon a social actor's desire to identify with a particular racial or ethnic group. These are not limited to rational calculation of the benefits accompanying such a choice. They interact, moreover, with a range of historical, cultural, and social structural variables that affect the social actor's *ability* to choose a particular identity. Nagel's (1996; *American Indian Ethnic Renewal*) sophisticated work on "ethnic renewal" has been an important contribution to this perspective, especially as it applies to American Indians. The reader may also consider Nathan Glazer and Daniel Moynihan, "Introduction," in *Ethnicity: Theory and Experience,* ed. Nathan Glazer and Daniel P. Moynihan (Cambridge, Mass.: Harvard University Press, 1975), 1–26; and Philip Gleason, "The Melting Pot: Symbol of Fusion or Confusion?" *American Quarterly* 16, no. 1 (1964): 20–46.

29. See, for instance, Susan E. Smith and Dennis G. Willms with Nancy A. Johnson, *Nurtured by Knowledge: Learning to Do Participatory Action-Research* (Ottawa, Ont.: IDRC, 1997); or William Foote Whyte, ed., *Participatory Action Research* (Newbury Park, Calif.: Sage, 1991).

1. Enrollees and Outalucks

1. Louis Owens, "Motion of Fire and Form," in *Native American Literature,* ed. Gerald Vizenor (Berkeley: Harper Collins, 1995), 83, 88.

2. Some of Owens's recent novels include *Nightland* (New York: Signet, 1997) and *Bone Game: A Novel,* American Indian Literature and Critical Studies Series, vol. 10 (Norman: University of Oklahoma Press, 1994). His works of literary criticism include *Mixed Blood Messages: Literature, Film, Family, Place,* American Indian Literature and Critical Studies Series, vol. 26 (Norman: University of Oklahoma Press, 1998), and *Other Destinies: Understanding the American Indian Novel,* American Indian Literature and Critical Studies Series, vol. 3 (Norman: University of Oklahoma Press, 1992).

3. Kent Carter, "Wantabees and Outalucks," *Chronicles of Oklahoma* 66, no. 1 (1988): 94–104.

4. A tribe's right to create its own legal definition of identity was determined in the 1905 court case *Waldron v. United States* and later clarified in a celebrated 1978 lawsuit, *Martinez v. Santa Clara Pueblo.* However, as with nearly every other rule in Indian country, there are exceptions. A small handful of tribes *are* federally required to hold to specific criteria in defining tribal membership — for instance, by maintaining a specific blood quantum standard for citizenship. This situation is, however, rare.

5. Thornton surveyed 302 of the 317 tribes in the lower forty-eight states that enjoyed federal acknowledgment in 1997. He found that 204 tribes had some minimum blood quantum requirement, while the remaining 98 had none. Russell Thornton, "Tribal Membership Requirements and the Demography of 'Old' and 'New' Native Americans," *Population Research and Policy Review* 16 (1997): 37.

6. To view a variety of tribal constitutions and their citizenship requirements, see http://thorpe.ou.edu/.

7. The two mentions of "Indians" in the Constitution appear in passages regarding the regulation of commerce and the taking of a federal census. The word "tribe" also appears once in the Constitution, in the Commerce Clause.

8. Sharon O'Brien, "Tribes and Indians: With Whom Does the United States Maintain a Relationship?" *Notre Dame Law Review* 66 (1991): 1481.

9. One particularly important law that provides no definition of "Indian" is the Major Crimes Act of 1885 (23 Stat. 385, U.S.C. Sec. 1153). It subjects reservation Indians to federal prosecution for certain offenses for which non-Indians would face only state prosecution.

10. For a detailed discussion of legal cases bearing on the definition of "Indian," see Felix S. Cohen, *Handbook of Federal Indian Law* (Charlottesville, Va.: Michie/Bobbs-Merrill, 1982).

11. Wilcomb E. Washburn, *Red Man's Land/White Man's Law: A Study of the Past and Present States of the American Indian* (New York: Charles Scribner's Sons, 1971).

12. These agencies administer resources and programs in areas such as education, health, social services, tribal governance and administration, law enforcement, nutrition, resource management, tribal economic development, employment, and the like. The most recently published source describing various programs and the requirements for participation is Roger Walk, *Federal Assistance to Native Americans: A Report Prepared for the Senate Select Committee on Indian Affairs of the US Senate* (Washington, D.C.: Government Printing Office, 1991). In fiscal year 2001, recognized tribes and their members had access to approximately four billion dollars of federal funding for various social programs. U.S. Government Accounting Office, *Indian Issues: Improvements Needed in Tribal Recognition Process,* Report to Congressional Requesters, Washington D.C.: Government Printing Office, November 2001.

13. Non-Indian students in my classes sometimes tell me that Indians also regularly receive such windfalls as free cars and monthly checks from the government strictly because of their race. It is my sad duty to puncture this fantasy; there is no truth in it. The common belief that Indians receive "free money" from the government probably stems from the fact that the government holds land in trust for certain tribes. As part of its trust responsibility, it may then lease that land, collect the revenue, and distribute it to the tribal members. Thus, some Indians do receive government checks, but these do not represent some kind of manna from heaven; they are simply the profits derived from lands which they own. For details on the special, political-economic relationship of Indians to the federal government in relation to taxation and licensure, see Gary D. Sandefur, "Economic Development and Employment Opportunities for American Indians," in *American Indians: Social Justice and Public Policy,* ed. Donald E. Green and Thomas V. Tonneson, Ethnicity and Public Policy Series, vol. 9 (Milwaukee: University of Wisconsin System Institute on Race and Ethnicity, 1991), 208–22.

14. Robert Bensen, *Children of the Dragonfly: Native American Voices on Child Custody and Education* (Tucson: University of Arizona Press, 2001), 13.

15. Suzan Shown Harjo, "The American Indian Experience," in *Family Ethnicity: Strength in Diversity,* ed. Harriet Pipes McAdoo (Newbury Park, Calif.: Sage, 1993), 199–207. See further R. B. Jones, "The Indian Child Welfare Act: The Need for a Separate Law," available online at http://www.abanet.org/gen-practice/compleat/f95child.html (1995); Aileen Redbird and Patrick Melendy, "Indian Child Welfare in Oregon," in *The Destruction of American Indian Families,* ed. Steven Unger (New York: Association on American Indian Affairs, 1978), 43–46; and Bensen, *Children of the Dragonfly.* For a discussion of similar problems with the Canadian child welfare system, see Patrick Johnston, *Native Children and the Child Welfare System* (Toronto: Canadian Council on Social Development and James Lorimer, 1983).

16. To be specific, the Commerce Department estimated in 1985 that specious "Indian art" imported from foreign countries meant $40–80 million in lost income for genuine Indian artists every year, or 10–20 percent of annual Indian art sales. *Congressional Record,* 101st Cong., 1st sess., 1990: 4–5.

17. An excellent, detailed discussion of this legislation appears in Gail K. Sheffield, *The Arbitrary Indian: The Indian Arts and Crafts Act of 1990* (Norman: University of Oklahoma Press, 1997).

18. The relevant case is *Morton v. Mancari,* 417 U.S. 535 (1974). The decision explained: "The preference is not directed towards a 'racial' Group consisting of 'Indians'; instead, it applies only to members of 'federally recognized' Tribes. This operates to exclude many individuals who are racially to be classified as 'Indians.' In this sense, the preference is political rather than racial in nature" (554 n. 24).

Related cases, also considered by the U.S. Supreme Court in the 1970s, include *Fisher v. District Court,* 424 U.S. 382 (1976) (related to adoption procedures) and *United States v. Antelope,* 430 U.S. 641 (1977) (concerning issues of criminal jurisdiction).

19. Department of Health and Human Services, Indian Health Service Circular no. 87–2 (Rockville, Md.: 9 July 1987).

20. "Mixed Marriages Present Some Property Problems," *Indian Country Today,* 26 May–2 June 1997.

21. For an explanation of the Santa Clara law of patrilineality, see Bruce B. MacLachlan, "Indian Law and Puebloan Tribal Law," in *North American Indian Anthropology: Essays on Society and Culture,* ed. Raymond J. DeMallie and Alfonso Ortiz (Norman: University of Oklahoma Press, 1994), 340–54.

22. *Akwesasne Notes* 6 (autumn 1974).

23. It is likewise possible for children whose parents belong to the same *tribe,* but who are from different *reservations,* to encounter enrollment prohibitions. See David Reed Miller, "Definitional Violence and Plains Indian Reservation Life: Ongoing Challenges to Survival," in *Violence, Resistance, and Survival in the Americas,* ed. William B. Taylor and Franklin Pease (Washington, D.C.: Smithsonian Institution, 1994), 237.

24. Russell Thornton, *American Indian Holocaust and Survival: A Population History* (Norman: University of Oklahoma Press, 1987), 190.

25. Bureau of Indian Affairs, *Tribal Enrollment* (Washington, D.C.: Bureau of Indian Affairs, 1979, handbook). The General Allotment Act of 1887 provided for the creation of some base rolls, but most were compiled in response to the Indian Reorganization Act of 1934. Tribes have continued to create membership listings, which they use as base rolls, after 1934 as well. Some tribes created their base rolls only a few years ago. This is true, for instance, with the Passamaquoddy of Maine, who (having only enjoyed federal acknowledgment for two decades) use a 1990 census for their base roll.

26. Kent Carter, *The Dawes Commission and the Allotment of the Five Civilized Tribes* (Orem, Utah: Ancestry.com, 1999), 147.

27. Kent Carter, "Deciding Who Can Be Cherokee: Enrollment Records of the Dawes Commission," *Chronicles of Oklahoma* 69, no. 2 (1991): 174–205.

28. Theodore Roosevelt, quoted in Robert F. Berkhofer, Jr., *The White Man's Indian* (New York: Vintage Books, 1979), 175. Contrast Roosevelt's optimism about allotment with the opinion of U.S. Commissioner of Indian Affairs John Collier, who would later call it "the greatest single practical evil" ever perpetrated upon American Indians. John Collier, quoted in Fergus Bordewich, *Killing the White Man's Indian* (New York: Doubleday, 1996), 124.

29. Angie Debo, *And Still the Waters Run: The Betrayal of the Five Civilized Tribes* (Princeton: Princeton University Press, 1972), 53.

30. In Oklahoma, the Creeks were especially resistant. Under the leadership of Chitto Harjo, or "Crazy Snake," the Creek full bloods set up their own government and council in 1901. They also appointed a cadre of law enforcement officers known as "lighthorsemen" to deal with tribal citizens who had accepted allotments, and to warn those who might be considering a similar action. The lighthorsemen roamed the countryside, confiscating enrollment papers and sometimes arresting and whipping those who possessed them. After being arrested by federal marshals and found guilty of such activities, Chitto Harjo and his followers continued to defy allotment through legal means, hiring lawyers and sending lobbyists to Washington.

The Oklahoma Cherokees used their own strategies, often under the guidance of traditionalist leader Redbird Smith. When field parties from the Dawes Commission "came to a full blood settlement, they found amusements planned in remote places to call the Indians away. When they tried to secure the names [of Cherokees eligible for allotment] from their neighbors, witnesses were threatened with bodily harm." Debo, *Waters Run*, 45. For further discussion of tribal resistance to allotment, see D. S. Otis, *The Dawes Act and the Allotment of Indian Lands* (Norman: University of Oklahoma Press, 1973), especially pp. 40–46.

31. Although other tribes created their base rolls in different circumstances and at different times than did the Oklahoma tribes, they too had their own irregularities and often met with their own resisters. See, for instance, Thomas Biolsi's description of allotment among the Lakota of the Rosebud Reservation in "The Birth of the Reservation: Making the Modern Individual among the Lakota," *American Ethnologist* 22, no. 1 (February 1995): 28–49; or Alexandra

Harmon's discussion of allotment among the Puget Sound tribes of Washington State in *Indians in the Making: Ethnic Relations and Indian Identities around Puget Sound* (Berkeley: University of California Press, 1998).

32. Modern tribes do realize that some of their proper members are excluded from legal citizenship, and most have created a mechanism for dealing with this. Many tribal constitutions allow for legally adopting individuals who do not meet formally specified identity criteria. The adoption provision, sometimes called selective enrollment, allows for a safety net to protect persons judged by some criterion to have a claim on tribal citizenship, but who, for whatever reason, cannot satisfy the usual requirements. Isleta Pueblo, for example, allows for the adoption of individuals with one-half Indian blood of *other* tribes besides its own, but forbids the adoption of non-Indians. Some tribal constitutions even provide for the adoption of non-Indians. Sharon O'Brien, *American Indian Tribal Governments* (Norman: University of Oklahoma Press, 1989), 175.

In practice, however, adoptions tend to be rather rare and to be limited to certain categories of people — members' spouses, reservation residents, children who meet a blood quantum requirement but whose parents are not enrolled, and so on. Angela Gonzales, "The (Re)Articulation of American Indian Identity: Maintaining and Regulating Access to Ethnically-Tied Resources," *American Indian Culture and Research Journal* 22, no. 4 (1998): 199–225. See further Bureau of Indian Affairs, *Tribal Enrollment*. And in most cases adoption is only partial salvation. Adopted individuals may not enjoy full privileges in the tribe, such as voting rights or the right to pass tribal citizenship on to their offspring. Perhaps even more significantly, the federal government refuses to recognize as Indian, for any purposes, anyone who cannot demonstrate at least *some* ancestral connection to a tribe, even if the tribe agrees to enroll her. Thus even with the safety net of tribal adoption in place, many people still cannot achieve an Indian identity within all of the legal definitions that are likely to be important to them. Stephen L. Pevar, *The Rights of Indians and Tribes: The Basic ACLU Guide to Indian and Tribal Rights,* 2d ed. (Carbondale: Southern Illinois University Press, 1992), 13.

33. David Melmer, "Enrollment Orphans: Does Adoption Help?" *Indian Country Today,* 25 March 1996.

34. Details on events at Keeweenaw Bay are available online at http://www.edwards1.com/rose/native/ffj/ffj.htm and at http://www.yvwiiusdinvnohii.net/news/thebayup.htm. The reader may also consult David Melmer, "Fred Dakota Pleads Not Guilty," *Indian Country Today,* 29 July–5 August 1996; David Melmer, "Enrollment Orphans: Does Adoption Help?" *Indian Country Today,* 25 March 1996; David Melmer, "FFJ Leader Jailed," *Indian Country Today,* 11–18 June 1996.

35. Henry E. Burks is an example of a white child who became Indian in this way. Both his mother and his father were whites who had been adopted by the Chickasaws through marriage. Henry was nevertheless granted tribal enrollment by the Dawes Commission in 1907. The legal petition of Mary Martin and many others in similar circumstances to Burks were denied, however, and several

Oklahoma tribes eventually passed laws preventing adopted whites from conferring citizenship privileges upon children with no Indian blood. Carter, "Wantabees and Outalucks," 90–91.

36. It is clear that some of the freedmen did have Indian ancestry. However, no effort was made (either when they were granted tribal citizenship after the Civil War or later, when freedmen and their descendants became eligible to receive land allotments under the General Allotment Act) to document any such ancestry. The Dawes Rolls were divided into separate categories: Cherokees by blood, freedmen, and intermarried whites. Individuals with identifiable black ancestry were placed in the freedmen category, which did not allow for a specification of blood quantum. Accordingly, there is no documentary record of tribal ancestry for the freedmen, even where it exists, and modern-day freedmen descendants are regularly denied rights, services, and benefits that are available to those who can show that they are citizens by blood. Circe Sturm, *Blood Politics: Race, Culture, and Identity in the Cherokee Nation of Oklahoma* (Berkeley: University of California Press, 2002).

The treatment of freedmen, however, could conceivably change. For the past several years, two groups of freedmen have been engaged in legal struggles with the Seminole Nation (Oklahoma). A central issue has been their right to share in a 56-million-dollar settlement that the tribe received in a land claims case. Seminoles enrolled in the tribe as descendants by blood were not eager to include the freedmen, and in 2000, the tribe stripped them of their tribal membership. The Department of the Interior, however, has declared the action illegal. As of this writing, the final outcome of the dispute is uncertain. Herb Frazier, "Black Seminoles Seek $100M in Retribution from Government," *Charleston Post and Courier,* 3 December 1999, available online at http://www.charleston.net/news/seminole/semsidea0706.htm; William Glaberson, "Who Is a Seminole, and Who Gets to Decide?" *New York Times,* 29 January 2001; Wilhelm Murg, "BIA Announces Position on Seminole Disputes," *Native American Times,* January 2002. Available online at http://www.okit.com/news/2002/january/biaposition.html.

The Cherokee Nation, likewise, has struggled for decades, in and out of court, with the issue of freedmen rights. Freedmen have sometimes shared (by dint of considerable struggle) in some economic benefits of Cherokee citizenship, including land allotments and monetary settlements, but they have been denied other benefits. For an excellent history of the Cherokee freedmen, see Sturm, *Blood Politics*.

37. Debo, *Waters Run*, 38.

38. Biolsi, "Birth of the Reservation," 28–49.

39. The word "acknowledgment" is the more technically correct word for the act by which the American government establishes formal relationships with an Indian tribe. However, the word "recognition" is also commonly used and will seem more familiar to many readers. The two words are therefore used interchangeably throughout this book.

40. State-recognized tribes may gain nothing more than a mention in a legislative memorial highlighting the contributions that their group made during

particular historic periods. On the other hand, in certain cases, state recognition can provide for access to significant funding sources and benefits, or even for a reservation. It allows tribal members to be included under some federal legislation (including the Indian Arts and Crafts Act, discussed earlier). State recognition may also be a stepping-stone to federal recognition.

If the rights and benefits conferred by state recognition are sometimes minimal and sometimes significant, they are also sometimes simply unclear. Just such a lack of clarity led to the 1996 armed standoff with state troopers that resulted from a disagreement, relating to taxation of Indian-owned commercial enterprises, between a citizen of the Golden Hill Paugussett, a state-recognized tribe, and the state. See further David Melmer, "Connecticut Continues Paugussett Recognition," *Indian Country Today*, 4 April 1996.

41. Important court cases that first began to grapple with the meaning of tribal sovereignty are *Cherokee Nation v. Georgia* (1831) and, even more important, *Worcester v. Georgia* (1832). The former includes the earliest description of the status of tribes as "domestic dependent nations." The latter clarified what this meant for the relationship of tribes to the federal government. It specified that tribes were to be considered as nations that enjoyed the status of protectorates but had not made their citizens subordinate to U.S. domination. For a more detailed discussion of legal cases pertaining to tribal sovereignty, see O'Brien, *Tribal Governments*.

42. This expansive understanding of tribal sovereignty is complicated by other legal decisions. Of particular significance is Public Law 280 (1953), which specifies that states may enforce criminal and civil law on reservations. Tribes, however, have continued to maintain that they properly have government-to-government relationships with the U.S. As O'Brien (1989) asserts: "The relationship between Indian nations and the federal government is based on Indian nations' status as inherent sovereigns. This status means that tribes have a higher legal status than states. States, therefore, can exert jurisdiction over tribes only with Congressional approval. . . . Indian nations, whose powers spring from their own sovereignty, are only partially under the authority of the U.S. Constitution." O'Brien, *Tribal Governments*, 277.

43. Sandefur, "Economic Development and Employment Opportunities for American Indians," 213-14.

44. William C. Canby, Jr., *American Indian Law in a Nutshell*, 2d ed. (St. Paul, Minn.: West Publishing Co., 1989); Pevar, *Rights of Indians;* U.S. General Accounting Office, *Indian Issues.*

45. U.S. Senate Committee on Governmental Affairs, Permanent Subcommittee on Investigations, *Efforts to Combat Fraud and Abuse in the Insurance Industry: Hearings before the Permanent Subcommittee on Investigations of the Committee on Governmental Affairs,* 102d Cong., 1st sess., part 3, 19 July 1991, 112.

46. American Indian Policy Review Commission (Task Force Ten), *Final Report: Report on Terminated and Nonfederally Recognized Indians* (Washington, D.C.: Government Printing Office, 1976), 1695.

47. Paul Shukovsky, "Samish Fight for Existence," *Seattle Post-Intelligencer,* 5 May 1992.

48. Terry Anderson, "Federal Recognition: The Vicious Myth," *American Indian Journal* 5 (1978): 7–19; Jack Campisi, "The New England Tribes and Their Quest for Justice," in *The Pequots in Southern New England: The Fall and Rise of an American Indian Nation.*, ed. Laurence J. Hauptman and James D. Wherry (Norman: University of Oklahoma Press, 1990), 179–80.

49. For instance, the Poarch Creeks and Jamestown S'Klallams (also spelled Clallams) appeared on the list of federally recognized tribes issued by the Department of the Interior in 1972 (*American Indian Tribes and Their Federal-Tribal Relations,* Commissioner of Indian Affairs Louis Bruce) but were dropped from the *Federal Register* listing issued only a few years later, in 1979. Both tribes were forced to endure the rigors of the acknowledgment process, by which both finally succeeded in reclaiming recognition, although the Poarch decision dragged out over nine years after they had submitted their letter of intent to petition. Bureau of Indian Affairs, "List of Petitioners by State (as of September 8, 1997)" (Washington, D.C.: Branch of Acknowledgment and Research, 1997).

50. The version of 25 CFR 83 revised in 1994 is published in the *Federal Register* 59, no. 38 (25 February 1994): 9289–300. See further Bureau of Indian Affairs, *The Official Guidelines to the Federal Acknowledgment Regulations, 25 CFR 83* (Washington, D.C.: Branch of Acknowledgment and Research, September 1997).

51. William W. Quinn, Jr., "The Southeast Syndrome: Notes on Indian Descendant Recruitment Organizations and Their Perceptions of Native American Culture," *American Indian Quarterly* 14, no. 2 (spring 1990): 152.

Formally, the final decision about acknowledgment does not rest with the Branch of Acknowledgment and Research. It make its judgments based on the evidence they receive and then make a recommendation to the assistant secretary for Indian affairs to grant or deny recognition. Tribes may also receive recognition by means of executive order or an act of Congress, without passing through the FAP. For a detailed discussion of the process by which tribes become federally recognized, see U.S. General Accounting Office, *Indian Issues.*

52. In 2001, federal judges recognized the problem of delayed recognition decisions and issued court orders that three tribes in Connecticut and one in California must receive their decisions within a specific time frame. The ruling required, for instance, that the Schaghticoke Tribal Nation (Connecticut), which reported filing its application in 1994, must receive its decision by September of 2003. Jim Adams, "Fed-up Tribes Want Recognition Schedules," *Indian Country Today*, 23 May 2001. Tribes, however, cannot depend on such good fortune. A recent report by the Government Accounting Office predicts that the Branch of Acknowledgment and Research may require as long as fifteen years to respond to all of the completed petitions now on hand. U.S. General Accounting Office, *Indian Issues.*

53. Bureau of Indian Affairs, *Federal Acknowledgment Regulations,* 54. For a detailed discussion of the FAP and its implications from a variety of perspectives, see Peter Beinart, "Lost Tribes: Native Americans and Anthropologists Feud over Indian Identity," *Lingua Franca* 9, no. 4 (May/June 1999). Available online at http://www.linguafranca.com/9905/beinart.html. For a detailed exploration of

forcible dispersion of Indian communities in California, and the consequences for tribal recognition efforts, see James Collins, *Understanding Tolowa Histories: Western Hegemonies and Native American Responses* (New York: Routledge, 1998).

54. Sue Alexander, letter to the editor, *Cherokee Phoenix and Indian Advocate* (spring 2002).

55. The Certificate of Degree of Indian Blood, or CDIB, is a federal document showing the precise amount of Indian ancestry an individual is believed to possess. It is discussed further in chapter 2.

56. Annie Cecilia Yallup, letter to the editor, "What Is Not Indian Enough?" *Indian Country Today,* 16 August 1999.

57. Thornton, "Tribal Membership Requirements," 37.

58. The Five Eastern Tribes to which Fleming refers are the Cherokee, Creek, Seminole, Choctaw, and Chickasaw.

59. For an excellent discussion of the process by which tribal peoples came to adopt legal definitions of identity, founded in ideas of blood quantum, see Melissa L. Meyer, "American Indian Blood Quantum Requirements: Blood Is Thicker than Family," in *Over the Edge: Remapping the American West,* ed. Valerie J. Matsumoto and Blake Allmendiger (Berkeley: University of California Press, 1999).

60. Thomas J. Morgan, U.S. Commissioner of Indian Affairs, *Sixty-First Annual Report of the Commissioner of Indian Affairs to the Secretary of the Interior* (Washington, D.C.: Government Printing Office, 1892), 37.

61. Terry P. Wilson, "Blood Quantum: Native American Mixed Bloods," in *Racially Mixed People in America,* ed. Maria P. P. Root (Newbury Park, Calif.: Sage Press, 1992).

62. Morgan, *Annual Report,* 36.

63. Wilson, "Blood Quantum"; William T. Hagan, "Full Blood, Mixed Blood, Generic and Ersatz," *Arizona and the West* 27 (1985): 309-26. For a discussion of the related struggles of Native Alaskan communities to be included in the provisions of legislation applying to American Indians, see Washburn, *Red Man's Land/White Man's Law,* 167.

2. "If He Gets a Nosebleed, He'll Turn into a White Man"

1. Aside from the issue of adopted children, the legal requirements for establishing legal status as Indian in Canada have generally been even more complicated and peculiar than the U.S. ones, and the tensions related to them even more severe. Until 1985, a Canadian Indian woman who married a legally non-Indian man lost her legal status as an Indian, and her children (who might have a blood quantum of one-half) could never be recognized as Indian under Canadian law. A non-Indian woman who married an Indian man, however, gained Indian status for herself and her children. Men could neither gain nor lose Indian status through marriage. When a 1985 bill amended the Indian Act, which governed

such matters, the issue of "real Indianness" came to a head. Many Canadian Indian women and children sought and received Indian legal status, but when they attempted to return to the reservations, they often got a chilly welcome from Indian communities already overburdened with financial obligations to their existing population. Like their American counterparts, Canadian Indian bands continue to struggle with the issue of how to conceive the boundaries of their membership. For a good discussion of Canadian Indian identification policies, see Eugeen Roosens, *Creating Ethnicity: The Process of Ethnogenesis* (Newbury Park, Calif.: Sage, 1989).

2. Shania Twain quoted in Jackie Bissley, "Country Star Shania Twain's Candor Is Challenged," *Indian Country Today,* 9–16 April 1996.

3. Quoted in Jackie Bissley, "Country Singer Says Stories Robbing Her of Her Native Roots," *Indian Country Today,* 16–23 April 1996. Even Twain's unusual situation does not exhaust the intricate aspects of the Canadian legal system as it struggles with matters of Indian identity. Roosens describes other fine points of Indian identity in force north of the border over a period of several decades:

Since 1951, to be registered as an Indian one has to be the legitimate child of an Indian father. The ethnic origin of the mother is irrelevant. . . . Furthermore, if the grandmother on the Indian side of a mixed marriage (the father's mother) is a non-Indian by descent, then the grandchild loses his or her status at the age of 21. Thus, one can be officially born an Indian and lose this status at the age of maturity. (Roosens, *Creating Ethnicity*, 24)

4. Roosens, *Creating Ethnicity,* 41–42. Roosens is discussing the situation of Canadian Indians, but the same remarks apply to American Indians.

5. G. William Rice, "There and Back Again — An Indian Hobbit's Holiday: Indians Teaching Indian Law," *New Mexico Law Review* 26, no. 2 (1996): 176.

6. Melissa L. Meyer, "American Indian Blood Quantum Requirements: Blood Is Thicker than Family," in *Over the Edge: Remapping the American West,* ed. Valerie J. Matsumoto and Blake Allmendiger (Berkeley: University of California Press, 1999).

7. Historians such as Grace Steele Woodward and Marion Starkey have made this argument. But see also Julia Coates, "None of Us Is Supposed to Be Here" (Ph.D. diss., University of New Mexico, 2002) for a revisionist understanding of Cherokee history.

8. C. Matthew Snipp, "Who Are American Indians? Some Observations about the Perils and Pitfalls of Data for Race and Ethnicity," *Population Research and Policy Review* 5 (1986): 249. For excellent and intriguing discussions of the evolution of ideas about blood relationships among European and Euro-American peoples over several centuries, and transference of these ideas into American Indian tribal populations, see Meyer, "Blood Quantum Requirements," and Circe Sturm, *Blood Politics: Race, Culture, and Identity in the Cherokee Nation of Oklahoma* (Berkeley: University of California Press, 2002). See further Peggy

Pascoe, "Miscegenation Law, Court Cases, and Ideologies of 'Race' in Twentieth Century America," *Journal of American History* 83, no. 1 (June 1996): 44–69. For the processes by which some of these theories were rejected by scientists, see Elazar Barkan, *Retreat of Scientific Racism: Changing Concepts of Race in Britain and the United States between the World Wars* (Cambridge: Cambridge University Press, 1992).

9. Thomas Biolsi, "The Birth of the Reservation: Making the Modern Individual among the Lakota," *American Ethnologist* 22, no. 1 (February 1995): 28–49; Patrick Limerick, *The Legacy of Conquest: The Unbroken Past of the American West* (New York: W. W. Norton, 1988).

10. Naomi Zack, "Mixed Black and White Race and Public Policy," *Hypatia* 10, 1 (1995): 120–32; Ariela J. Gross, "Litigating Whiteness: Trials of Racial Determination in the Nineteenth-Century South," *Yale Law Journal* 108 (1998): 109–88.

11. Studies of other trials of racial determination in the nineteenth and early twentieth centuries illustrate how considerations aside from ancestry might also intrude into actual trial rhetoric at times. In determinations of race, judges and juries might also consider the claimant's behavior, physiological attributes (such as cranial measurements), or claims to identity. Such behavioral or physiological evidence tended to be invoked, however, as the observable manifestations of the underlying and invisible, biological, racial "essence" rather than as an argument against the biological basis of race. Gross, "Litigating Whiteness"; Pascoe, "Miscegenation Law."

12. F. James Davis, *Who Is Black? One Nation's Definition* (University Park: Pennsylvania State University Press, 1991).

13. Calvin Trillin, "American Chronicles: Black or White," *New Yorker,* 14 April 1986, 62–78.

14. Susie Phipps's suit, it should be noted, did create a change in the legal definition of racial identity that was to have a practical effect for others, if not for herself. In view of her original suit, the Louisiana legislature did reject the 1/32 legal standard of blackness in favor of allowing parents, from then on, to designate the race of their newborns on their birth certificates as they chose. But the court insisted that this decision did not allow anyone to alter a birth certificate that had *already* been issued, unless the information it contained was shown to be in error. Mrs. Phipps failed to do this in 1985, and the court ruled to hold her, and her birth certificate, to the norms of racialization in effect when it was originally prepared.

Yet even if laws about racial attribution by means of the one-drop rule have changed significantly, social practice has not followed suit. This is nowhere more clearly demonstrated than in a tragic event that transpired in 1996 in Thomasville, Georgia. A white woman gave birth to a baby who died shortly after birth. She chose to lay the infant to rest in her family cemetery plot, next to her grandfather, so the baby "would have company." A few days after the burial, however, the deacons of the church learned that the child's father was black. They demanded that the infant be disinterred and reburied elsewhere because the cemetery (as is still frequently the case in many places) was for whites only. Clearly, race is still assigned, in social practice, according to a rule of hypodescent. The child, although biracial, was automatically designated black because its father was black. (Or, it should be said, the father was *judged* to be black. The deacons apparently did not ask him how he identified himself, but classified him themselves, on the grounds that he appeared to have black ancestry — thus making him, too, subject of a rule of hypodescent.) Rick Bragg, "Just a Grave for a Baby but Anguish for a Town," *New York Times,* 31 March 1996.

15. Jack D. Forbes, "The Manipulation of Race, Caste, and Identity: Classifying AfroAmericans, Native Americans and Red-Black People," *Journal of Ethnic Studies* 17, no. 4 (1990): 24; original emphasis. Indians are "lost," in Forbes' sense, both to black *and* to white racial classifications, but at differing rates. Popular conventions of racial classification in America tend to prevent individuals with any discernible black ancestry from identifying themselves as Indians. As an interview respondent quoted by anthropologist Circe Sturm observes, "This is America, where being to any degree Black is the same thing as being to any degree pregnant." Sturm, *Blood Politics,* 188.

By contrast, individuals with discernible white ancestry are *sometimes* allowed by others to identify as Indian. In their case the legitimacy of their assertion is likely to be evaluated with reference to the *amount* of white ancestry, and with beliefs about whether that amount is enough to merely *dilute* or to entirely *compromise* Indian identity. Other factors, such as culture and upbringing, may also be taken into account. People of partial white ancestry, in other words, are typically somewhat more free (although not entirely free) to negotiate a legitimate identity as Indian than are people of partial black ancestry.

16. For further details on the historical impact of blood quantum on individuals' legal rights, see Felix S. Cohen, *Cohen's Handbook of Federal Indian Law* (Charlottesville, Va.: Michie/Bobbs-Merrill, 1982).

17. For a listing of the blood quantum requirements that different tribes require for tribal citizenship, see Edgar Lister, "Tribal Membership Rates and Requirements," unpublished table (Washington, D.C: Indian Health Service, 1987). An edited version of the table appears in C. Matthew Snipp, *American Indians: The First of This Land* (New York: Russell Sage Foundation, 1989), appendix.

18. Devon A. Mihesuah, "Commonality of Difference: American Indian Women and History," in *Natives and Academics: Researching and Writing about American Indians,* ed. Devon A. Mihesuah (Lincoln: University of Nebraska Press, 1998), 42. For a fascinating and detailed discussion of the significance of appearance among contemporary Cherokees in Oklahoma, see Sturm, *Blood Politics,* 108-15.

19. Michael Dorris, *The Broken Cord* (New York: Harper Perennial, 1990), 22.

20. Eric Konigsberg, "Michael Dorris's Troubled Sleep," *New York Magazine,* 16 June 1997, 33. For a related article, see Jerry Reynolds, "Indian Writers: The Good, the Bad, and the Could Be, Part 2: Indian Writers: Real or Imagined," *Indian Country Today,* 15 September 1993.

21. Terry P. Wilson, "Blood Quantum: Native American Mixed Bloods," in *Racially Mixed People in America,* ed. Maria P. P. Root (Newbury Park, Calif.: Sage, 1992), 109.

22. This decision is reflected in Article III of the Passamoquoddy Draft Constitution of 1990, available online at http://thorpe.ok.edu/Constitution/Passama/. The Poarch Band of Creek Indians (Alabama) likewise constituted all registrants on their base rolls as full bloods.

23. Kent Carter, *The Dawes Commission and the Allotment of the Five Civilized Tribes, 1893–1914* (Orem, Utah: Ancestry.com, 1999), 49; see further Sturm, *Blood Politics.* For a related discussion of Indian enrollment in Washington State, see Alexandra Harmon, *Indians in the Making: Ethnic Relations and Indian Identities around Puget Sound* (Berkeley: University of California Press, 1998), 137–44.

24. *Inflation* of blood quanta has also sometimes occurred. Some mixed-blood Dawes applicants reported themselves as full bloods, hoping to increase their chances of receiving an allotment. Carter, *Dawes Commission,* 49. Wilson also reports how, in the 1930s, full-blood members of the Osage tribe addressed anxieties about their waning authority in the tribe by documentarily converting a number of mixed bloods into their own ranks:

Rather than allow a lower birthrate [among full bloods] and intermarriage with non-Indians to widen the numerical gap and erode their power entirely, the Osage full bloods . . . broadened their political base by identifying as "full blood" all tribal members of one-half or more blood quantum (and in some instances even less if the person's physical appearance seemed to warrant the designation) and accepting into their society — and politics — those whose attitudes and conduct coincided with the surviving traditional culture. (Wilson, "Blood Quantum," 120)

25. David Melmer, "Today American Indian, Tomorrow 'Multiracial'?" *Indian Country Today,* 29 March 1996.

26. Snipp, *First of This Land,* 309.

27. Jamaica Kincaid, *Lucy* (New York: Farrar Straus Giroux, 1990), 40–41.

28. Jimmie Durham, quoted in M. Annette Jaimes, "Federal Indian Identification Policy: A Usurpation of Indigenous Sovereignty in North America," in *The State of Native America: Genocide, Colonization, and Resistance,* ed. M. Annette Jaimes (Boston: South End, 1992), 123.

29. Snipp, "Who Are American Indians?" 249.

30. Jace Weaver, "Native Americans in U.S. Society," *Challenge Racism: Christian Perspectives on Social Issues* 5 (1994): 47. While calculations of blood quantum are quite clearly an invention of the European colonizers, Ray DeMallie even raises the question, by means of an interesting linguistic analysis of tribal dialects, whether Sioux Indians used "blood" as the symbol of familial relationship before European contact. See DeMallie, "Kinship and Biology in Sioux Culture," in *North American Indian Anthropology: Essays on Society and Culture,* ed. Ray DeMallie and Alfonso Ortiz (Norman: University of Oklahoma Press), 1994.

31. The Indigo Girls (Amy Ray and Emily Saliers) are a musical group that

has often taken up issues of concern to indigenous peoples. This song is included on the compact disk *Honor: A Benefit For the Honor the Earth Campaign.*

32. Elizabeth Cook-Lynn, "Literary and Political Questions of Transformation: American Indian Fiction Writers," *Wicazo Sa Review* 11, no. 1 (spring 1995): 49. Cook-Lynn is professor emerita of English and Native American Studies at Eastern Washington University.

33. Wilson, "Blood Quantum," 108–25; Clara Sue Kidwell, "Indian Women as Cultural Mediators," *Ethnohistory* 39 (1992): 97–107; Margaret Connell Szasz, *Between Indian and White Worlds: The Cultural Broker* (Norman: University of Oklahoma Press, 1994).

34. Michael Dorris and Louise Erdrich, *The Crown of Columbus* (New York: Harper Collins, 1991), 123–24.

35. Cook-Lynn, "Political Questions," 48.

36. Snipp, *First of This Land,* 157.

37. Russell Thornton, "Tribal Membership Requirements and the Demography of 'Old' and 'New' Native Americans," *Population Research and Policy Review* 16 (1997): 37.

38. Lenore A. Stiffarm and Phil Lane, Jr., "The Demography of Native North America: A Question of American Indian Survival," in *The State of Native America: Genocide, Colonization, and Resistance,* ed. M. Annette Jaimes (Boston: South End, 1992), 45. For specific details on blood quantum levels among American Indians, see also C. Matthew Snipp, *Indian Health Care* (U.S. Office of Technological Assessment, 1989), p. 167.

39. Races, in popular American thought, are assumed to be natural biological categories. Most people suppose that individuals can be grouped into races in the same way they are grouped into sexes. This is not the case. Student of race Naomi Zack summarizes the nature of racial difference as most scientists presently understand it: "Biologically there is no general genetic marker for race. There are genes associated with particular physical traits that have been socially designated as racial traits, but no gene for white race, black race, Asian race, or any other race has been scientifically identified."

Things are different in the case of sex: "X and Y [chromosomes] are identifiable as general sexual markers that determine more specific sexual characteristics. . . . This general XX-ness or XY-ness causes or explains less general physical characteristics, which themselves have underlying genes. For example, the presence of XX predicts the presence of the gene for ovaries. If it were the case that all of the specific physical sexual characteristics varied along continua and that XX and XY did not exist, then there would be no general genetic basis for sex. That is the situation with race." In short, "the ordinary concept of race in the United States, which purports to be about something hereditary and physical, has no scientific foundation." Zack, "Mixed Black and White Race," 120. See further Audrey Smedley, *Race in North America: Origin and Evolution of a Worldview,* 2d ed. (Boulder, Colo.: Westview Press, 1999).

40. Terry Anderson, "Federal Recognition: The Vicious Myth," *American Indian Journal* 5 (1978): 11. See further, Wilson, *Blood Quantum,* 121; and David

L. Beaulieu, "Curly Hair and Big Feet: Physical Anthropology and the Implementation of Land Allotment on the White Earth Chippewa Reservation," *American Indian Quarterly* 8, no. 4 (1984): 281–314.

41. Anderson, "Federal Recognition," 11 n.

42. Seltzer's efforts followed earlier attempts by Ales Hrdlicka, a Czechoslovakian anthropologist at the Smithsonian, and his University of Minnesota colleague Albert Jenks to determine racial admixture among the Ojibwe of the White Earth Reservation (Minnesota). Hrdlicka and Jenks had used a micrometer to analyze cross sections of hair, which they thought would show distinctive racial characteristics. So devoted were these researchers to their method that they persevered with it even after it suggested (in what must have been a truly surprising turn of events) that they themselves were both of African ancestry. Meyer, "Blood Quantum Requirements," 240; Beaulieu, "Curly Hair and Big Feet," 305.

43. H. Annette Jaimes, "Some Kind of Indian: On Race, Eugenics, and Mixed-Bloods," in *American Mixed Race,* ed. Naomi Zack (Lanham, Md.: Rowman and Littlefield, 1995), 134.

44. Teresa Olwick Grose, "Reading the Bones: Information Content, Value, and Ownership Issues Raised by the Native American Graves Protection and Repatriation Act," *Journal of the American Society for Information Science* 47, no. 8 (1996): 625.

45. Walter R. Echo-hawk and Roger C. Echo-hawk, "Repatriation, Reburial, and Religious Rights," in *Handbook of American Indian Religious Freedom,* ed. Christopher Vecsey (New York: Crossroad Publishing Co., 1991), 72; similarly, Roger Echo-hawk, *Battlefields and Burial Grounds* (Minneapolis: Lerner, 1994).

46. Minik's previously fruitless efforts finally came to resolution nearly one hundred years after his little party had traveled to New York. In 1993, the American Museum of Natural History finally relented and shipped Qisuk's remains, and those of his fallen comrades, back to Greenland. There the bodies were interred under a plaque reading, "They have come home." Minik himself had long since gone to his own rest in a grave in Pittsburg, New Hampshire, where he still lies. For a fuller retelling of the tragic lives of Qisuk and Minik (who lived for many years in the United States because Robert Peary promptly forgot his promise to return the group of Inuits to their homeland within a year), see Kenn Harper, *Give Me My Father's Body: The Life of Minik, the New York Eskimo,* 2d ed. (South Royalton, Vt.: Steerforth Press, 2000).

3. What If My Grandma Eats Big Macs?

1. *Mashpee Tribe v. Town of Mashpee* 447 F. Supp. (D. Mass. 1978), aff'd sub nom. *Mashpee Tribe v. New Seabury Corp.*, 592 F.2d 575 (1st Cir.), cert. denied, 444 US 866 (1979).

2. The act states, in part: "No sale of lands made by any Indians, or any

nation or tribe of Indians within the United States, shall be valid to any person or persons, or to any state . . . unless the same shall be made and duly executed at some public treaty, held under the authority of the United States." Quoted in Felix Cohen, *Handbook of Federal Indian Law* (Charlottesville, Va.: Michie/Bobbs-Merrill, 1982), 511.

3. James Clifford, "Identity in Mashpee," in *The Predicament of Culture*, ed. James Clifford (Cambridge: Harvard University Press, 1988), 323.

4. Don Monet and Skanu'u [Ardythe Wilson], *Colonialism on Trial: Indigenous Land Rights and the Gitksan and Wet'suwet'en Sovereignty Case* (Philadelphia: New Society, 1992). For the reaction of Canadian anthropologists to the court decision, see Ken McQueen, "A Landmark Ruling Shocks Anthropologists," *Vancouver Sun*, 13 July 1991.

5. The agricultural lifestyle of the Pueblo tribes was significant to the court because "land was intended and designed by Providence for the use of mankind, and the game that it produced was intended for those too lazy and indolent to cultivate the soil." *United States v. Jose Juan Lucero*, 1 NM 422, 425–26 (Su Ct NM 1869).

6. *United States v. Jose Juan Lucero* (1869).

7. *United States v. Joseph*, 94 US 614 (1876). Given the discrimination to which those classified as Indians were subjected, one might think that it would have been a boon to the Pueblos to be legally classified as a category separate from the "wild Indians." Ironically, however, this meant that the government was not required to protect Pueblo lands, and the pueblos were soon overrun with homesteaders.

8. *United States v. Sandoval*, 231 US 28 (1913).

9. The relevant portion of the bill H.R. 3275, in its unamended form, may be viewed online at: http://www.alt.net/~waltj/shea/icwia.html.

10. Senator John McCain, quoted in "Panel Passes ICWA Amendments," *Indian Country Today*, 11 August 1997.

11. Even given the failure of H.R. 3286, there have been individual cases in which courts have refused to abide by the ICWA's dictates on grounds related to cultural practice. In one such case, involving twin infants born to Mississippi Choctaw parents (*Mississippi Band of Choctaw Indians v. Holyfield*, 490 US 30 [1989] 49), the ruling appeared to follow the logic that the ICWA should apply only to children of a certain age — specifically, to children old enough to have acquired a Native culture at the time of their adoption. The parents had given the children up to a non-Indian family, but the tribe had not received the requisite notice of adoption. When the tribe learned of the adoption some weeks later, it sought to invalidate it and to obtain jurisdiction over the children. The state court ruled against the tribe, arguing that the children in question were adopted at too young an age to have formed cultural, social, or political ties to a tribe. The implication is clearly that the children were not "really" Indian, by virtue of their lack of familiarity with Indian culture. The U.S. Supreme Court, however, later overturned the state's decision, reasoning that the children's cultural experiences were irrelevant to the appli-

cation of the ICWA. For a thorough discussion of the events in this case, see Jose Monsivais, "A Glimmer of Hope: A Proposal to Keep the Indian Child Welfare Act of 1978 Intact," *American Indian Law Review* 22, no. 1 (1997): 1–36. For other cases in which nontribal courts have made judgments about Indian culture significant to decisions about child placement, see *Matter of Adoption of Baby Boy L.,* 64333 P.2d 168 (Kan. 1982) and *In re Crews,* 825 P.2d 305 (Wash. 1992).

12. Russell Thornton, *The Cherokees: A Population History* (Lincoln: University of Nebraska, 1990), 174–75.

13. Jack D. Forbes, "The Manipulation of Race, Caste, and Identity: Classifying AfroAmericans, Native Americans and Red-Black People," *Journal of Ethnic Studies* 17, no. 4 (1990): 23–24.

14. For an outstanding study of modern cultural revivals across American Indian communities since the 1960s, see Joane Nagel, *American Indian Ethnic Renewal: Red Power and the Resurgence of Identity and Culture* (New York: Oxford University Press, 1996). For a more focused work on cultural revival, see John Bean Lowell, ed., *The Ohlone Past and Present: Native Americans of the San Francisco Bay Region* (Menlo Park, Calif.: Ballena Press, 1994).

15. Clifford, "Identity in Mashpee," 341. It is not, of course, strictly the Mashpee who are accused of fraud and disingenuousness when they attempt to restore lapsed elements of their cultures. Many other groups are accused of simply masquerading as Indians, as when James A. Clifton (not to be confused with James Clifford, cited in this note) condemns "North Carolina's born again 'Lumbee Indians'" and their attempts at cultural renewal. James A. Clifton, *The Invented Indian: Cultural Fictions and Government Policies* (New Brunswick: Transaction, 1990), 6.

16. For instance, the Code of Federal Regulations (CFR), the set of definitions now used in decisions related to federal recognition of tribes, enshrines a similar logic. It offers an instance in which a tribe entirely disperses except for one family, but the same tribal members later return, re-form the original community, and again take up their former way of life. The CFR uses this as an example of a group that would be denied federal recognition. Like Judge Skinner, these regulations appear to assume that a tribal culture, once abandoned, cannot be resuscitated.

17. Clifford, "Identity in Mashpee," 338.

18. *United States v. Rogers,* in *Federal Cases and Circuit and District Courts 1789–1880,* vol. 27, Ark. Cir.Ct. D (1845) (St. Paul: West Publishing Co., 1894–1897), 886–890; emphasis mine.

19. In this regard racial/ethnic identification is strikingly unlike another aspect of cultural experience, namely, religion. That is, Americans generally accept accounts of religious conversion and even expect them as a normal part of life. A social actor's religious sentiments are not typically dismissed as inauthentic simply because she is a proselyte rather than a member of the faith from birth. There are, of course, unusual circumstances that cast doubt on the truthfulness of a particular conversion narrative; nevertheless, the possibility of religious conversion is widely accepted. By contrast, the possibility of "genuinely" identifying

with an ethnic or racial group other than the one assigned by others at birth is rather uniformly disallowed by popular convention.

20. Alvin Josephy, "New England Indians: Then and Now," in *The Pequots in Southern New England: The Fall and Rise of an American Indian Nation,* ed. Laurence Hauptman and James D. Wherry (Norman: University of Oklahoma Press, 1990), 7.

21. Ramona Peters is the daughter of John Peters, cited earlier in the chapter as a witness in the Mashpee trial. On a separate occasion she donated her time in an interview for this book, and she is quoted elsewhere as a respondent.

22. Bureau of Indian Affairs, *The Official Guidelines to the Federal Acknowledgment Regulations, 25 CFR 83* (Washington, D.C.: Bureau of Indian Affairs, Branch of Acknowledgment and Research, September 1997), 45.

23. Bureau of Indian Affairs, *Official Guidelines,* 36, 45.

24. Anne Merline McCulloch and David E. Wilkins, "Constructing Nations within States: The Quest for Federal Recognition by the Catawba and Lumbee Tribes," *American Indian Quarterly* 19, no. 3 (1995): 369.

25. House Committee on Interior and Insular Affairs, *Indian Federal Acknowledgment Process: Hearing before the Committee on Interior and Insular Affairs,* 102nd Cong., 2d sess., 15 September 1992, 68–69. For a discussion of the relationship of the Indian Reorganization Act to tribal recognition, see Government Accounting Office, *Indian Issues: Improvements Needed in Tribal Recognition Process,* Report to Congressional Requesters (Washington, D.C., November 2001).

26. Jace Weaver, "From I-Hermeneutics to We-Hermeneutics: Native Americans and the Post-Colonial," in *Native American Religious Identity: Unforgotten Gods,* ed. Jace Weaver (Maryknoll, N.Y.: Orbis Books, 1998): 20.

27. Gregory A. Cajete, *Look to the Mountain: An Ecology of Indigenous Education* (Durango, Colo.: Kivaki, 1994), 83.

28. Geary Hobson, "Introduction: Remembering the Earth," in *The Remembered Earth: An Anthology of Contemporary Native American Literature,* ed. Geary Hobson (Albuquerque: University of New Mexico Press, 1990), 11.

29. Donald Grinde and Quintard Taylor, "Slaves, Freedmen, and Native Americans in Indian Territory (Oklahoma), 1865–1907," in *Peoples of Color in the American West,* ed. Sucheng Chan et al. (Lexington, Mass.: D. C. Heath, 1994), 291. *The WPA Oklahoma Slave Narratives,* collected in the 1930s, include some limited material on "black Indians." T. Lindsay Baker and Julie P. Baker, *The WPA Oklahoma Slave Narratives* (Norman: University of Oklahoma Press, 1996). More recent interviews are reported in Circe Sturm, *Blood Politics: Race, Culture, and Identity in the Cherokee Nation of Oklahoma* (Berkeley: University of California Press, 2002).

30. The respondent gave the full name of her relative. However, since the person is now deceased and cannot give permission for her name to be used, I have used only her first name.

31. Tahlequah, Oklahoma, is the capital of the Cherokee Nation. The stomp dance is an important ceremony practiced by traditional Cherokee people.

32. Gail K. Sheffield, *The Arbitrary Indian: The Indian Arts and Crafts Act of 1990* (Norman: University of Oklahoma Press, 1997), 103.

33. See further Howard Harrod's interesting book, *Becoming and Remaining a People: Native American Religions on the Northern Plains* (Tucson: University of Arizona Press, 1995).

34. Elizabeth Cook-Lynn, "Literary and Political Questions of Transformation: American Indian Fiction Writers," *Wicazo Sa Review* 11, no. 1 (1995): 49.

35. Alfred W. Crosby, Jr., *The Columbian Exchange: Biological and Cultural Consequences of 1492* (Westport, Conn.: Greenwood Press, 1972).

36. Paul Brodeur, *Restitution: The Land Claims of the Mashpee, Passamaquoddy, and Penobscot Indians of New England* (Boston: Northeastern University Press, 1985).

37. Wendy Rose, "Neon Scars," in *I Tell You Now: Autobiographical Essays by Native American Writers,* ed. Brian Swann and Arnold Krupat (Lincoln: University of Nebraska Press, 1987), 260–61.

38. Tom Hill and Richard W. Hill, Sr., *Creation's Journey: Native American Identity and Belief* (Washington, D.C.: Smithsonian Institution, 1994), 23.

39. Christina West, *Inner Circles* (Tulsa: University of Tulsa Press, 1996), 15.

40. For a description of tribal efforts in this direction, see Les Field, "Complicities and Collaborations: Anthropologists and the 'Unacknowledged Tribes' of California," *Current Anthropology* 40, no. 2 (April 1999): 193–201. See further Alan Leventhal, Les Field, Hank Alvarez, and Rosemary Cambra, "The Ohlone: Back from Extinction," in *The Ohlone Past and Present,* ed. Lowell J. Bean (Menlo Park, Calif.: Ballena Press, 1994).

41. Clifford, "Identity in Mashpee," 338.

4. If You're Indian and You Know It (But Others Don't)

1. Zug G. Standing Bear, "To Guard against Invading Indians: Struggling for Native Community in the Southeast," *American Indian Culture and Research Journal* 18, no. 4 (1994): 305–6, 310.

2. Zug G. Standing Bear, "Questions of Assertion, Diversity, and Spirituality: Simultaneously Becoming a Minority and a Sociologist," *American Sociologist* 20 (1988): 363–71.

3. Russell Thornton, *The Cherokees: A Population History* (Lincoln: University of Nebraska Press, 1990), 175.

4. Standing Bear, "To Guard against Invading Indians," 305–6.

5. Standing Bear, "To Guard against Invading Indians," 305–6.

6. For instance, retired Oklahoma Cherokee chief Wilma Mankiller has testified, in a federal hearing, that the Delilah Whitecloud United Cherokee Indian Tribe of Kentucky (a group that does not enjoy federal acknowledgment) at one time received federal funds earmarked for Indian employment training through the Department of Labor. U.S. Senate Committee on Indian Affairs,

Federal Recognition Administrative Procedures Act: Hearing before the Committee on Indian Affairs, 104th Cong., 1st sess., 13 July 1995, 212.

7. "The Cherokee Name and Sovereignty are in Danger," report compiled under the administration of Principal Chief Wilma Mankiller by the Cherokee Nation Tribal Registrar and entered into the Congressional record. U.S. Senate Committee on Indian Affairs, *Federal Recognition Act,* 38.

The word *Tsalagi* is the Cherokee people's traditional name for themselves. The word "oukah" is presumably an Anglicized attempt at the Cherokee word *uku* or *ugvwiyuhi,* translatable as "chief." If Mr. Robinson's larger-than-life self-presentation illustrates how a claim to an Indian identity may be used as a kind of social capital, it reveals something else important: the tendency to attach exotic, self-aggrandizing associations to Indianness is not *only* a foible of misguided non-Indians. However remarkable his claims to "chieftainship" (not to mention divinity), Mr. Robinson appears (from information provided on his website) to be a legally enrolled citizen of the Cherokee Nation.

8. Some researchers use the term "ethnic switching" somewhat differently than I do. Hopi sociologist Angela Gonzales (Cornell University), for example, defines it as the process of changing one's explicit ethnic identification *specifically for reasons of personal gain.* Angela Gonzales, "The (Re)Articulation of American Indian Identity: Maintaining and Regulating Access to Ethnically-Tied Resources," *American Indian Culture and Research Journal* 22, no. 4 (1998): 199–225. This definition does adequately characterize at least *some* subset of those who switch racial identities, but I do not think that it characterizes all of them. Given that all identifications can be, or at least can be constructed as, advantageous in certain circumstances and ways, Gonzales's usage, while perfectly sensible given the goals of her article, could be problematic if applied universally; it potentially places a negative label on anyone who asserts an ethnic re-identification. For my purposes, I have tried to establish a terminology that allows for a more neutral construction of racial re-identification, one that simply observes the behavior without implying speculation about the motivation for it.

9. Betty L. Bell, *Faces in the Moon* (Norman: University of Oklahoma Press, 1995), 57–58.

10. Alfonso Ortiz, quoted in Jerry Reynolds, "Indian Writers: Real or Imagined," *Indian Country Today,* 8 September 1993.

11. Lorelie Decora (Means), quoted in M. Annette Jaimes, "Federal Indian Identification Policy: A Usurpation of Indigenous Sovereignty in North America," in *The State of Native America,* ed. M. Annette Jaimes (Boston: South End Press, 1992), 130–31.

12. The Association of American Indian and Alaska Native Professors is a national organization devoted to the needs and interests of the current and future American Indian and Alaska Native professoriate. Their Statement on Ethnic Fraud is available at http://www.niti.net/~michael/AIANP/default.htm.

13. Here I am using the word "rational" in the sense that sociologist Max

Weber intended when he used it to describe a form of social organization in which authority derives from written rules.

14. Charles Wilkinson, *The Eagle Bird: Mapping a New West* (New York: Pantheon, 1992).

15. Elizabeth Cook-Lynn, "Who Stole Native American Studies?" *Wicazo Sa Review* 12, no. 1 (1997): 15.

16. U.S. Senate Committe on Indian Affairs, *Federal Recognition Act*. Some nonrecognized tribal groups have pursued other illegal actions, such as opening gambling facilities or Indian smoke shops, and even issuing their own "official tribal" currency. "Another Bogus Cherokee Group Exposed," *Cherokee Advocate*, 3 August 2000. Available online at http://www.cherokee.org/NewsArchives/August2000.asp.

17. David Melmer, "Plastic Medicine Man Exposed," *Indian Country Today*, 26 August 1996; David Melmer, "Plastic Indian Jailed for Sexual Misconduct," *Indian Country Today*, 13 January 1997.

18. I have deliberately omitted the title and author of this book, on the grounds that I believe it to be pornographic. The reader can only be mystified why Reagan is not subject to legal prosecution for this published admission of criminal behavior.

19. Melmer, "Plastic Medicine Man Exposed."

20. Into the early decades of the twentieth century the BIA enforced a set of regulations, known as the Religious Crimes Code, upon Indian tribes, in order to prevent them from maintaining traditional worship practices. Activities targeted for destruction included sacred dances, medicine men's practices, and the "give aways" in which a number of tribes (especially Plains tribes) redistributed wealth. Also forbidden were "any frequent or prolonged periods of celebration which bring the Indians together from remote points to the neglect of their crops, livestock and home interests," thereby threatening the accumulation of goods necessary for the capitalist economy to which the Americans were attempting to convert tribal subsistence economies.

Those who attempted to continue in their spiritual practices were tried in specially created courts for Indian offenses and punished with denial of food rations and with jail sentences. Government officials also confiscated and burned religious objects. Some of the original documents issued by the Department of the Interior and distributed to BIA area superintendents and the commissioner of Indian affairs are reprinted and discussed in American Indian Historical Society, "The Facts of History: The Denial of Indian Civil and Religious Rights," *The Indian Historian* 8, no. 3 (1975): 43–46; and in Francis Paul Prucha, ed., *Documents of United States Indian Policy*, 3rd ed. (Lincoln: University of Nebraska Press, 2000). For discussion see David E. Witheridge, "No Freedom of Religion for American Indians," *Journal of Church and State* 18, no. 1 (1976): 5–19; and Clyde Ellis, "We Don't Want Your Rations, We Want This Dance: The Changing Use of Song and Dance on the Southern Plains," *Western Historical Quarterly* 30, no. 1 (1999): 137–41.

Today Indian people must satisfy certain strict legal definitions of identity in order to participate in ceremonial practices related to the Native American Church or "peyote way" — and even then, they may find themselves subject to arrest and prosecution. In another department of religious freedom, American Indian prison inmates continually complain that although individuals of other beliefs are allowed to exercise their faiths, they are denied access to traditional spiritual leaders and worship activities.

21. Mary Pierpont, "Cherokee Members Spread across Nation," *Indian Country Today*, 2 August 2000. Delaware/Peoria respondent Billy S. offers an interpretation similar to Pierpont's about the Cherokee ancestor-princess professed to lurk in the genealogies of so many individuals who would, by any other measure, be judged non-Indians: given the number of her putative descendants, he speculates, "there's somebody back there [in history] that was damn *busy!*"

22. Advertisement reprinted in David Melmer, "Become Indian, Buy Your Own Indian Name," *Indian Country Today*, 2–9 September 1996.

23. Susan Smith's video, *Sweating Indian Style*, offers a compelling and balanced look at one such New Age group operating in California. The group combines elements of mainstream feminism, goddess worship, and a variety of other non-Indian cultural traditions with a version of the sweat lodge, which is used in various forms by a number of tribes. *Sweating Indian Style*, prod. Susan Smith, 56 min., University of Southern California, Center for Visual Anthropology, 1994, videocassette.

Joseph Bruchac also documents and evenhandedly discusses a "medicine wheel" gathering in the Catskills that offers a version of American Indian ceremonies to a New Age audience. Joseph Bruchac, "Spinning the Medicine Wheel: The Bear Tribe in the Catskills," *Akwesasne Notes* 15, no. 5 (1983).

24. Philip Deloria, *Playing Indian* (New Haven: Yale University Press, 1998), 393.

25. Clearly, not all New Age practitioners, not even all of the many who are interested in Indian cultures, actually claim Indian identity in one sense or another. My intention here is to show some of the ways that such a self-identification, where it does exist, can function.

26. Jack D. Forbes, "The Manipulation of Race, Caste, and Identity: Classifying AfroAmericans, Native Americans and Red-Black People," *Journal of Ethnic Studies* 17, no. 4 (1990): 49; original emphasis.

27. N. Scott Momaday, *The Names: A Memoir* (New York: Harper and Row, 1976), 23–25.

28. James A. Clifton, "Introduction: Memoirs, Exegesis," in *The Invented Indian: Cultural Fictions and Government Policies*, ed. James A. Clifton (New Brunswick: Transaction, 1990), 5.

29. Russell Thornton, *American Indian Holocaust and Survival* (Norman: University of Oklahoma Press, 1987), 224.

30. Taiaiake Alfred, *Peace, Power, Righteousness: An Indigenous Manifesto* (Don Mills, Ont.: Oxford University Press, 1999), 55.

31. Alfred, *Peace, Power, Righteousness*, 57, 56.

32. Greg Sarris, quoted in Dinitia Smith, "The Indian in Literature Is Catching Up," *New York Times*, Living Arts section, 21 April 1997.

33. Joane Nagel, "American Indian Ethnic Renewal: Politics and the Resurgence of Identity," *American Sociological Review* 60, no. 6 (December 1995): 961.

34. Greg Sarris, *Keeping Slug Woman Alive* (Berkeley: University of California Press, 1993).

35. Craig Calhoun, *Social Theory and the Politics of Identity* (Cambridge, Mass.: Blackwell, 1994), 24.

5. "Whaddaya Mean 'We,' White Man?"

1. M. Annette Jaimes, "Some Kind of Indian: On Race, Eugenics, and Mixed-Bloods," in *American Mixed Race,* ed. Naomi Zack (Lanham, Md.: Rowman and Littlefield, 1995), 139; Rayna Green, "Enrolled or Not, Green Still Says She's Cherokee," *Indian Country Today,* 26 January 1994; Jackie Bissley, "Canadian Singer's Status Charges Ancestry Debate," *Indian Country Today,* 30 April–7 May 1996.

2. I have deliberately omitted the publication information for this quotation, so as to discourage further circulation of such rumors and the unpleasant motivations that fuel them.

3. Ever since the emergence of the ethnic and women's studies programs in universities, a debate has raged over whether there can be unique ethnic and gender perspectives. Can we, in any meaningful sense, speak about a "black" or "women's" history, a "Hispanic voice" in literature, and so on? Most recently, these questions have even been extended, in sociology, to consider whether there is a perspective unique to the physically disabled. See, for instance, James I. Charlton, *Nothing about Us without Us: Disability Oppression and Empowerment* (Berkeley: University of California Press, 1998). The discussion in this chapter is intended to carry these debates further.

4. In this rationale for choosing the word "radical," I am borrowing from a similar argument used by scholars who identify as radical feminists.

5. The field of postcolonial theory is extremely diverse. For a useful overview, see Peter Childs and R. J. Patrick Williams, *An Introduction to Post-Colonial Theory* (New York: Prentice-Hall, 1999).

6. Walter D. Mignolo, "Afterword: Writing and Recorded Knowledge in Colonial and Postcolonial Situations," in *Writing without Words: Alternative Literacies in Mesoamerica and the Andes,* ed. Elizabeth Hill Boome and Walter D. Mignolo (Durham: Duke University Press, 1994), 309.

7. Les W. Field, "Complicities and Collaborations: Anthropologists and the 'Unacknowledged Tribes' of California," *Current Anthropology* 40, no. 3 (April 1999); Florencia E. Mallon, *Peasant and Nation: The Making of Postcolonial Mexico and Peru* (Berkeley: University of California Press, 1995).

8. These include such questions as: What happens to oral traditions in the academic context, where the written word is the coin of the realm? And how can we can think about the irony that colonized peoples, if they are to succeed in the life-and-death task of communicating about themselves to their colonizer, are

driven to use *his* language, and *his* means of recording ideas? On this latter subject, see *Writing without Words: Alternative Literacies in Mesoamerica and the Andes,* edited by Elizabeth Hill Boone and Walter D. Mignolo (Durham: Duke University Press, 1994). For discussions of doing scholarship related to indigenous peoples in a "foreign" language, see Walter D. Mignolo, "On the Colonization of Amerindian Languages and Memories: Renaissance Theories of Writing and Discontinuity of the Classical Tradition," *Comparative Studies in Society and History* 34, no. 2 (April 1992): 301–330; Ngugi Wa Thiong'o, *Decolonising the Mind: The Politics of Language in African Literature* (Portsmouth, N.H.: Heineman, 1986); and also the essays in *The Surreptitious Speech: Presence Africaine and the Politics of Otherness 1947–1987,* ed. V. Y. Mudimbe (Chicago: University of Chicago Press, 1992). For investigations of related issues as they concern North American Native peoples specifically, see the extremely insightful essays in Phyllis Morrow and William Schneider, eds., *When Our Words Return: Writing, Hearing, and Remembering Oral Traditions of Alaska and the Yukon* (Logan: Utah State University Press, 1995).

9. Mignolo, "Afterword," 310.

10. There are various versions of this critique. One of the very few efforts to assess the utility of postcolonial theory specifically in regard to American Indian concerns is Jace Weaver, "From I-Hermeneutics to We-Hermeneutics: Native Americans and the Post-Colonial," in *Native American Religious Identity: Unforgotten Gods,* ed. Jace Weaver (Maryknoll, N.Y.: Orbis Books, 1998).

11. Kwame Anthony Appiah, *In My Father's House: Africa in the Philosophy of Culture* (New York: Oxford University Press, 1993), 107–36. Appiah's discussion is mostly interested in contemporary academic disciplines that explicitly constitute themselves as sciences, but other authors argue that even disciplines that do not do this have been influenced by many of the same assumptions. See, for instance, Gonzáles's argument that the modern worldview has created an increasingly "de-mythologized" theology. Justo Gonzáles, *Out of Every Tribe and Nation: Christian Theology at the Ethnic Roundtable* (Nashville: Abingdon Press, 1992), 48.

12. Appiah, *In My Father's House,* 116.

13. Appiah, *In My Father's House,* 135.

14. Some readers will object to the idea that the new scholarship proposed here can include both Native and non-Native people. I incline, however, toward Stover's opinion: "If a postcolonial discourse is going to move beyond reactive response in order to effect a decolonizing of both the colonized 'other' and the colonizing 'self,' the voice of the postmodern 'self' may need to be included in the decolonizing process." To say this more simply: Given the history of violence toward Native communities, real healing probably needs to include everyone. Failure to include aggressors (or beneficiaries of aggression) in the process of healing invites further violence. Dale Stover, "Postcolonial Sun Dancing at Wakpamni Lake," *Journal of the American Academy of Religion* 69, no. 4 (December 2001): 817–36.

15. See further Sam Gill, "The Academic Study of Religion," *Journal of the*

American Academy of Religion 62, no. 4 (1994): 965–75; Christopher Jocks, "American Indian Religious Traditions and the Academic Study of Religion: A Response to Sam Gill," *Journal of the American Academy of Religion* 65, no. 1 (1997): 169–76; Sam Gill, "Rejoinder to Christopher Jocks," *Journal of the American Academy of Religion* 65, no. 1 (1997): 177–81. Additionally, see Lee Irwin's capable and thoughtful summary of the debate, "Response: American Indian Religious Traditions and the Academic Study of Religion," *Journal of the American Academy of Religion* 66, no. 4 (1998): 887–92.

16. Gill, "Rejoinder," 169.

17. Gill, "Academic Study," 966, 968.

18. Gill, "Rejoinder," 169.

19. Gill, "Academic Study," 967–68.

20. Jocks, "Religious Traditions," 172.

21. Jocks, "Religious Traditions," 173.

22. Jocks, "Religious Traditions," 173.

23. Jocks, "Religious Traditions," 173.

24. Gill, "Academic Study."

25. Jocks, personal communication, 22 March 1999.

26. Paul Radin, in *Primitive Man as Philosopher* (Minneola, N.Y.: Dover Publications, 1957), made one of the early arguments that indigenous people possessed sophisticated, coherent, logically ordered philosophies that allow for critical engagement with the world, and subsequent researchers have enlarged on these ideas. See further Appiah, *In My Father's House;* Barry Hallen, "Robin Horton on Critical Philosophy and Traditional Thought," *Second Order* 1 (1977): 81–92; Robin Horton, "African Traditional Religion and Western Science," *Africa* 37, nos. 1 and 2 (1967): 50–71, 155–87; and Bruno Latour, *Science in Action: How to Follow Scientists and Engineers through Society* (Cambridge: Harvard University Press, 1987). Another book that contributes to the same general conversation examines the logic of folk beliefs in rural France. See Jeanne Favret-Saada, *Deadly Words: Witchcraft in the Bocage* (New York: Cambridge University Press, 1980).

27. Robert Allen Warrior, *Tribal Secrets: Recovering American Indian Intellectual Traditions* (Minneapolis: University of Minnesota Press, 1995), 112.

28. Ideas about community-centered scholarship in literature that Weaver discusses are related to some expressed in this section; he summarizes them under the rubric of "communitism," a literary perspective that constantly returns to the relevance of authorial endeavor to community survival. As he remarks, "Native writers, in their commitment to Native communities, write to and for Native peoples. They take cultural endurance as a priority. . . . They write that the People might live." This commitment must, I think, also ground Radical Indigenism. Jace Weaver, *That the People Might Live: Native American Literatures and Native American Communities* (New York: Oxford University Press, 1997), 161.

29. Linda Tuhiwai Smith, *Decolonizing Methodologies: Research and Indigenous Peoples* (New York and London: Zed Books, 1999). Related comments about the

disjunction between Native American studies and Native communities appear in Mary Katharine Duffie and Ben Chavis, "American Indian Studies and Its Evolution in Academia," *The Social Science Journal* 34, no. 4 (1997): 435–46.

30. Faith Smith, "I See an Incredible Force within Native People," in *Messengers of the Wind: Native American Women Tell Their Life Stories,* ed. Jane Katz (New York: Ballantine, 1995), 128.

6. Allowing the Ancestors to Speak

1. For instance, Field usefully describes the evolution of the discipline of anthropology in its approach to tribal communities. See Les Field, "From Applied Anthropology to Applications of Anthropology for Tribal Goals: Examples from Indian Country," in *A Companion to the Anthropology of North American Indians,* ed. Thomas Biolsi (Malden, Mass.: Blackwell Publishers, in press).

2. By no means do I imply, in the discussion that follows, that the many diverse tribal philosophies are somehow "the same" in their teachings about tribal belonging and tribal boundaries, or about anything else. If the postcolonial theorists who have helped to lay out a direction for a Radical Indigenous scholarship have taught us anything, it is that there *is* no "primal mind," no "indigenous psyche," no "tribal society." For this reason there can be no generic "American Indian philosophy" either, and I hope not to be read to suggest that there is. Instead, I merely observe that there are certain *themes* that appear repeatedly across different American Indian philosophies, in the same way that there are themes that reappear in Amer-European philosophies that also display significant differences. For further treatment of themes common across various tribal philosophies, see Peggy V. Beck, Anna Lee Walters, and Nia Francisco, *The Sacred: Ways of Knowledge, Sources of Life* (Tsaile, Ariz.: Navajo Community College, 1992); or Gregory A. Cajete, *Look to the Mountain: An Ecology of Indigenous Education* (Durango, Colo.: Kivaki, 1994).

3. Christopher Jocks, "Combing Out Snakes: Violence and the Construction of Knowledge in Longhouse Tradition" (paper presented at the 1994 annual meeting of the American Academy of Religion, Native Traditions in the Americas Group, session on "Knowing the World: Native American Epistemologies," Chicago, 21 November 1994), 2. Similarly, Cajete, *Look to the Mountain,* 127.

4. Beck, Walters, and Francisco, *The Sacred,* 49. See further Herbert John Benally, "Navajo Philosophy of Learning," *Journal of Navajo Education* 12, no. 1 (1994): 23–31.

5. Linda Clarkson, Arun Kumar, and Jaime Martinez, *Our Responsibility to the Seventh Generation* (Winnipeg, Manitoba: International Institute for Sustainable Development, 1992), 44.

6. Vine Deloria, Jr., *God Is Red: A Native View of Religion,* 2d ed. (Golden, Colo.: Fulcrum, 1994), 88.

7. Ann Lee Walters, "Come, My Sons," quoted in Geary Hobson,

"Introduction: Remembering the Earth," in *The Remembered Earth: An Anthology of Contemporary Native American Literature* (Albuquerque: University of New Mexico Press, 1990), 10.

8. Ella Deloria, *Speaking of Indians* (New York: Friendship Press, 1994): 27.

9. Elizabeth Cook-Lynn, *Why I Can't Read Wallace Stegner and Other Essays: A Tribal Voice* (Madison: University of Wisconsin Press, 1996): 94. The word *tiospaye* has been glossed in various ways. This translation follows Eugene Buechel, *A Lakota-English Dictionary* (Pine Ridge, S.D.: Red Cloud Indian School, 1970).

10. DeMallie, "Kinship," 135.

11. William Harlen Gilbert, Jr., *The Eastern Cherokees* (New York: AMS Press, 1978); Joseph Maxwell, "Biology and Social Relationship in the Kin Terminology of an Inuit Community," in *North American Indian Anthropology: Essays on Society and Culture,* ed. Raymond J. DeMallie and Alfonso Ortiz (Norman: University of Oklahoma Press, 1994); Anne S. Straus, "Northern Cheyenne Kinship Reconsidered," in *North American Indian Anthropology: Essays on Society and Culture,* ed. Raymond J. DeMallie and Alfonso Ortiz (Norman: University of Oklahoma Press, 1994).

12. N. Scott Momaday, "A Conversation with N. Scott Momaday," interview by Lawrence J. Evers, quoted in *Conversations with N. Scott Momaday,* ed. Matthias Schubnell (Jackson: University Press of Mississippi, 1997): 40.

13. N. Scott Momaday, "The Center Holds," interview by Charles L. Woodard, in *Ancestral Voice: Conversations with N. Scott Momaday* (Lincoln: University of Nebraska Press, 1989), 21.

14. Edward W. Said, *Culture and Imperialism* (New York: Alfred A. Knopf, 1993), 16; Salman Rushdie, "'Commonwealth Literature' Does Not Exist," in *Imaginary Homelands: Essays and Criticism 1981–1991* (London: Granta Books, 1991), 67. Wole Soyinka, *Myth, Literature and the African World* (Cambridge: Cambridge University Press, 1976), 136.

15. Jack David Eller and Reed M. Coughlan, "The Poverty of Primordialism: The Demystification of Ethnic Attachment," *Ethnic and Racial Studies* 16, no. 2 (April 1993): 183–202. For a history of essentialism as a concept, see Ann Laura Stoler, "Racial Histories and Their Regimes of Truth," *Political Power and Social Theory* 11 (1997): 186.

16. Eugeen E. Roosens, *Creating Ethnicity: The Process of Ethnogenesis* (Newbury Park, Calif.: Sage, 1989): 18.

17. Arnold Krupat, *The Voice in the Margin: Native American Literature and the Canon* (Berkeley: University of California Press, 1989), 14.

18. The Tewa language is spoken in the pueblos of Nambe, Pojoaque, San Ildefonso, Santa Clara, San Juan, and Tesuque, and Cajete reports that versions of this story are still told in some of them. For the full text of the story, see Cajete, *Look to the Mountain,* 125–27. Another version appears in David Leeming and Jake Page, *Myths, Legends, and Folktales of America: An Anthology* (New York: Oxford University Press, 1999).

19. For the text of this Cherokee story, see James Mooney, *History, Myths, and*

Sacred Formulas of the Cherokee (Asheville, N.C.: Historical Images, 1992): 311–15. Another version appears in Jack Frederick Kilpatrick and Anna Gritts Kilpatrick, "Eastern Cherokee Folktales: Reconstructed from the Field Notes of Frans M. Olbrechts," *Bureau of American Ethnology Bulletin* 196, no. 80: 393–97.

20. A version of the Hopi story appears in Richard Erdoes and Alfonso Ortiz, eds., *American Indian Myths and Legends* (New York: Pantheon Books, 1984), 145–50; several other Hopi stories with a similar theme appear in Ekkehart Malotki and Ken Gary, *Hopi Stories of Witchcraft, Shamanism, and Magic* (Lincoln: University of Nebraska Press, 2001).

21. David Schneider, *A Critique of the Study of Kinship* (Ann Arbor: University of Michigan Press, 1984), 165–66; original emphasis.

22. Schneider, *A Critique of the Study of Kinship,* 173.

23. Gilbert, *Eastern Cherokees,* 207.

24. John Gambolds to the Rev. John Herbst, 10 November 1810, M-412, Moravian Archives, Salem, N.C.

25. Jack D. Forbes, "The Manipulation of Race, Caste, and Identity: Classifying AfroAmericans, Native Americans and Red-Black People," *Journal of Ethnic Studies* 17, no. 4 (1990): 38–39. The illustration is useful even recognizing that some tribes do not have such unilineal descent groups. For detailed examinations of the social organization of many different tribes, see DeMallie and Ortiz, *North American Indian Anthropology.*

26. At the same time as the tribal essentialisms discussed here do not attend to genealogical distance, Forbes's example suggests that they may introduce a factor neglected by social scientific models of kinship, namely, gender. In the matrilineal tribes to which Forbes refers, children born to white mothers and Indian fathers lacked a defining social location, regardless of their half-Indian genetics, because they had no clan. Because clan membership determined so many of one's obligations and expectations, such children might be treated as non-Indian. The same Moravian missionaries quoted in the text continued in their remarks on the matrilineal Cherokees' philosophy of kinship: "If the father is a full Indian and the mother is a white person, then the children belong to the white people and don't concern the Indians at all."

Yet it is not clear that such an observation exhausts the richness of understandings of kinship in traditional, tribal philosophies. Anthropologist Raymond Fogelson notes that the Cherokee clearly understood that mothers alone transmitted the blood that linked the child to a clan. But there is evidence that ancient Cherokee philosophies suggest a physical bond that also connects *fathers* and children in fundamental substance: "The Cherokee theory of procreation holds, in common with the beliefs of other Iroquoians, that the female contributes blood and flesh to the fetus, while the father provides the skeleton through the agency of sperm, which can be considered a form of uncongealed bone." Raymond Fogelson, "On the 'Petticoat Government' of the Eighteenth Century Cherokee," in *Personality and the Cultural Construction of Society: Papers in Honor of Melford E. Spiro,* ed. David K. Jordan and Marc J. Swartz (Tuscaloosa: University of Alabama Press), 174.

Circe Sturm tentatively but plausibly suggests that this understanding of both parents' literal, bodily connection to the child may explain why children traditionally could not marry into the clan of *either* parent. She also proposes an interesting idea for future exploration: perhaps, in traditional Cherokee philosophy, "fathers may have been understood as kin, but as kin of a different sort [than mothers]." The question of the significance of gender in determining essential relationships is an obvious issue for explorations of tribal identity within indigenous philosophies to take up. Circe Sturm, *Blood Politics: Race, Culture and Identity in the Cherokee Nation of Oklahoma* (Berkeley: University of California Press, 2002), 216 n. 6.

27. David Reed Miller, "Definitional Violence and Plains Indian Reservation Life: Ongoing Challenges to Survival," in *Violence, Resistance, and Survival in the Americas,* ed. William B. Taylor and Franklin Pease (Washington, D.C.: Smithsonian Institution, 1994), 226–27.

28. Colin Calloway provides an index of the commonplace nature of adoption for some historic tribes when he writes: "Among some of the Iroquois tribes to the west, adoption became such a vital means of replenishing the losses occasioned by constant warfare that adoptees came to outnumber pure-blooded Iroquois." Colin G. Calloway, "An Uncertain Destiny: Indian Captivities on the Upper Connecticut River," *Journal of American Studies* 17 (1983): 194.

29. Frederick W. Hodge, ed., *Handbook of American Indians North of Mexico, Part 1,* Smithsonian Institution Bureau of American Ethnology Bulletin 30 (Washington, D.C.: Government Printing Office, 1912; St. Clair Shores, Mich.: Scholarly Press, 1968), 15.

30. Hartland's early yet extensive study of kinship philosophies argues that similar ideas were present in many of the "primitive" cultures he examined:

Descent is the normal, the typical cause of kinship and a common blood. . . . But kinship may also be acquired; and when once it is acquired by a stranger he ranks thenceforth for all purposes as one descended from a common ancestor. To acquire kinship a ceremony must be undergone: the blood of the candidate must be mingled with that of the kin. The ceremony, no less than the words made use of in various languages to describe the members of the kind and their common bond, renders it clear that the bond is the bond of blood. (Edwin Sidney Hartland, *Primitive Paternity: The Myth of Supernatural Birth in Relation to the History of the Family* [London: D. Nutt, 1909–1910], 258)

For many specific examples of tribal adoption, see James Axtell, "The White Indians of Colonial America," *William and Mary Quarterly* 32 (1975): 55–88; and Robert L. Hall, *An Archaeology of the Soul: North American Indian Belief and Ritual* (Urbana: University of Illinois Press, 1997).

31. I am not suggesting, in this discussion, that tribes or tribal members *frequently* adopt people today (as some tribes once did). Nor am I suggesting that they *ought* to do so. I offer the example of the adoption process only to illuminate some of the meanings that may attach to tribal versions of "essential" relationship.

32. Melissa Nelson, "Becoming Métis," in *At Home on the Earth: Becoming*

Native to Our Place, edited by David Landis Barnhill (Berkeley: University of California Press, 1999), 119.

33. Christopher Jocks, "American Indian Religious Traditions and the Academic Study of Religion: A Response to Sam Gill," *Journal of the American Academy of Religion* 65, no. 1 (1997): 172.

34. A number of such stories appear, with discussion, in Howard Harrod, *The Animals Came Dancing: Native American Sacred Ecology and Animal Kinship* (Tucson: University of Arizona Press, 2000); in David Rockwell, *Giving Voice to Bear: North American Indian Rituals, Myths, and Images of the Bear* (Niwot, Colo.: Roberts Rinehart Publishers, 1991); and in Stith Thompson, *Tales of the North American Indians* (Cambridge: Harvard University Press, 1929).

35. The original name of the Thompson River Indians is the Ntlakyapamuk or Nhlakapmuh tribe. They are of Salishan linguistic stock. Stories sharing the theme of human-deer marriage are reported among the Tsimshian, Kwakiutl, Southern Paiute, Micmac, and other tribes. See further Thompson, *Tales.*

36. Thompson, *Tales,* 173.

37. Hodge, *Handbook,* 16.

38. Daniel K. Richter, *The Ordeal of the Longhouse: The Peoples of the Iroquois League in the Era of European Colonization* (Chapel Hill: University of North Carolina Press, 1992), 69.

39. Richter, *Ordeal,* 72.

40. Richter, *Ordeal,* 70, quoting treaty minutes, 10 November 1680, Massachusetts Archives Series 30, Massachusetts State Archives, Boston, 254.

41. Richter, *Ordeal,* 69.

42. Ella Deloria, *Speaking of Indians* (Lincoln: University of Nebraska Press, 1998), 73; original parentheses.

43. On the importance of behavior for defining tribal identity among the Sioux, see further DeMallie, "Kinship and Biology in Sioux Culture."

44. See, for instance, Fred Eggan, *Essays in Social Anthropology and Ethnology* (Chicago: Department of Anthropology, University of Chicago, 1975).

45. Bronislaw Malinowski, "The Role of Magic and Religion," in *Reader in Comparative Religion: An Anthropological Approach,* ed. William A. Lessa and Evon Z. Vogt, 4th ed. (New York: Harper and Row, 1979), 43.

46. Herbert John Benally, "Navajo Philosophy of Learning and Pedagogy," *Journal of Navajo Education* 12, no. 1 (1994): 23–31, 28.

47. Herbert John Benally, "Navajo Ways of Knowing," in *Traversing Philosophical Boundaries,* ed. Max O. Hallman (Belmont, Calif.: Wadsworth Publishing Company, 1998), 244.

48. Julio Valladolid and Frédérique Apffel-Marglin, "Andean Cosmovision and the Nurturing of Biodiversity," in *Indigenous Traditions and Ecology: The Interbeing of Cosmology and Community,* ed. John A. Grim (Cambridge: Harvard University Press, 2001), 656.

49. Valladolid and Apffel-Marglin, 660.

50. Said, "'Commonwealth Literature,'" 67.

51. Raymond D. Fogelson, "Perspectives on Native American Identity," 43.

52. For detailed explorations of the way ideas and practices related to tribal belonging have changed over time in particular tribal groups, see Sturm, *Blood Politics;* and Alexandra Harmon, *Indians in the Making: Ethnic Relations and Indian Identities around Puget Sound* (Berkeley: University of California Press, 1998).

53. Gerald R. Alfred, *Heeding the Voices of Our Ancestors: Kanhawake Mohawk Politics and the Rise of Native Nationalism* (Toronto: Oxford University Press, 1995), 188. Stover's discussion of the Lakota concept of *Lakol wicoh'an* ("doing things in a Lakota way") emphasizes this idea of simultaneous continuity and dynamism in traditional thought and practice. Dale Stover, "Postcolonial Sun Dancing at Wakpamni Lake," *Journal of the American Academy of Religion* 69, no. 4 (December 2001), 830. Howard L. Harrod provides another careful, and more extended, discussion of how tribal spirituality simultaneously changes and stays the same in his *Becoming and Remaining a People: Native American Religions on the Northern Plains* (Tucson: University of Arizona Press, 1995).

54. Stover, "Postcolonial Sun Dancing," 823.

Conclusion

1. Letter from Mrs. Domenica Pallister to Donald B. Smith, 4 July 1977, quoted in Donald B. Smith, *Long Lance: The True Story of an Impostor* (Lincoln: University of Nebraska Press, 1983), 207.

2. Joane Nagel, "Constructing Ethnicity: Creating and Recreating Ethnic Identity and Culture," in *New Tribalisms: The Resurgence of Race and Ethnicity,* ed. Michael W. Hughey (New York: New York University Press, 1998), 237–72.

3. Gregory A. Cajete, *Igniting the Sparkle: An Indigenous Science Education Model* (Skyand, N.C.: Kivaki Press, 1999), 85; see further Herbert John Benally, "Navajo Philosophy of Learning and Pedagogy," *Journal of Navajo Education* 12, no. 1 (1994): 23–31; and Duane Champagne and Joseph H. Stauss, eds. *Native American Studies in Higher Education: Models for Collaboration between Universities and Indigenous Nations* (Walnut Creek, Calif.: Altamira Press, 2002).

4. Julio Valladolid and Frédérique Apffel-Marglin, "Andean Cosmovision and the Nurturing of Biodiversity," in *Indigenous Traditions and Ecology: The Interbeing of Cosmology and Community* (Cambridge: Harvard University Press, 2001), 645. See further Frédérique Apffel-Marglin with PRATEC [Andean Project of Peasant Technologies], ed. *The Spirit of Regeneration: Andean Cultures Confronting Western Notions of Development* (London: Zed Books, 1998).

5. Melissa Nelson and Philip M. Klasky, "Storyscape: The Power of Song in the Protection of Native Lands," *Orion Afield* (autumn 2001), 23.

6. Jace Weaver, "From I-Hermeneutics to We-Hermeneutics: Native Americans and the Post-Colonial," in *Native American Religious Identity: Unforgotten Gods,* ed. Jace Weaver (Maryknoll, N.Y.: Orbis Books, 1998), 22. See

further Jace Weaver, *That the People Might Live: Native American Literatures and Native American Community* (New York: Oxford University Press, 1997).

7. For more detailed discussions of fundamental differences between American Indian and scientific models of inquiry, see Eva Garroutte, "American Indian Science Education: The Second Step," *American Indian Culture and Research Journal* 23, no. 4 (1999): 91–114; James Keith, ed., *Science and Native American Communities: Legacies of Pain, Visions of Promise* (Lincoln: University of Nebraska Press, 2001); Laurie Anne Whitt, "Indigenous Peoples and the Cultural Politics of Knowledge," in *Issues in Native American Cultural Identity,* ed. Michael K. Green (New York: Peter Lang, 1995).

8. John C. Whittaker, "Red Power Finds Creationism," review of *Red Earth, White Lies: Native Americans and the Myth of Scientific Fact,* by Vine Deloria, Jr., in *The Skeptical Inquirer,* January/February 1997: 48. For a much broader critique of related issues, see Paul R. Gross and Norman Levitt, *Higher Superstition: The Academic Left and Its Quarrrels with Science* (Baltimore: Johns Hopkins University Press, 1994).

9. There is now a large literature that problematizes the fundamental assumptions of the sciences and the apparent necessity of their conclusions. See, for instance, Michael Edward Lynch, *Art and Artifact in Laboratory Science: A Study of Shop Work and Shop Talk in a Research Laboratory* (Irvine: University of California Press, 1979); Karin Knorr-Cetina and Michael Mulkay, eds., *Science Observed: Perspectives on the Social Studies of Science* (London: Sage Publications, 1983); G. Nigel Gilbert and Michael Mulkay, *Opening Pandora's Box: A Sociological Analysis of Scientists' Discourse* (New York: Cambridge University Press, 1984); Bruno Latour and Steve Woolgar, *Laboratory Life: The Construction of Scientific Facts* (Princeton: Princeton University Press, 1986); Bruno Latour, *Science in Action: How to Follow Scientists and Engineers through Society* (Cambridge: Harvard University Press, 1987); H. M. Collins and T. J. Pinch, *The Golem: What You Should Know about Science* (New York: Cambridge University Press, 1998); Jay A. Labinger and H. M. Collins, *The One Culture? A Conversation about Science* (Chicago: University of Chicago Press, 2001).

10. Jack Weatherford, *Indian Givers: How the Indians of the Americas Transformed the World* (New York: Fawcett Columbine, 1988).

11. Payson D. Sheets, "Dawn of a New Stone Age in Eye Surgery," in *Applying Anthropology: An Introductory Reader,* ed. Aaron Podolefsky and Peter J. Brown (Mountain View, Calif.: Mayfield Publishers, 1989), 112.

12. Anthony F. Aveni, ed., *Native American Astronomy* (Austin: University of Texas Press, 1977); Anthony F. Aveni, *Skywatchers* (Austin: University of Texas Press, 2001); John P. Hart, ed., *Current Northeast Paleoethnobotany* (Albany: University of the State of New York, State Education Department, 1999); Weatherford, *Indian Givers;* Ray A. Williamson, *Living the Sky: The Cosmos of the American Indian* (Boston: Houghton Mifflin Company, 1984).

13. Taiaiake Alfred, *Peace, Power, Righteousness* (Don Mills, Ontario: Oxford University Press, 1999), 142.

14. Alfred, *Peace, Power, Righteousness,* 142–43.

Appendix

1. Devon Mihesuah, "Commonality of Difference: American Indian Women and History," in *Natives and Academics: Researching and Writing about American Indians,* ed. Devon Mihesuah (Lincoln: University of Nebraska Press, 1998), 47.

Selected Bibliography

Alcoff, Linda. "Mestizo Identity." In *American Mixed Race,* edited by Naomi Zack. Lanham, Md.: Rowman and Littlefield, 1995.

Alfred, Gerald R. *Heeding the Voices of Our Ancestors: Kanhawake Mohawk Politics and the Rise of Native Nationalism.* Toronto: Oxford University Press, 1995.

Alfred, Taiaiake [Gerald R. Alfred]. *Peace, Power, Righteousness: An Indigenous Manifesto.* Don Mills, Ont.: Oxford University Press, 1999.

Allen, Paula Gunn. "Problems in Teaching Leslie Marmon Silko's *Ceremony.* In *Natives and Academics: Researching and Writing about American Indians,* edited by Devon A. Mihesuah. Lincoln: University of Nebraska Press, 1998.

American Indian Policy Review Commission (Task Force Ten). *Final Report: Report on Terminated and Nonfederally Recognized Indians.* Washington, D.C.: Government Printing Office, 1976.

Anders, Gary C. "A Critical Analysis of the Alaska Native Land Claims and Native Corporate Development." In *Native Americans and Public Policy,* edited by Fremont J. Lyden and Lyman H. Legters. Pitt Series in Policy and Institutional Studies 6. Pittsburgh: University of Pittsburgh Press, 1992.

Anderson, Terry. "Federal Recognition: The Vicious Myth." *American Indian Journal* 5 (1978): 7–19.

Andrade, Ron. "Are Tribes Too Exclusive?" *American Indian Journal* 6, no.7 (July 1980): 12–13.

Apffel-Marglin, Frédérique, with PRATEC [Andean Project of Peasant Technologies], ed. *The Spirit of Regeneration: Andean Cultures Confronting Western Notions of Development.* London: Zed Books, 1998.

Appiah, Kwame Anthony. *In My Father's House: Africa in the Philosophy of Culture.* New York: Oxford University Press, 1993.

Atchison, Sandra D. "Who Is an Indian, and Why Are They Asking?" *Business Week* (26 December 1988): 71.

Axtell, James. "The White Indians of Colonial America." *William and Mary Quarterly* 32 (1975): 55–88.

Baird, W. David. "Are There 'Real' Indians in Oklahoma? Historical Perceptions of the Five Civilized Tribes." *Chronicles of Oklahoma* 6 (1990): 4–23.

Banton, Michael. *Racial and Ethnic Competition.* Cambridge: Cambridge University Press, 1983.

Barkan, Elazar. *The Retreat of Scientific Racism: Changing Concepts of Race in Britain and the United States between the World Wars.* Cambridge: Cambridge University Press, 1992.

Barth, Frederick, ed. *Ethnic Groups and Boundaries: The Social Organization of Cultural Difference.* Boston: Little, Brown, 1969.

Beale, Calvin. "American Tri-Racial Isolates: Their Status and Pertinence to Genetic Research." *Eugenics Quarterly* 4, no. 4 (1957): 187–96.

———. "An Overview of the Phenomenon of Mixed Racial Isolates in the United States." *American Anthropologist* 74 (1972): 704–10.

Beaulieu, David L. "Curly Hair and Big Feet: Physical Anthropology and the Implementation of Land Allotment on the White Earth Chippewa Reservation." *American Indian Quarterly* 8, no. 4 (1984): 281–314.

Beck, Peggy V., Anna Lee Walters, and Nia Francisco. *The Sacred: Ways of Knowledge, Sources of Life.* Tsaile, Ariz.: Navajo Community College, 1992.

Beinart, Peter. "Lost Tribes: Native Americans and Anthropologists Feud over Indian Identity." *Lingua Franca* 9, no. 4 (May/June 1999).

Bell, Daniel. *The Winding Passage: Essays and Sociological Journeys (1960–1980).* Cambridge, Mass.: Abt Books, 1980.

Benally, Herbert John. "Navajo Philosophy of Learning and Pedagogy." *Journal of Navajo Education* 12, no. 1 (1994): 23–31.

———. "Navajo Ways of Knowing." In *Traversing Philosophical Boundaries,* edited by Max O. Hallman. Belmont, Calif.: Wadsworth Publishing Company, 1998.

Benedict, Jeff. *Without Reservation: The Making of America's Most Powerful Indian Tribe and Foxwoods, the World's Largest Casino.* New York: Harper Collins, 2000.

Berkhofer, Robert F., Jr. *The White Man's Indian.* New York: Vintage, 1979.

Berry, Brewton. *Almost White.* New York: Macmillan, 1963.

Biolsi, Thomas. "The Birth of the Reservation: Making the Modern Individual among the Lakota." *American Ethnologist* 22, no. 1 (February 1995): 28–49.

Blu, Karen I. *The Lumbee Problem: The Making of an American Indian People.* Cambridge: Cambridge University Press, 1980.

Boissevain, Ethel. "The Detribalization of the Narrangansett Indians: A Case Study." In *The Emergent Native Americans: A Reader in Culture Contact,* edited by Deward E. Walker, Jr. Boston: Little Brown, 1972.

Brascoupe, Simon. "Indigenous Perspectives on International Development." *Akwe:kon Journal* 9, no. 2 (1992): 6–17.

Brodeur, Paul. *Restitution: The Land Claims of the Mashpee, Passamaquoddy, and Penabscot Indians of New England.* Boston: Northeastern University Press, 1985.

Bruchac, Joseph. "Spinning the Medicine Wheel: The Bear Tribe in the Catskills." *Akwesasne Notes* 15, no. 5 (1983): 20–22.

Bureau of Indian Affairs. *Tribal Enrollment.* Washington, D.C.: Bureau of Indian Affairs, 1979.

Cajete, Gregory A. *Look to the Mountain: An Ecology of Indigenous Education.* Durango, Colo.: Kivaki, 1994.

———. *Igniting the Sparkle: An Indigenous Science Education Model.* Skyand, N.C.: Kivaki Press, 1999.

Calhoun, Craig. *Social Theory and the Politics of Identity.* Cambridge, Mass.: Blackwell, 1994.

Calloway, Colin G. "An Uncertain Destiny: Indian Captivities on the Upper Connecticut River." *Journal of American Studies* 17 (1983): 189–210.

Campisi, Jack. "The New England Tribes and Their Quest for Justice." In *The Pequots in Southern New England: The Fall and Rise of an American Indian Nation,* edited by Laurence J. Hauptman and James D. Wherry. Norman: University of Oklahoma Press, 1990.

Canby, William C., Jr. *American Indian Law in a Nutshell.* 2d ed. St. Paul: West Publishing Co., 1989.

Carillo, Jo. "Identity as Idiom: *Mashpee* Reconsidered." *Indiana Law Review* 28, no. 3 (1995): 511–45.

Carter, Kent. "Wantabees and Outalucks." *Chronicles of Oklahoma* 66, no. 1 (1988): 94–104.

———. "Deciding Who Can Be Cherokee: Enrollment Records of the Dawes Commission." *Chronicles of Oklahoma* 69, no. 2 (1991): 174–205.

———. *The Dawes Commission and the Allotment of the Five Civilized Tribes, 1893–1914.* Orem, Utah: Ancestry.com, 1999.

Champagne, Duane, and Joseph H. Stauss, eds. *Native American Studies in Higher Education: Models for Collaboration between Universities and Indigenous Nations.* Walnut Creek, Calif.: Altamira Press, 2002.

Clifford, James. "Identity in Mashpee." In *The Predicament of Culture,* edited by James Clifford. Cambridge: Harvard University Press, 1988.

Clifton, James A. "Cultural Fictions." *Society* 27, no. 4 (1990): 19–28.

———. *The Invented Indian: Cultural Fictions and Government Policies.* New Brunswick: Transaction, 1990.

———, ed. *Being and Becoming Indian: Biographical Studies of North American Frontiers.* Chicago: Dorsey Press, 1989.

Cohen, Felix S. *Handbook of Federal Indian Law.* Charlottesville, Va.: Michie/Bobbs-Merrill, 1982.

Cook-Lynn, Elizabeth. "The Rise of the Academic 'Chiefs.'" *Wicazo Sa Review* 2, no. 1 (1986): 38–40.

———. "Who Gets to Tell the Stories?" *Wicazo Sa Review* 9, no. 1 (1994): 60–64.

———. "Literary and Political Questions of Transformation: American Indian Fiction Writers." *Wicazo Sa Review* 11, no. 1 (1995): 46–51.

———. *Why I Can't Read Wallace Stegner and Other Essays: A Tribal Voice.* Madison: University of Wisconsin Press, 1996.

——. "Who Stole Native American Studies?" *Wicazo Sa Review* 12, no. 1 (1997): 9–28.

——. "American Indian Intellectualism and the New Indian Story." In *Natives and Academics: Researching and Writing about American Indians,* edited by Devon A. Mihesuah. Lincoln: University of Nebraska Press, 1998.

Cornell, Stephen. "The Transformations of Tribe Organization and Self-Concept in Native American Ethnicities." *Ethnic and Racial Studies* 11, no. 1 (November 1988): 27–47.

Cottrell, Gretchen Louise. "Americans of Indian and European Descent: Ethnic Identity Issues: Twelve Lives in the Annal of Modern Mixed Bloods." Ph.D diss., University of California, Berkeley, 1993.

Davis, F. James. *Who Is Black? One Nation's Definition.* University Park: Pennsylvania State University Press, 1991.

Debo, Angie. *And Still the Waters Run: The Betrayal of the Five Civilized Tribes.* Princeton: Princeton University Press, 1972.

Deloria, Philip J. *Playing Indian.* New Haven: Yale University Press, 1998.

Deloria, Vine, Jr. "Comfortable Fictions and the Struggle for Turf: An Essay Review of *The Invented Indian: Cultural Fictions and Government Policies.*" *American Indian Quarterly* 16, no. 3 (1990): 397–410.

DeMallie, Ray. "Kinship and Biology in Sioux Culture." In *North American Indian Anthropology: Essays on Society and Culture,* edited by Ray DeMallie and Alfonso Ortiz. Norman: University of Oklahoma Press, 1994.

DeMallie, Ray, and Alfonso Ortiz, eds. *North American Indian Anthropology: Essays on Society and Culture.* Norman: University of Oklahoma Press, 1994.

Dempsey, Hugh A. "Sylvester Long, Buffalo Child Long Lance: Catawba-Cherokee and Adopted Blackfoot, 1891–1932." In *American Indian Intellectuals,* edited by Margot Liberty. St. Paul: West Publishing, 1978.

Eipper, Chris. "The Magician's Hat: A Critique of the Concept of Identity." *Australian and New England Journal of Sociology* 19, no. 3 (November 1983): 427–46.

Eschbach, Karl. "Changing Identification among American Indians and Alaska Natives." *Demography* 30, no. 4 (November 1993): 635–47.

Fee, Margery. "What Use Is Ethnicity to Aboriginal Peoples in Canada?" *Canadian Review of Comparative Literature/Revue Canadienne de Litterature Comparee* 22, no. 3/4 (1 September 1995): 683–91.

Feraca, Stephen E. "Inside BIA: Or, 'We're Getting Rid of All These Honkies.'" In *The Invented Indian: Cultural Fictions and Government Policies,* edited by James A. Clifton. New Brunswick: Transaction, 1990.

——. *Why Don't They Give Them Guns? The Great American Indian Myth.* Lanham, Md.: University Press of America, 1990.

Ferrante, Joan, and Prince Browne, Jr., eds. *The Social Construction of Race and Ethnicity in the United States.* 2d ed. Upper Saddle River, N.J.: Prentice Hall.

Field, Les. "From Applied Anthropology to Applications of Anthropology for Tribal Goals: Examples from Indian Country." In *A Companion to the Anthropology of North American Indians,* edited by Thomas Biolsi. Malden, Mass.: Blackwell Publishers, in press.

Fixico, Donald L. "The Persistence of Identity in Indian Communities of the Western Great Lakes." In *American Indians: Social Justice and Public Policy,* edited by Donald E. Green and Thomas V. Tonneson. Ethnicity and Public Policy Series, vol. 9. Milwaukee: University of Wisconsin, System Institute on Race and Ethnicity, 1991.

Flacks-Jatta, JoHanna. "Constructive Race: The Interaction of Personal, Social, and Legal Identity in an American Indian Experience with Title VII: *Perkins v. Lake County Department of Utilities.*" *American Indian Law Review* 19, no. 2 (1994): 473–98.

Fogelson, Raymond D. "Perspectives on Native American Identity." In *Studying Native America: Problems and Prospects,* edited by Russell Thornton. Madison: University of Wisconsin Press, 1998.

Forbes, Jack D. "Mulattoes and People of Color in Anglo-North America: Implications for Black-Indian Relations." *Journal of Ethnic Studies* 12, no. 2 (1984): 17–60.

———. "The Manipulation of Race, Caste, and Identity: Classifying AfroAmericans, Native Americans and Red-Black People." *Journal of Ethnic Studies* 17, no. 4 (1990): 1–51.

Friedman, Daniel J., Bruce B. Cohen, Abigail R. Averbach, and Jennifer M. Norton. "Race/Ethnicity and OMB Directive 15: Implications for State Public Health Practice." *American Journal of Public Health* 90, no. 11 (November 2000): 1714–19.

Garroutte, Eva. "American Indian Science Education: The Second Step." *The American Indian Culture and Research Journal* 23, no. 2 (1999): 91–96.

Gill, Sam. "The Academic Study of Religion." *Journal of the American Academy of Religion* 62, no. 4 (1994): 965–75.

———. "Rejoinder to Christopher Jocks." *Journal of the American Academy of Religion* 65, no. 1 (1997): 177–81.

Glazer, Nathan. "American Diversity and the 2000 Census." *The Public Interest* 144 (2001): 3–18.

Glazer, Nathan, and Daniel P. Moynihan. *Beyond the Melting Pot: The Negroes, Puerto Ricans, Jews, Italians, and Irish of New York City.* 2d ed. Cambridge: MIT Press, 1963.

Gonzales, Angela. "The (Re)Articulation of American Indian Identity: Maintaining Boundaries and Regulating Access to Ethnically-Tied Resources." *American Indian Culture and Research Journal* 22, no. 4 (1998): 199–225.

Green, Michael K. *Issues in Native American Cultural Identity.* New York: Peter Lang, 1995.

Greenbaum, Susan. "What's in a Label? Identity Problems of Southern Indian Tribes." *The Journal of Ethnic Studies* 19, no. 2 (1991): 107–26.

Grinde, Donald, and Quintard Taylor. "Slaves, Freedmen, and Native Americans in Indian Territory (Oklahoma), 1865–1907." In *Peoples of Color in the American West,* edited by Sucheng Chan et al. Lexington, Mass.: D. C. Heath & Co., 1994.

Grose, Teresa Olwick. "Reading the Bones: Information Content, Value, and Ownership Issues Raised by the Native American Graves Protection and

Repatriation Act." *Journal of the American Society for Information Science* 47, no. 8 (1996): 624–31.

Gross, Ariela J. "Litigating Whiteness: Trials of Racial Determination in the Nineteenth-Century South." *Yale Law Journal* 108 (1998): 109–88.

Hagan, William T. "Full Blood, Mixed Blood, Generic, and Ersatz: The Problem of Indian Identity." *Arizona and the West* 27 (1985): 309–26.

Hajda, Yvonne. "Creating Tribes." *Anthropology Newsletter* 28, no. 2 (October 1987): 2.

Hallen, Barry. "Robin Horton on Critical Philosophy and Traditional Thought." *Second Order* 1 (1977): 81–92.

Halliburton, R., Jr. *Red over Black: Black Slavery among the Cherokee Indians.* Westport, Conn.: Greenwood Press, 1977.

Hallman, Max O., ed. 1998. *Traversing Philosophical Boundaries.* Belmont, Calif.: Wadsworth Publishing Company, 1998.

Hanson, Allan. "The Making of the Maori: Culture Invention and Its Logic." *American Anthropologist* 91 (1989): 890–902.

Harjo, Suzan Shown. "The American Indian Experience." In *Family Ethnicity: Strength in Diversity,* edited by Harriet Pipes McAdoo. Newbury Park, Calif.: Sage, 1993.

———. "Tribal and Cultural Identity." *Artpaper* 13, no. 2 (1993): 9–11.

Harmon, Alexandra. "When Is an Indian Not an Indian? The 'Friends of the Indian' and the Problems of Indian Identity." *Journal of Ethnic Studies* 18, no. 2 (1990): 95–123.

———. *Indians in the Making: Ethnic Relations and Indian Identities around Puget Sound.* Berkeley: University of California Press, 1998.

Harrod, Howard. *Becoming and Remaining a People: Native American Religions on the Northern Plains.* Tucson: University of Arizona Press, 1995.

Hechter, Michael. *Principles of Group Solidarity.* Berkeley: University of California Press, 1987.

Henige, David. "Origin Traditions of American Racial Isolates: A Case of Something Borrowed." *Appalachian Journal* 11 (1984): 201–14.

Hill, Tom, and Richard W. Hill, Sr. *Creation's Journey: Native American Identity and Belief.* Washington, D.C.: Smithsonian Institution, 1994.

Hobsbawn, Eric, and Terence Ranger, eds. *The Invention of Tradition.* Cambridge: Cambridge University Press, 1983.

Hodge, Frederick Webb, ed. *Handbook of American Indians North of Mexico. Part 1.* Smithsonian Institution Bureau of American Ethnology Bulletin 30. Washington, D.C.: Government Printing Office, 1912; St. Clair Shores, Mich.: Scholarly Press, 1968.

Horowitz, D. *Ethnic Groups in Conflict.* Berkeley: University of California Press, 1985.

Horton, Robin. "African Traditional Religion and Western Science." Parts 1 and 2. *Africa* 37, no. 1 (1967): 50–71; no. 2 (1967): 155–87.

Irwin, Lee. "Response: American Indian Religious Traditions and the Academic Study of Religion." *Journal of the American Academy of Religion* 66, no. 4 (1998): 887–92.

Jaimes, M. Annette. "Federal Indian Identification Policy: A Usurpation of Indigenous Sovereignty in North America." In *The State of Native America: Genocide, Colonization, and Resistance,* edited by M. Annette Jaimes. Boston: South End, 1992.

———. "Some Kind of Indian: On Race, Eugenics, and Mixed-Bloods." In *American Mixed Race,* edited by Naomi Zack. Lanham, Md.: Rowman and Littlefield, 1995.

Jaimez, Vicki. "White Eyes, Red Heart: Mixed-Blood Indians in American History." M.A. thesis, University of Arizona, 1995.

Jarvenpa, Robert. "The Political Economy and Political Ethnicity of American Indian Adaptations and Identities." *Ethnic and Racial Studies* 8 (1985): 29–48.

Jocks, Christopher. "American Indian Religious Traditions and the Academic Study of Religion: A Response to Sam Gill." *Journal of the American Academy of Religion* 65, no. 1 (1997): 169–76.

———. "Combing Out Snakes: Violence and the Construction of Knowledge in Longhouse Tradition." Paper presented at the 1994 annual meeting of the American Academy of Religion, Native Traditions in the Americas Group, session on "Knowing the World: Native American Epistemologies." Chicago, 21 November 1997.

Johansen, Bruce Eliot, ed. *The Encyclopedia of Native American Legal Tradition.* Westport, Conn.: Greenwood Press, 1998.

Josephy, Alvin. "New England Indians: Then and Now." In *The Pequots in Southern New England: The Fall and Rise of an American Indian Nation,* edited by Laurence Hauptman and James D. Wherry. Norman: University of Oklahoma Press, 1990.

Kasee, Cynthia R. "Identity, Recovery, and Religious Imperialism: Native American Women and the New Age." *Women and Therapy* 2/3 (1995): 83–93.

Kidwell, Clara Sue. "Indian Women as Cultural Mediators." *Ethnohistory* 39 (1992): 97–107.

Krupat, Arnold. "Scholarship and Native American Studies: A Response to Daniel Littlefield, Jr." *American Studies* 34, no. 2 (1993): 81–100.

Limerick, Patricia. *The Legacy of Conquest: The Unbroken Past of the American West.* New York: W. W. Norton, 1988.

Linnekin, Jocelyn. "Cultural Invention and the Dilemma of Authenticity." *American Anthropologist* 93, no. 2 (1 June 1991): 446–49.

Littlefield, Daniel F., Jr. *The Cherokee Freedmen: From Emancipation to American Citizenship.* Westport, Conn.: Greenwood, 1978.

Lockman, Paul T., and William Hawk. "Black Native Americans on the East Coast: The Case of the Algonkian Remnants of Long Island." *Free Inquiry in Creative Sociology* 23, no. 1 (May 1995): 11–14.

Lomayesva, Frederick K. "Indian Identity and Degree of Indian Blood." *Red Ink* 3 (1995): 33–37.

Long Lance, Buffalo Child. *Chief Buffalo Child Long Lance.* 1928. Jackson: University Press of Mississippi, 1995.

Lurie, Nancy Oestereich. "An American Indian Renascence?" In *The American*

Indian Today, edited by Stuart Levine and Nancy Oestereich Lurie. Deland, Fla.: Everett/Edwards, Inc., 1968.

Lyman, Stanford M., and William A. Douglas. "Ethnicity: Strategies of Collective and Individual Impression Management." *Social Research* 40, no. 2 (1973): 344–65.

McCulloch, Anne Merline, and David E. Wilkins. "'Constructing Nations within States: The Quest for Federal Recognition by the Catawba and Lumbee Tribes." *American Indian Quarterly* 19, no. 3 (1995): 361–88.

Meyer, Melissa L. *The White Earth Tragedy: Ethnicity and Dispossession at a Minnesota Anishinaabe Reservation 1889–1920.* Lincoln: University of Nebraska Press, 1994.

———. "American Indian Blood Quantum Requirements: Blood Is Thicker Than Family." In *Over the Edge: Remapping the American West,* edited by Valerie J. Matsumoto and Blake Allmendiger. Berkeley: University of California Press, 1999.

Mignolo, Walter D. "Afterword: Writing and Recorded Knowledge in Colonial and Postcolonial Situations." In *Writing without Words: Alternative Literacies in Mesoamerica and the Andes,* edited by Elizabeth Hill Boome and Walter D. Mignolo. Durham: Duke University Press, 1994.

Miller, Bruce. "After the F.A.P.: Tribal Reorganization after Federal Recognition." *The Journal of Ethnic Studies* 17, no. 2 (1989): 89–100.

Miller, David Reed. "Definitional Violence and Plains Indian Reservation Life: Ongoing Challenges to Survival." In *Violence, Resistance, and Survival in the Americas,* edited by William B. Taylor and Franklin Pease. Washington, D.C.: Smithsonian Institution, 1994.

Monet, Don, and Skanu'u [Ardythe Wilson]. *Colonialism on Trial: Indigenous Land Rights and the Gitksan and Wet'suwet'en Sovereignty Case.* Philadelphia: New Society, 1992.

Moore, John H. "Truth and Tolerance in Native American Epistemology." In *Studying Native America,* edited by Russell Thornton. Madison: University of Wisconsin Press, 1998.

Mudimbe, V. Y. *The Invention of Africa: Gnosis, Philosophy, and the Order of Knowledge.* Bloomington: Indiana University Press, 1984.

Nagel, Joane. "American Indian Ethnic Renewal: Politics and the Resurgence of Identity." *American Sociological Review* 60, no. 6 (December 1995).

———. *American Indian Ethnic Renewal: Red Power and the Resurgence of Identity and Culture.* New York: Oxford University Press, 1996.

———. "Constructing Ethnicity: Creating and Recreating Ethnic Identity and Culture." In *New Tribalisms: The Resurgence of Race and Ethnicity,* edited by Michael W. Hughey. New York: New York University Press, 1998.

Nelson, Melissa. "Becoming Métis." In *At Home on the Earth: Becoming Native to Our Place,* edited by David Landis Barnhill. Berkeley: University of California Press, 1999.

Nelson, Melissa, and Philip M. Klasky, "Storyscape: The Power of Song in the Protection of Native Lands." *Orion Afield* (2001): 22–25.

Norment, Lynn. "The New Ethnicity: Who's Black and Who's Not?" *Ebony* 45, no. 5 (1990): 134–37.

O'Brien, Sharon. *American Indian Tribal Governments.* Norman: University of Oklahoma Press, 1989.

The Official Guidelines to the Federal Acknowledgment Regulations, 25 CFR 83. Washington: BIA Branch of Acknowledgment and Research, September 1997.

Omi, Michael, and Harold Winant. "Racial Formations." In *Race, Class, and Gender in the United States,* edited by Paula S. Rothenberg. 3d ed. New York: St. Martin's, 1995.

Otis, D. S. *The Dawes Act and the Allotment of Indian Lands.* Norman: University of Oklahoma Press, 1973.

Owens, Louis. "Motion of Fire and Form." In *Native American Literature,* edited by Gerald Vizenor. New York: Harper Collins, 1995.

Paredes, Anthony. "The Emergence of Contemporary Eastern Creek Indian Identity." In *Social and Cultural Identity: Problems of Persistence and Change,* edited by Thomas K. Fitzgerald. Southern Anthropological Society Proceedings no. 8. Athens: University of Georgia Press, 1974.

———. "Federal Recognition and the Poarch Creek Indians." In *Indians of the Southeastern United States in the Late Twentieth Century,* edited by Anthony J. Paredes. Tuscaloosa: University of Alabama Press, 1992.

———. "Paradoxes of Modernism and Indianness in the Southeast." *American Indian Quarterly* 19, no. 3 (1995): 341–60.

Pascoe, Peggy. "Miscegenation Law, Court Cases, and Ideologies of 'Race' in Twentieth-Century America." *The Journal of American History* 83, no. 1 (June 1996): 44–69.

Pevar, Stephen L. *The Rights of Indians and Tribes: The Basic ACLU Guide to Indian and Tribal Rights.* 2d ed. Carbondale: Southern Illinois University Press, 1992.

Porter, Frank W., ed. *Strategies for Survival: American Indians in the Eastern United States.* New York: Greenwood, 1986.

Prucha, Francis Paul. *The Great Father: The United States Government and the American Indians.* Lincoln: University of Nebraska Press, 1986.

———. *American Indian Treaties: The History of a Political Anomaly.* Berkeley: University of California Press, 1994.

Quinn, William W., Jr. "The Southeast Syndrome: Notes on Indian Descendant Recruitment Organizations and Their Perceptions of Native American Culture." *American Indian Quarterly* 14, no. 2 (1990): 147–54.

———. "Ethnic Communities: Southeastern Indians: The Quest for Federal Acknowledgment and a New Legal Status." *Ethnic Forum* 13, no. 1 (1993): 34–52.

Rice, G. William. "There and Back Again — An Indian Hobbit's Holiday: Indians Teaching Indian Law." *New Mexico Law Review* 26, no. 2 (1996): 169–90.

Rice, Julian. *Lakota Storytelling: Black Elk, Ella Deloria, and Frank Fools Crow.* New York: Peter Lang, 1989.

Roosens, Eugeen E. *Creating Ethnicity: The Process of Ethnogenesis.* Newbury Park, Calif.: Sage, 1989.

Root, Maria P. P., ed. *Racially Mixed People in America*. Newbury Park, Calif.: Sage, 1992.

Rose, Wendy. "The Great Pretenders: Further Reflections on Whiteshamanism." In *The State of Native America,* edited by M. Annette Jaimes. Boston: South End, 1992.

Roth, George. "Overview of Southeastern Tribes Today." In *Indians of the Southeastern United States in the Late Twentieth Century,* edited by Anthony J. Paredes. Tuscaloosa: University of Alabama Press, 1992.

Sheffield, Gail K. *The Arbitrary Indian: The Indian Arts and Crafts Act of 1990.* Norman: University of Oklahoma Press, 1997.

Smedley, Audrey. *Race in North America: Origin and Evolution of a Worldview.* 2d ed. Boulder, Colo.: Westview Press, 1999.

Smith, Andy. "For All Those Who Were Indian in a Former Life." *Ms* 11, no. 3 (November/December 1991): 44–45.

Smith, Donald B. *Long Lance: The True Story of an Imposter.* Lincoln: University of Nebraska Press, 1983.

Smith, Linda Tuhiwai. *Decolonizing Methodologies: Research and Indigenous Peoples.* New York and London: Zed Books, 1999.

Smith, Susan. *Sweating Indian Style.* 56 min. University of Southern California, Center for Visual Anthropology, 1994. Videocassette.

Snipp, C. Matthew. "Who Are American Indians? Some Observations about the Perils and Pitfalls of Data for Race and Ethnicity." *Population Research and Policy Review* 5 (1986): 247–52.

———. *American Indians: The First of This Land.* New York: Russell Sage Foundation, 1989.

———. Review of "Why Don't They Give Them Guns?" by Stephen E. Feraca. *Rural Sociology* 56, no. 1 (1991): 144–46.

Sprott, Julie E. "'Symbolic Ethnicity' and Alaska Natives of Mixed Ancestry Living in Anchorage: Enduring Group or a Sign of Impending Assimilation?" *Human Organization* 53, no. 4 (1994): 311–22.

Standing Bear, Zug G. "Questions of Assertion, Diversity, and Spirituality: Simultaneously Becoming a Minority and a Sociologist." *American Sociologist* 20 (1988): 363–71.

———. "To Guard against Invading Indians: Struggling for Native Community in the Southeast." *American Indian Culture and Research Journal* 18, no. 4 (1994): 301–20.

Starna, William A. "The Southeast Syndrome: The Prior Restraint of a Non-Event." *American Indian Quarterly* 15, no. 4 (1991): 493–502.

Steinberg, Stephen. *The Ethnic Myth: Race, Ethnicity, and Class in America.* Boston: Beacon, 1981.

Stiffarm, Lenore A., and Phil Lane, Jr. "The Demography of Native North America: A Question of American Indian Survival." In *The State of Native America: Genocide, Colonization, and Resistance,* edited by M. Annette Jaimes. Boston: South End, 1992.

Stoler, Ann Laura. "Racial Histories and Their Regimes of Truth." *Political Power and Social Theory* 11 (1997): 183–206.

Stover, Dale. "Postcolonial Sun Dancing at Wakpamni Lake." *Journal of the American Academy of Religion* 69, no. 4 (December 2001), 817–36.

Strong, Pauline Turner. Review of *The Invented Indian,* by James Clifton. *American Ethnologist* 21, no. 4 (1994): 1052–53.

Strong, Pauline Turner, and Barrik Van Winkle. "'Indian Blood': Reflections on the Reckoning and Refiguring of Native North American Identity." *Cultural Anthropology* 11 (1996): 547–76.

Sturm, Circe. *Blood Politics: Race, Culture, and Identity in the Cherokee Nation of Oklahoma.* Berkeley: University of California Press, 2002.

Szasz, Margaret Connell. *Between Indian and White Worlds: The Cultural Broker.* Norman: University of Oklahoma Press, 1994.

Thompson, Bobby, and John H. Peterson, Jr. "Mississippi Choctaw Identity: Genesis and Change." In *The New Ethnicity: Perspectives from Ethnology,* edited by John W. Bennett. St. Paul: West Publishing, 1975.

Thornton, Russell. *American Indian Holocaust and Survival.* Norman: University of Oklahoma Press, 1987.

———. *The Cherokees: A Population History.* Lincoln: University of Nebraska Press, 1990.

———. "Tribal Membership Requirements and the Demography of 'Old' and 'New' Native Americans." *Population Research and Policy Review* 16 (1997): 33–42.

———, ed. *Studying Native America: Problems and Prospects.* Madison: University of Wisconsin Press, 1998.

Toelken, Barre. "Ethnic Selection and Intensification in the Native American Powwow." In *Creative Ethnicity,* edited by Stephen Stern and John Allan Cicala. Logan: Utah State University Press, 1991.

Torres, Gerald, and Kathryn Milun. "Translating Yonnondino by Precedent and Evidence: The Mashpee Indian Case." *Duke Law Journal* 4 (September 1990): 625–59.

Trask, Haunani-Kay. "Politics in the Pacific Islands: Imperialism and Native Self-Determination." *Amerasia* 16 (1990): 1–19.

Tsosie, Rebecca. "Changing Women: The Cross-Currents of American Indian Feminine Identity." *American Indian Culture and Research Journal* 12, no. 1 (1988): 1–37.

Tuller, Cheyenne. "The Politics and Perfidy of Federal Recognition." M.A. thesis, Washington State University, 1997.

U.S. Government Accounting Office. *Indian Issues: Improvements Needed in Tribal Recognition Process.* Report to Congressional Requesters. Washington, D.C., November 2001.

U.S. House Committee on Interior and Insular Affairs. *Provide for the Recognition of the Lumbee Tribe of Cheraw Indians of North Carolina: Joint Hearing before the Committee on Interior and Insular Affairs and the Select Committee on Indian Affairs.* 102d Cong., 1st sess., 1 August 1991.

———. *Indian Federal Acknowledgment Process: Hearing before the Committee on Interior and Insular Affairs.* 102d Cong., 2d sess., 15 September 1992.

U.S. Office of Management and Budget. "Revisions to the Standards for the

Classification of Federal Data." *Federal Register* 62, no. 210 (30 October 1997): 58781–90.

U.S. Senate Committee on Governmental Affairs. Permanent Subcommittee on Investigations. *Efforts to Combat Fraud and Abuse in the Insurance Industry: Hearing before the Permanent Subcommittee on Investigations of the Committee on Governmental Affairs.* 102d Cong., 1st sess., pt. 3, 19 July 1991.

U.S. Senate Committee on Indian Affairs. *Federal Recognition Administrative Procedures Act: Hearing before the Committee on Indian Affairs.* 104th Cong., 1st sess., 13 July 1995.

U.S. Senate Select Committee on Indian Affairs. *Federal Acknowledgment Process: Hearing before the Select Committee on Indian Affairs.* 100th Cong., 2d sess., 26 May 1988.

———. *Indian Federal Recognition Administrative Procedures Act of 1991: Hearing before the Select Committee on Indian Affairs.* 102d Cong., 1st sess., 22 October 1991.

Valladolid, Julio, and Frédérique Apffel-Marglin. "Andean Cosmovision and the Nurturing of Biodiversity." In *Indigenous Traditions and Ecology: The Interbeing of Cosmology and Community,* edited by John A. Grim. Cambridge: Harvard University Press, 2001.

Vizenor, Gerald. "Socioacupuncture: Mythic Reversals and the Striptease in Four Scenes." In *The American Indian and the Problem of History,* edited by Calvin Martin. New York: Oxford, 1987.

Warrior, Robert Allen. *Tribal Secrets: Recovering American Indian Intellectual Traditions.* Minneapolis: University of Minnesota Press, 1995.

Washburn, Wilcomb E. *Red Man's Land/White Man's Law: A Study of the Past and Present Status of the American Indian.* New York: Charles Scribner's Sons, 1971.

Waters, Mary C. *Ethnic Options: Choosing Identities in America.* Berkeley: University of California Press, 1990.

Weaver, Jace. "From I-Hermeneutics to We-Hermeneutics: Native Americans and the Post-Colonial." In *Native American Religious Identity: Unforgotten Gods,* edited by Jace Weaver. Maryknoll, N.Y.: Orbis Books, 1998.

Weibel-Orlando, Joan. *Indian Country, LA: Maintaining Ethnic Community in Complex Society.* Urbana: University of Illinois Press, 1991.

Whitt, Laurie Anne. "Indigenous Peoples and the Cultural Politics of Knowledge." In *Issues in Native American Cultural Identity,* edited by Michael K. Green. New York: Peter Lang, 1995.

Wilkins, David. "Convoluted Essence: Indian Rights and the Federal Trust Doctrine." *Native Americas* 14, no. 1 (1997): 24–31.

Wilkinson, Charles F. *American Indians, Time, and the Law: Native Societies in a Modern Constitutional Democracy.* New Haven: Yale University Press, 1987.

Wilson, Terry. "Blood Quantum: Native American Mixed Bloods." In *Racially Mixed People in America,* edited by Maria P. P. Root. Newbury Park, Calif.: Sage, 1992.

Zack, Naomi. "Mixed Black and White Race and Public Policy." *Hypatia* 10, no. 1 (1995): 120–32.

Index

Text: 10/13 Galliard
Display: Galliard
Indexer: Barbara Roos
Compositor: BookMatters, Berkeley

CPSIA information can be obtained at www.ICGtesting.com
Printed in the USA
LVOW11s0524230816

501339LV00002B/8/P

9 780520 229778